'It's hard to imagine a tougher ur[...] gangsters and addicts of Manenberg. Whoever you are, [...] you minister, Pete Portal's vivid, tough account of keeping faith in the face of seemingly overwhelming odds will teach you something about developing a rigorous theology appropriate to your local needs.'

Thabo Makgoba, Archbishop of Cape Town

'Pete's book is a combination of inspiring stories, wild faith and insightful challenge. It will stretch your views of prayer – both answered and unanswered – and of the deeply transformative power of love.'

Pete Greig, Author and Founder of 24–7 Prayer

'Never have I met a more authentic follower of Christ – his stories, confessions and reflections will draw you into the reality of the time we live in and the possibility that you and I just might be the ones the prophets of old told about! Yes, we might just be that link that has been missing in completing the Master's piece – "a wave of Spirit-fuelled revival spreading like fire throughout Africa towards the North!"'

Nkosinathi Mbuyazi, Director of 24–7 Prayer South Africa

'Pete and Sarah Portal are a remarkable couple. They have made their home amongst gangsters and addicts in the heart of one of the most dangerous places in South Africa. Following Jesus, Pete and Sarah have moved into the neighbourhood and are demonstrating God's love through their daily lives.'

Nicky Gumbel, Vicar of Holy Trinity Brompton,
Pioneer of The Alpha Course

'Wow. Honest, inspiring, heartbreakingly convicting, spirit-infused, humble and holy. This book reeks of Jesus and the invitation he still gives to lose our lives for something so much better. Pete writes and lives with both skill and passion and reading this book inspires me to actively participate in God's Kingdom coming to our world!'

Danielle Strickland, Speaker, Author, Justice Advocate

'Written with fierce intelligence and disarming humility, Pete Portal's testimony vividly demonstrates the wealth in those we call poor and the poverty in those we call rich. What is presented as a journey of discovery is in fact one long Magnificat – a celebration of the God who is Christ meets us in the faces of those on whom the world turns its back.'

Sam Wells, Author, Vicar of St Martin-in-the-Fields, London

'Pete Portal is a revivalist and an activist, an unusual and powerful combination. This book is the story of how he holds together the great hope of cultural transformation and spiritual revival. He does so while facing the painful realities of day-to-day life in one of the most troubled communities in South Africa. This book will be a huge encouragement to the many people who work against the odds in some of the harshest and most difficult parts of the Kingdom, but it will also inspire every reader faced with the sacrifices required to fulfil God's calling on their lives. I cannot recommend it more highly, but don't expect to be unmoved by the stories – the deep human tragedies and the joy and hope that they live for.'

Ken Costa, Author and Dean of the Leadership College, London

'This is a shocking book. It's full of exorcism and demons, wounds and healing and a genuine pilgrimage of grace . . . Combining evangelical confession with sociological analysis it gives an intense analysis of the structures of sin that the world as it is imposes and the redemption that indicates the world as it should be. Swinging easily between globalisation and healing the sick this is the most interesting book I have read this year. It certainly bears witness to the durability of love in a fallen world. It is a testament to good faith.'

Lord Maurice Glasman, Labour Peer and
Director of The Common Good Foundation

'For anyone like me who loves Jesus, but every so often fears they've embraced a spirituality that has less to do with the teachings of Jesus and the example of the early church, and more to do with the culture we find ourselves in, you have to read this book. It is rammed with kingdom stories and profound insights that will simultaneously wound and heal you, disturb you and birth fresh hope, and leave you with an unshakable vision of what is possible when ordinary people follow the promptings of the Spirit and recklessly follow the way of Jesus.'

Pete Hughes, Lead Pastor at King's Cross Church, London

'Portal compels us to lay down our pursuit of comfort, security and quality of life and follow Jesus not just to places like Manenberg, but to the edges of ourselves. *No Neutral Ground* is a glimpse into a story of our mutual liberation and it is not without cost.'

Idelette McVicker, Founder and Editor-in-Chief at *SheLoves* Magazine

'I have been in Manenberg with Pete many times. When people muse over God's presence in these fearful places, I can say "I have seen him walking in the garden of Manenberg bringing back Eden through his persistent servants". Reading this compelling account combines the raw lashes of disappointment and stings of loss with a faith-fuelled optimism as real tangible stories, solid biblical insights and vividly revealing thoughts are laid bare. In this book is a calculation – what it costs in joy and tears, in mind and money, in diligent study and politically astute policy creation, in the letting-go and holding-tight – so that talk of hope has real names and faces on it and not just ideals to serve, to love, to live, to give, to grow, to lead. I could rave forever for herein is true wisdom from lived life, making my many visits pale by the actuality of Pete and Sarah's incarnation of grace that just by knowing them and this story lets me grow in the shadow of their sacrifices and their honour.'

Lord Dr Hastings of Scarisbrick CBE, Chancellor, Regents University London

'*No Neutral Ground* is not only riveting, inspiring and hope-filled, it is a mandate for how to live out the revolutionary words of Jesus. It tells the story of a people born in to systemic poverty, violence and injustice. What makes it so powerful for me is that it tells the story of my people; born as a "coloured" into an apartheid system that used a "divide and conquer" strategy along lines of race and socio-economic status, I remember hearing the stories of Manenberg. This book is a provocation to marry the power of God with his loving justice. It's a call to live as agents of change through simply loving the ones in front of you and sometimes moving into the places where the unloved are . . . This book is not just for the "die-hard" missionary types. It's for the everyday Christian who needs to discover again the incredible power of a life laid down. This book has changed me profoundly.'

Julian Adams, Author, International Speaker and
Director of Frequentsee

'This book is inspiring and challenging and will likely challenge many of your convictions about how we are to live if we follow Jesus. Pete tells of his own journey from security and comfort to a life full of adventure. It's obvious that he's found it to be completely worth it and pulls no punches in explaining why we should all embark on our own journey of risk and sacrifice.'

Jay Pathak, Pastor of the Mile High Vineyard

'I remember very well the first time I met Pete and his wife; that in Cape Town one Thursday evening I was meeting modern-day heroes. But you will not have to travel there to meet them: you will meet them in the pages of this book. Real-life stories jump from its pages – intelligently written and thoughtful, with more than a passing knowledge of theology and history. With me you will most likely feel challenged and ask yourself "do I do enough?", "could I live more on the edge?", "is my life touching the broken and making a difference?"'

Paul Manwaring, Author, Bethel Church Senior Leadership Team

NO NEUTRAL GROUND

FINDING JESUS IN A CAPE TOWN GHETTO

Pete Portal

HODDER &
STOUGHTON

First published in Great Britain in 2019 by Hodder & Stoughton
An Hachette UK company

1

A CIP catalogue record for this title is available from the British Library

ISBN 978 1 473 69737 9
eBook ISBN 978 1 473 69739 3

Typeset in Celeste by Palimpsest Book Production Limited, Falkirk, Stirlingshire

Printed and bound in Great Britain by Clays Ltd, Elcograf S.p.A.

Hodder & Stoughton policy is to use papers that are natural, renewable
and recyclable products and made from wood grown in sustainable forests.
The logging and manufacturing processes are expected to conform to
the environmental regulations of the country of origin.

Hodder & Stoughton Ltd
Carmelite House
50 Victoria Embankment
London EC4Y 0DZ

www.hodderfaith.com

. . . for all those seeking to live their lives
for something worth dying for.

Contents

Preface

There is no neutral ground in the universe: every square inch, every split second, is claimed by God and counterclaimed by Satan.
(C. S. Lewis, *Christian Reflections*)[1]

This is war, and there is no neutral ground. If you're not on my side, you're the enemy; if you're not helping, you're making things worse.
(Jesus, Matthew 12:30, MSG)

Robben Island is a peculiar place. Just 14 kilometres from the mainland, accessible only by boat, it is another world compared to Cape Town's bustling waterfront. Famous for being where Nelson Mandela was incarcerated for eighteen years (along with Oliver Tambo and scores of other apartheid freedom fighters and activists), these days on the island the main traffic is tortoises, the main flora hardy shrubs, and the main resistance attempting to stay out of the fairly constant wind. It is a strange mix of extremely busy (with ferries of tourists chugging over multiple times a day for bus tours of the prison) and, well . . . kind of abandoned. Simultaneously a revered icon and a forgotten landscape. A funny mix indeed.

In January 2016 I took the Robben Island ferry to take part in a rather grandly named Writers Symposium. Really it was just a bunch of us who wanted to learn to write, learning from a few theologians and authors. We walked round to the lime quarry where fifty years earlier prisoners had been made to chip away at rock, as they did so being slowly blinded by the sun reflecting off the bright white stone. I sat in what had been PAC activist Robert Sobukwe's kitchen and reflected on the six years he spent in enforced isolation during which time his vocal chords packed up and he forgot how to speak, the insidious torture of atrophy disabling such a bright voice. I began to scribble down thoughts and feelings about life and power, faith and freedom. And I began to think about how to make a start on the book I wanted to write – the one you are now holding.

For over half my life I've given more time to trying to work out my faith in Jesus than anything else. I've thought and prayed and sought advice and read books all with this in mind: finding my own answer to the implications of saying I follow him, and how this will affect the way I spend my short life here on earth.

I get the impression I'm not the only one asking this question. Many conversations I have had and continue to have with people – whether those close to me or those I hardly know, whether rich and privileged, poor and disempowered, or anywhere in between – orient around this question. Everyone is searching for answers to the questions the onlookers asked the disciples at Pentecost: 'What does this mean?' and 'What should we do?' Is there a God? What is my purpose? What does believing Jesus is God mean, for me, today? And what should I do in response?

If what you believe translates into how you live, then your worldview will necessarily affect your lifestyle. And for those of us who profess faith in Jesus, he left us with no doubt that it's in spending our lives serving the poor, the lost, the hurting, the broken and the forgotten, that we will discover the heart of God and, along the way, our own true self. Life can be tough. Brutal, even. But Jesus' message of hope, though difficult (for it demands everything of us) is really quite simple – that in losing your life you will find it. There is no better way to live than for others, and in surrendering our own broken plans for ourselves we discover God's perfect ones.

Cartoon truth

Midway through my first year as an undergraduate theology student I once saw a notice on the office door of one of my university lecturers. It was a cartoon of two people chatting. Though visually unremarkable, it made me stop in my tracks. The first character is posing a well-known conundrum to his friend – 'If God exists then why doesn't he do anything about all the people who are hurting and hungry?' The wistful-looking second character replies, 'I'm just worried he might ask me the same question.'

God's plans for anyone he ever created is 'life in its fullness' (John 10:10), yet for many around the world this is far from their reality. Walking back to my halls of residence that day, I couldn't get this cartoon out of my head. I began to reflect on how cynical I had become, chatting to intellectually proud students dismissing the existence of God based on the very same sentiments of the first character in the cartoon (there is nothing like cynicism to paralyse and anaesthetise against hope-filled vision and active engagement with the world). I began to see there is another option to simply blaming God for the mess the world is in and that, beyond the cop-out of mere academic debate, my relationship with Jesus gave me something precious that many of my friends didn't have. I had the opportunity to give my life in response to the glaring gulf between Jesus' promise of abundant life and the lived reality of so many. I could hardly believe it had taken me so long to see. What an unbelievable privilege! I suddenly experienced a profound joy at the thought of playing even just a tiny part in helping others who were hungry and hurting to discover fullness of life in Jesus.

What has this got to do with the book you're holding?

Well, everything really. This book is the kind of 'what happened next' after this fairly obvious realisation I had as a student. This is the story of how, six months after graduating, I moved to Cape Town and, soon after, moved into a township called Manenberg – a place most fear and few will voluntarily go. It tells about why my wife Sarah and I have chosen to live with drug addicts and gangsters. It tells of the emergence of a house-church-planting movement there, and the subsequent cultivating of a family of faith. It's a story of how (often quite accidentally) following the call of Jesus on my life, I ended up in places I would never have guessed going, met people I would never have dreamt meeting, seen things I could never have imagined, and experienced his power and love interlaced throughout. My hope is that as you read you will be inspired to know Jesus better, encouraged that he really is the hope for a hurting world, and that he can use absolutely anyone to spread his message of hope, and so be challenged to step out of the ordinary and mundane into a life of faith-filled adventure.

Roughly speaking, I have tried to incorporate three strands together: story, confession and reflection. The stories are a recounting of what happened; the confession part focuses on personal doubts, fears and inadequacies experienced along the way; and the reflection seeks to relate both to the journey of faith and the process of learning to depend on the faithfulness and goodness of God.

It's time

If you spend any time in South African churches it won't be long before you hear about the oft-prophesied move of the Holy Spirit that will spread throughout Africa, from the tip to the top, from Cape to Cairo. This continent-wide revival-in-the-making is heady stuff, and it seems clear that the Spirit of God has been speaking about it for over a century through various means and people. From John G. Lake, renowned seer and healer, through Lonnie Frisbee of the Jesus People movement, Indonesian revivalist Mel Tari, and mega-evangelist Reinhardt Bonnke – quite apart from innumerable South African and African prophets – the word has gone out time and time again: *a wave of Spirit-fuelled revival will spread throughout Africa towards the north, the fires having been stoked and started in Cape Town.* My sense is that this is not some kind of fringe, charismatic hysteria – but that God has spoken, and is speaking. In his kindness, he has not given up telling us, over and over, about his heart for continent-wide transformation. But working out how we, the Church, collaborate with bringing about this groundbreaking word seems to have been almost entirely neglected.

This book tells some of the story of how a small group of us are trying to respond. By giving God our everything in light of the potential for widespread revival, by living in generative contradiction to an apartheid hangover and a dislocated past, by seeking the wholeness of one troubled community, by committing to those others reject, and by taking Jesus' gospel at face value, we believe we are doing our bit in ploughing the ground in readiness.

This coming move of God isn't just going to fall into our laps. As God said to Moses in the book of Exodus prior to liberating his people via miraculous deliverance through the Red Sea, 'Why are you crying out to me? Tell the Israelites to move on.' In other words, 'Shut up and start doing what I've told you about!' The state and fate of communities and nations depend on the people of God giving their whole selves to this work. It's all or nothing. There is no neutral ground. It's time to reframe the narrative, to stop talking and start doing.

It's time.

Introduction

There's really no such thing as the 'voiceless'. There are only the
deliberately silenced, or the preferably unheard.
(Arundhati Roy)[2]

Power is the ability not just to tell the story of another person, but to
make it the definitive story of that person.
(Chimamanda Ngozi Adichie)[3]

The book you have in your hand is primarily a book of stories.
Within these pages are stories that are happy, stories that are sad,
disturbing stories and funny stories. There may be stories that
challenge you, or stories of pain that make you instinctively thump
the table with your fist. There may be some stories that will make
you think and reflect, and lead you to pray. Mainly, there are
stories about God and people, people and the world, and the
potential for a beautiful relationship between all three. That all
sounds OK, right?

The thing is, all the stories will be told by me.

And that's just fine – but it does come with its challenges.
That's because I tend to make assumptions. My assumptions are
often based on presuppositions, and I carry these with me wherever I go. We all do it. Even if we're open to these suppositions
being challenged and redefined, we need to be aware that each
of us carries them. I have my own presuppositions about the
people I think might read this book, and to an extent that has
influenced the way I've written. And no doubt you, who are
reading these words, have also made some assumptions about me
or the stories I will tell. Again, that's not a problem. But as a
result I've tried to ensure that the stories in this book do not fall

into the trap of perpetuating what Nigerian author Chimamanda Ngozi Adichie calls the 'single story'.

Let me explain. We are all aware of various stereotypes – whether religious, racial, gender-based or whatever. The single story is based upon, and seeks to maintain caricatures based upon, stereotypes. In this way, it brings division, misunderstanding and distance between those it categorises. And, of course, no single story is ever true.

What about you?

It is possible to construct a single story about some of the people, issues or places that will come up in the book you are about to read. So, let me ask you: evangelical Christians – right leaning, obsessed with polarising issues such as abortion, gay marriage and Bible bashing?; South Africa – a democratic rainbow nation that has miraculously moved on from apartheid and racism?; Cape Town – problem free and as close to heaven on earth as a city could be?; Manenberg – a morally nihilistic, godforsaken hellhole?; British people – colonial supremacists adept in the art of manipulation?; God – imaginary, angry, cruel?

The 'single story' is (consciously or not) directly related to power and the assertion of *our* superiority over *those people*. So the fact that much of the history of Africa has been written by non-Africans should trouble us – because where the story starts, and how it is told, necessarily shapes perceptions of truth and reality. Does the story of modern Africa start with post-independence crises riddled with the corruption and self-interest of tyrannical dictators masquerading as revolutionaries? Or does it begin centuries earlier with the terror wrought by genocidal European colonisers? Or does it originate centuries before that, with indigenous art such as the Benin Bronzes crafted by the Ogiso dynasty in the thirteenth century, which left the West dumbfounded that African culture was so advanced and cutting edge so early on? Where does it start, and who decides?

Single stories emphasise differences rather than similarities. Unless nuanced, balanced stories are told, the subjects of these stories will be robbed of dignity. Because the fact is, *single stories simply do not exist*. The telling of single stories is ignorant at best, and catastrophic at worst. An example of one such single story is the foundational myth on which apartheid was built – the myth of white superiority based upon a bastardised ideology of racial purity and God's supposed blessing on a particular people group. What J. Kameron Carter describes as 'the theological problem of whiteness . . . how whiteness came to function as a substitute for the Christian doctrine of creation, thus producing a reality into which all else must enter'.[4]

A prevailing single story told about a period in history called the Enlightenment generally emphasises the intellectual advances made for the direct benefit of humanity. It certainly must have been an exciting time to have been alive. Yet, digging slightly deeper it emerges that, pretty ironically in an age of criticism, intellectualism, and desire for truth, the great Enlightenment thinkers produced and circulated such unenlightened dross around race and racialisation. Immanuel Kant, for example, wrote extensively on notions of a Eurocentric 'normative gaze' that, Cornel West notes, 'would provide an authoritative cultural norm of white supremacy, which would become the basis for modern racism'.[5]

Since then, many, many stories have been written about Africa by white people. This has meant that that which is *normative* and that which is *different* has pretty much always been defined by the white Westerner, usually male.

I am white, a male, and a Westerner.

I celebrate how God made me and who he made me to be. Genuinely. Yet I cannot but hold this truth alongside another truth that people who look and speak like me have historically caused huge harm to those who are 'different' to this white-centric, male-dominated narrative.

Get to the point

Manenberg is a community in Cape Town, 20 kilometres from the city centre. I call it home and it's my favourite place I've ever lived. But if you asked most Capetonians of any race or socio-economic standing what Manenberg is like, the response would make you wince. With very few exceptions, you would be told something along the lines of: 'It's full of gangsters'; 'There's no reason to go to Manenberg except to buy drugs'; 'Those people are violent'; 'It's full of poverty and hopelessness'; 'It's a . . . gang breeding ground/apartheid dumping ground/ godforsaken ghetto.' If you were to ask that same person if they have ever *been* to Manenberg, the likely response would be an emphatic 'No,' followed by a defiant 'and I wouldn't go if you paid me!'

I am, of course, generalising. But that's the nature of the single story. It is based upon generalisation and caricature. It's fear-induced, it breeds division and perpetuates ignorance. How Manenberg is widely viewed and spoken about – 'teeming with gangsters, poverty and drugs' – is the epitome of the single story. I'm not saying it doesn't have significant problems. But there would likely be no mention of close-knit community vibes, slap-stick Cape Flats humour, thriving local sports leagues, street *braais* and soccer games, colourful *klopse* bands, block parties with pumping music, and a prevailing and contagious friendliness.

And so I write this book with a degree of fear and trembling. Whether the words that follow are widely read or hardly read, the following should be taken into account:

- I make no claims to having a definitive, authoritative opinion on Manenberg, Cape Town or South Africa.
- Stories are, inevitably, told from the perspective of how I saw them as they happened. Where possible, I have consulted someone else who was present to check I'm not misrepresenting people or places.

- I love Jesus and I follow him. I believe that he is who he says he is – God. Does that make this a 'Christian' book? No more than if I sneeze, it makes it a 'Christian' sneeze. But it is written out of who I am and what's inside me. For some, it will be too 'Christian'. For others, it won't be 'Christian' enough. To use that overly used and slightly meaningless phrase; *it is what it is.*

Confession: I have an innate desire to come across better than I am. Maybe we all do, deep down. I'm not proud of it, but it's something I'm working on. The process of writing this book has afforded ample opportunity to exaggerate, lie, twist truth, and present myself better than I really am. Just know that I have battled against this, and hope that there's not too much of it in the pages that follow.

1: Early Days

This is my dilemma. I am dust and ashes, frail and wayward,
a set of predetermined behavioural responses . . . riddled with fear,
beset with needs . . . the quintessence of dust and unto dust shall I
return. But there is something else in me . . . Dust I may be, but
troubled dust, dust that dreams, dust that has strong premonitions of
transfiguration, of a glory in store, a destiny prepared, an inheritance
that will one day be my own . . . so my life is spread out in a painful
dialectic between ashes and glory, between weakness and
transfiguration. I am a riddle to myself, an exasperating enigma . . .
the strange duality of dust and glory.
(Richard Holloway)[1]

I grew up in south-east London in a conventional middle-class family. By that I mean we had a VW Passat, a modest back garden, went on summer holidays to Devon and always had food on the table. While we weren't 'rich' in a British sense of the word, we lacked very little – indeed, I've never known what it's like to go to bed hungry, or to not receive gifts for my birthday. My parents both worked full time. There was nothing particularly flashy or extravagant about our family's way of life, but it was, looking back, the epitome of comfort and safety. In many ways, it was all a kid could have asked for, and I'm deeply thankful for it.

I attended the local government primary school. Much as I enjoyed it there, I kept finding myself getting in fights with a much bigger boy called Andre. When, one day at a family lunch, my granddad heard about the clashes between me and my classmate nemesis, he decided to take it upon himself to teach me some boxing moves. It was an unconventional teaching method involving him tensing his stomach and telling me to hit him as

caught up with me, and was enough to persuade her to arrange
me a voice trial for Westminster Abbey Choir School.

hard as I could. The fact is, as a seven-year-old I couldn't hit very
hard (I'm not even sure I can now to be honest), but I would do
my utmost to pummel Granddad. Despite my best efforts, our
coaching sessions invariably ended up in him telling me I hit
'like a sissy'.

Like the good middle-class parents they were, my mum and
dad arranged for me to have piano lessons. My teacher was a
wrinkly old lady with a sense of humour failure but who somehow
cultivated a passion in me for music. I would return home with
various tunes in my head and sing myself to sleep night after
night.

During this time of musical and box-ical awakening, my mum
came across an advert in the newspaper that caught her attention.
It was a photo of a young boy dressed in cassock, surplice and
ruff, with a caption underneath that read 'Could This Be Your
Son?' and a phone number to call. My habit of getting in play-
ground scuffles combined with my new-found love of music had
caught up with me, and was enough to persuade her to arrange
me a voice trial for Westminster Abbey Choir School.

In preparation for this big event, which I was totally not up
for, I had to learn a couple of songs to sing. Again my granddad's
unconventional methods came into play. While staying with him
for a week during the school holidays, he harnessed my love for
the board game Monopoly (I hadn't yet grown to understand the
unjust, inequality-creating nature of unfettered capitalism) by only
agreeing to play if I learned to sing the Naval Hymn. I couldn't
believe my luck: limitless hours of one-on-one Monopoly guaranteed, and all I had to do was learn his dreary song.

The day finally arrived and we took the train to Charing Cross
station and walked to Westminster Abbey. There were a bunch of
other seven- and eight-year-old boys, all looking equally nervous
and clueless about the events of the day. When my time came,
I was called to the choirmaster's house, which was in a quiet
courtyard through the ancient abbey cloisters, whose worn stone
alleyways told a story of centuries of religious devotion. The

history was lost on me, however; I was more interested in the game of football going on outside.

After giving a rousing rendition of the Naval Hymn, and playing a pretty basic minuet on the piano, I returned to Mum and Dad. By mid-afternoon the auditions were finished. A group of us were asked to stay behind for one final chat with the choirmaster.

To my great horror, I had passed.

WACS

The next five years at Westminster Abbey Choir School were unique in the extreme. Despite needing to navigate a subconscious sense of rejection from my parents packing me off to boarding school at the age of eight, I began to really enjoy life at this peculiar place. Every morning as we got up and got dressed we would look out on to the Victoria Tower, Big Ben and the Houses of Parliament. Evensong was sung every day but one, and Sunday brought three choral services – all meticulously prepared for through hours a day in 'song school' learning different settings of the Magnificat and Nunc Dimittis. Regular concerts, tours abroad (most memorably to the USA, where we toured to twelve different cities in two weeks), performing in the occasional BBC Prom, making numerous CD recordings, as well as singing in historic events in the abbey such as Princess Diana's funeral, left little time for a regular primary school curriculum – but somehow we managed to fit it all in. An advantage of being in a school of just thirty-six boys meant that if you had any remote hand–eye coordination you were automatically in both the football and cricket teams. The highlight of the year was always the grudge match against St Paul's Cathedral, which we often lost – though we would console ourselves after losing by affirming our superior singing abilities.

As for any spiritual life, I had none – nor any remote interest in Christianity or Jesus. Being made to learn the Nicene Creed off by heart, rehearsing pace and diction, always emphasising the correct words, with no explanation as to what any of it meant, served as a very effective inoculation to true faith. We were being taught a disembodied denominational framework, devoid of any personal experience. Everything was a performance, liturgical in the extreme, and as far as relating to God was concerned, no emotion was ever to be shown. I remember watching Princes William and Harry processing up the aisle during their mother's funeral as we sang the words of the Funeral Sentences, 'the Lord gave and the Lord hath taken away', and thinking to myself how brave they were not to break down in tears. Everything, even the funeral of two young boys' mother, was a performance.

The mysterious man

The advantage of such a childhood was that we occasionally met some extraordinary people. If a head of state was coming through town, they often came to Westminster Abbey for a private visit. The choir would give a brief performance as these dignitaries laid a wreath or took a walk around. Nelson Mandela's state visit to the UK in 1996 was no exception. I still remember, as a ten-year-old, all of us getting ready in what was called 'song school', where we rehearsed. As we were putting on the red cassocks and white frilly ruffs, we were getting over-excited as we tried to piece together various bits of information we had been told by our parents or teachers about this mysterious man who used to be a criminal but was now everyone's hero.

We processed through the nave to below the organ loft, stood in front of the gold-leaf-lined screen to the quire, and waited for the cue from the choirmaster. Minutes passed, but eventually the great west door opened and the organ began the intro. We began to sing a rather dreary motet and Nelson Mandela, alongside the Dean of Westminster, walked towards us doing that kind of smiling, looking around and making polite chitchat to each other as they went.

Normally, they would stand and listen to a verse or two, and then move on to Poets' Corner or take a look at the dramatic vaulted ceiling of the Henry VII Chapel. But this time was a little different. Nelson Mandela left the dean standing on his own and walked up to us, assembled in two lines as we sang, and began to go down the line shaking each one of our hands. When he finished with the front row he then squeezed behind and made his way along the second row. To each of us, he said the same words, 'I am very honoured to shake your hand.' The moment we were out of the abbey we ran back to song school laughing and joking that we would never wash our right hands again.

Making it official

It was an expectation that those in their final year at WACS would be confirmed into the Church of England. I had no idea what this entailed, and the confirmation classes offered by one of the canons didn't much help, simply confirming my suspicions that Christianity was indeed mind-numbingly boring. Nonetheless, I did it. There was a mini-scandal when one of our classmates announced he didn't want to be confirmed as he 'wasn't sure God existed'. I hadn't realised God's existence was even up for debate. I was clueless in matters of faith, but seemed totally convinced that there was a God. The fact is, despite taking part in eight Christian services a week for five years, I can't remember it ever being preached that knowing Jesus was soul-transforming, sin-forgiving, joy-bringing, destiny-launching and world-changing – rather, faith in God was a cerebral, private matter, neatly compart-mentalised into hour-long rituals, and I didn't question it. Nor did I want much to do with it – though this had less to do with belief than just being plain bored by the seemingly irrelevant ceremony, outdated language and the fact that everyone looked so damn serious. It is only now, listening to some of the music we sang, that I can reflect on the life of Jesus through the beauty of Handel's *Messiah*, or imagine the throne room of God through William Harris's *Faire is the Heaven*. At the time, though, it went almost entirely over my head.

Teen angst

At thirteen I went to secondary school in Tonbridge, Kent. Though just fifteen minutes from where we then lived, I decided to board again. Moving from being the oldest in a school of thirty-six to being the youngest in a school of over seven hundred was daunting in the extreme. Whatever niche skills I may have picked up at Westminster Abbey, nothing prepared me for the intimidating teenage environment and unforgiving public school banter of Tonbridge. My parents could only afford the extortionate school fees because I was offered a 70 per cent music scholarship, meaning I was required to be in the choir, the band, the orchestra and a wind quintet – none of which were considered worthy of respect in my new environment. Mercifully, I was also in a couple of sports teams, which counterbalanced at least some of the uncool music vibes.

As time went on, weekends were spent under-age drinking, and while I wouldn't say I went off the rails much more than anyone else around me in the safety of our privileged cocoon, my teenage insecurities combined with the intense peer pressure of a school like that led to an event that I can now see God's fingerprints all over.

Aged fifteen, a bunch of us had managed to get our hands on some fake ID cards from an advert in the back of a lads mag. So the next Saturday night we trawled through the pubs and bars of our local high street, getting more and more out of control. The evening ended with the obligatory kebab at a shop down the road. We got chatting to the guy in front of us in the queue.

'You guys look pretty hammered – good night was it?!'

'You bet! We've been all over tonight.'

'You look a little young for that, though – you can't be eighteen, how old are you?'

'No, we're both fifteen! Check out these fake IDs – they get you in everywhere!'

Our new acquaintance took a look at our IDs. 'Well it's your unlucky night, I'm afraid, lads – I'm the manager of The Golden Lion, and you're now barred.'

Not the reply we'd expected.

When he wouldn't give our IDs back we began to get abusive. So he punched us both in the face. At that moment, a guy sitting in the corner got up and intervened. He split us up, managed to calm us down and got us to leave. And that was that.

For reasons I'm still unsure of, my mum had signed me up to the church youth camp the next week. I think she had seen that evangelical camps had helped my older sister Claire navigate the complexities of teenage life (or was at least more productive than smoking behind the bike sheds), and might do the same for me. I really don't know. And I honestly don't know why I went. But the next Saturday as I was getting on the bus, turning off my Nokia 5110 so none of my friends knew where I was (church camp was hardly earning of kudos at school), there was a guy there ticking people's names off a list. He looked up and we made eye contact – and I immediately went a deep shade of red. He was the same guy that had split me up from the scuffle with the manager of The Golden Lion the week before.

I didn't have a grid for it then, but subconsciously God had got my attention.

The next week was unlike any other in my life. I was an inse-cure teenager desperately looking for meaning and purpose, and found both that week as I heard about Jesus' life, death and resurrection. There was no emotional manipulation, no coercion, no strong-arming of repentance – just a simple presentation of the love of God in the person of Jesus. I had never actually read the Gospels before then, and I became captivated by the character of Jesus. He was strong and authoritative and yet gentle and kind. He did all the things he wasn't meant to do, broke all the rules, said some pretty heavy stuff, and he was scathing of the ritualistic religion that had bored me senseless at Westminster Abbey. That felt good, and it made me think he must understand where I was coming from. He seemed to be entirely different to how I had imagined and what I had associated with him. And here he was, apparently alive today and offering me the opportunity of a living relationship that would not only help me become a little more like him, but would enable me to share this amazing news with others. Before the week had even ended, as I heard the message of the talks and saw the congruence of the people around me, living and behaving in line with what they professed to believe, my heart made a shift. I had a whole bunch of issues, and a list of questions as long as my arm, but I prayed a prayer to Jesus and committed my life to following him.

I went back to school the next term and excitedly told everyone about my new-found faith. I just figured that when people heard what they were missing out on, they'd sign up too. I mean, why wouldn't you? But I wasn't remotely prepared for the reactions that followed. Jokes were made, insults were thrown, and some friendships were lost. Pivotally, though, I found one friend who also knew Jesus. Jack (who would later be the best man at my wedding) had also just come to faith, and when he heard I'd gone 'Jesus crazy' too, he suggested we hang out and pray together. Praying seemed to be something Jesus did a lot of, so it sounded like a good idea.

Jack and I met up once a week and prayed for our friends to come to know Jesus. It wasn't like wild all-night prayer or anything, just once a week together and five minutes alone after lunch. Soon our mate Dave signed up, along with a couple of others who had heard what we were doing, and gradually a small group of Jesus followers formed. We were all pretty unsure of what being a Christian meant and what we were meant to do, beyond being nice to people, not swearing or getting drunk, and praying for our unbelieving friends and family. So that's what we did. We would meet up in a classroom, play worship music on an old hi-fi, and pray together. It was bare-bones Christianity; we hadn't heard of the Holy Spirit, and nothing very dramatic ever happened. Except we were once accused of being a cult. That was it, really.

As I grew in faith, the next few years were immeasurably better than those previous ones had been. In my final year at school I was given the duty of being deputy head boy. The head boy was a friend called J. J. Waters. I figured I should begin praying for him to know Jesus, and a couple of years into university he too came to faith. Meanwhile, the more I experienced of life with Jesus, the hungrier I became to know and experience more. Now and then inspiring people would be invited to preach at church about mission trips aboard, and would tell exotic stories about people all across the world being changed through faith in Jesus. I couldn't think of anything more exciting, and decided I wanted to do the same – travel somewhere and tell people about Jesus. So during my gap year I went to an island in Indonesia called Sulawesi, and lived with students following the truth of the gospel in an entirely different context, some having come from backgrounds in the occult. It was all so new to me – we didn't have so much of that in south-east London, and it grew in me an evangelistic desire to travel the world and spread the gospel.

Upon my return home I had no idea what to study at university, so landed fairly arbitrarily on theology. It was while I was a student at Edinburgh University during the British summer of 2007 that God twisted my arm and got me on a plane to South Africa for the first time.

2: The Stirring

There are many more battles to be fought. It would be such
fun to be a part of them rather than just read of them. So go!
Write your own books. Go!
(Jackie Pullinger)[1]

Go.
(Jesus)

My friend Andy and I were studying theology together, and one morning after lectures he approached me and asked if I wanted to join his short-term mission trip to Cape Town. This caught me off-guard. Desperate not to be associated with anything to do with the Christian Union (I thought I was going through a 'cool' phase), I panicked and said an outright no. He then played the Christian trump card and asked, 'Will you at least pray about it?' According to the rules of good Christian etiquette, I now had no choice. So, that evening, I mumbled an uninterested prayer asking God to show me if he wanted me to go to South Africa. And then I forgot about it.

A week or so later I received a letter in the post. It was from the NHS confirming a date for a shoulder operation I had been waiting for. The date was right in the middle of the proposed mission trip, and having waited nine months for the letter, and with my shoulder dislocating with increasing regularity, I wasn't about to fanny around with arrangements. So I told Andy, God had answered my prayer with a clear 'No'.

'Why don't you phone them and just see if they'll change the date by a couple of weeks?'

'Well, I could do . . . But I think this is the answer God's given.'

'You'll never know for sure unless you phone them.'

Begrudgingly, I phoned the shoulder consultant's secretary.

'Hi, I'm phoning to see if it would be possible to change the date of my surgery.'

'I'm afraid that's not possible. Why do you ask?'

'I'm thinking about going on a trip.'

'What sort of trip?'

'A Christian mission trip.'

'Oh right. I'm a Christian too. Where are you thinking of going?'

'South Africa.'

'Ha, funny – I'm from South Africa. Whereabouts in South Africa are you heading?'

'We'd be staying in Cape Town, but volunteering in a prison in Paarl.'

'Wow – I'm from Paarl! I think God might want you to go on this trip – OK, what date should I change your operation to?'

So, just like that, God ambushed me to get me to go to South Africa.

I cried every day for six weeks

In July 2007 nine of us fresh-faced students in our late teens and early twenties arrived in Cape Town and were driven to the place we'd be staying for the next six weeks. I'd googled Cape Town and its surrounds (such was my ignorance – that comprised most of my pre-trip 'orientation'), so was looking forward to being somewhere near the ocean, or at least a place with some natural beauty. And having heard and read about the reconciliation process and transition to multiracial democracy just over a decade before, I was excited to taste a bit of the cultural diversity of the 'rainbow nation'.

I couldn't have been more wrong.

We arrived in Bonteheuwel, the community where we'd be staying for the duration of our trip. While there was a lively feel to the place, there was gang graffiti emblazoned on most of the vibracrete and corrugated iron walls, the streets were bare and badly paved and dimly lit, a mixture of sand and rubbish was blowing in the strong wind, and there was hardly a tree in sight. On top of that, I'd packed all the T-shirts, shorts and summer clothes I had – we were off to Africa, after all, so it would definitely be hot – but my Western blanket stereotyping of 'African weather' had failed to take into account that July in Cape Town is winter – wet, windy and cold.

Over the course of our time in Bonteheuwel, we got to know the youth group of the church in whose property we were staying. We were told story after story of family members and friends who were caught up in drug addiction and gangsterism. Looking back, we accidentally became unwitting (and completely useless) counsellors to these young local people, who offloaded years of trauma on to us. I'm not even sure I had ever experienced a trauma in my life at that stage. But this, combined with the fact that no one would let us walk a hundred yards down the road to buy a Coke from the bakery on the corner, 'because the *skollies* will mug you', didn't exactly cultivate a sense of feeling at home in our new surroundings.

There were three bedrooms in the house we were staying in. Clare and Becky, two of our team, had come across an organisation called 24–7 Prayer, and suggested that we have one bedroom for the guys, one for the girls, and the third room should be a prayer room. Dedicating a room to night and day prayer was a totally new concept to me. To be honest, it seemed a bit intense, probably unnecessary, and a questionable use of a third bedroom. But I figured that's just the sort of thing you do on short-term mission. As time wore on, however, we heard the gunshots fired between warring gangs fighting late into the night, and stared into the dull lifeless eyes of teenagers on heroin, as various items of ours went missing from the house, and after I was mugged by a bunch of crystal meth-addicted fourteen-year-olds, eyes popping out of their faces, brandishing kebab skewer-type weapons, I began to find myself drawn more and more to the protection and peace of our team prayer room. Night after night I would sit processing the events of the day – people I'd met, stories I'd heard, poverty I'd witnessed, violence I'd been threatened with, division and hopelessness that seemed endemic wherever we went; and I sat and wept.

As Søren Kierkegaard reminds us, we are never going to change the person of God through our prayers, but he seems to revel in using our prayers to change us. That was what happened to me as I sat in that prayer room. I'm not sure what we achieved in a practical sense in that six-week trip, but I now know that in those times we spent praying in what could have been a third bedroom, pressing into the presence of God, crying out for him to intervene in the lives of those we'd met, amid the chaos going on around us, he placed in me a significant deposit of love for those we had met and made friends with. I didn't know it then, but the memory of interceding for Cape Town during these late night-times would be the catalyst for me returning to the Cape Flats eighteen months later.

In the meantime, I returned to Edinburgh eager to share the stories and drama we'd witnessed in Bonteheuwel. While some friends did a good job of seeming vaguely interested, no one *really* cared. Or at least not as much as I felt they should. But I gradually began to realise it was unfair of me to expect others to share my emotions about my experiences. God had given me a unique window into a situation, Cape Town had left a deposit in my heart, and it was my responsibility (not anyone else's) to respond to what he had shown me.

Stepping out

He needs only enough faith to take a step. He needs only
enough faith to put his life on the line . . . he will not fall.
But he has to take the first step. If he does not take the step,
he will never know. (John Ortberg)[2]

People sometimes talk about the sacrifices that have to be made if one goes overseas to be a 'missionary' (I hate that word – it turns a very normal response to the gospel into something seemingly exceptional), but for me it kind of worked the other way round. If 'mission' work (I also dislike that term, but you get the point) did not quite save my faith, then it certainly made the gospel real to me in completely new ways – beautiful ways I'd never have imagined. It was a year after that trip to South Africa, I was fresh out of university and had a dormant longing within myself. I longed to travel the world, meet people different to me, share what I knew about Jesus, make some kind of difference in the lives of the poor, and try to play a part in changing the world.

I was going to a comfortable church in London. And I mean 'going to' – I was not part of the church community in any meaningful way, and nor was I ever particularly encouraged to be. My church attendance was oriented around listening to encouraging talks, watching flat screens, drinking smoothies and socialising with people who looked and spoke just like me. I had my weekly top-up of God and then went out and lived life like any other reasonably nice person. The church proved to be very popular – and the people who ran it and attended it were genuinely lovely. But I found it to lack any sense of sacrifice, grittiness or vulnerability. I suppose this is a difficulty of busy city-centre churches where people are commuting in from all over the place – it is exceptionally hard to cultivate deep, trusting relationships between people that would make them feel safe sharing what's really going on in their lives beyond the surface level, 'Yup, I'm well, thanks!' As a result, my church life resembled a pale reflection of secular London life and God became another product for me to use or consume as much or as little as I liked.

During the week I was working for CBBC. I was surrounded by dynamic, interesting people, and my entry-level job was a satisfying mix of easy and engaging. I found a certain kudos in working in television, and bought a pair of skinnyish jeans to look the part. I made friends with the presenters and producers, with the aim that they would all then circulate my show reel far and wide and I would become the next big thing in children's television. It wasn't a bad dream to have, though it gradually emerged that most of my junior colleagues had the same idea – I had no idea that so many people working in children's television did so in order to be the next *Blue Peter* presenter.

So my life consisted of assembling giant pogo sticks for the live broadcast show during the week, and attending a cozy, feel-good church service most Sunday evenings. It was quite an enjoyable way to live. I was giving some of my income away (nowhere near 10 per cent, but I wasn't accountable to anyone, so what did it matter), I was sharing the gospel with my colleagues and non-Jesus-following friends, I was going to church (in a fairly meaningless, me-centred way), doing a bit of armchair advocacy, and I wasn't sleeping around or doing drugs. In short, I was ticking the required boxes of a respectable middle-class evangelical guy in his early twenties living in London.

And yet, something in me just *knew* if I didn't do something – something that shifted my conception of Jesus from a white urban millennial to the Saviour of the world, whose main interest was not so much in making life easier for me but more about inspiring me to dream beyond my little world – I would end up missing the very purpose of my life, wasting my time climbing a career ladder I wasn't sure I wanted to be on in the first place, and seeking affirmation and significance through professional success that if it ever came I was worried would swallow me up, all the while enjoying a comforting high-five from a trendy London curate. My life had no problems whatsoever. I was nice. I had enough friends. I gave a bit to responsible Christian charities, sponsored a child in India, and got political after a couple of drinks. But ultimately I existed in a warm, fuzzy haze of self-centredness and passive indifference.

I began to look around and ask some questions. *Is it possible to love Jesus and not yearn to see the world changed? Is how I live congruent with what I believe to be true? What does a radical*

Christian life look like? I found myself determined to bust out of the safe and known, refusing to just shrug and become resigned to the 'way things are', in the face of desperate situations all around the world. It meant swimming against passive endorsement of the graduate-from-university-find-a-job-in-London-climb-a-corporate-ladder-you-never-wanted-to-be-on-and-maybe-get-a-ball-achingly-high-mortgage-if-you're-lucky-then-look-round-in-ten-years-and-ask-WTF-happened-to-my-dreams lifestyle.

Meanwhile, my obsession for South Africa was growing unabated. I would sit in front of my laptop until the early hours watching documentaries about apartheid and gangs and Desmond Tutu and the Truth and Reconciliation Commission. I began to long to be back in Bonteheuwel but this time actually staying long enough to learn the names of the young boys wanting to mug me, and having lunch together and hearing about how they ended up on heroin. I remember reading Francis Schaeffer's words for the first time, about how a Christian 'is the one whose imagination should fly beyond the stars',[3] and then allowing my own imagination to let rip, and literally fantasise about all sorts of different scenarios where addicts and gangsters were coming to know Jesus, and I'd even begin to dream about raising a family – somewhere less like Battersea and more like Bonteheuwel. I prayed a prayer of surrender to God and made a decision to return to Cape Town the following year. I was pretty confused about what even constituted a 'calling', but was adamant that my life should count for a cause, for people, beyond myself. I didn't have a plan, was woefully ignorant, and gloriously naive – but it was one of the best decisions I've ever made.

We've been duped

There is necessarily a clash between the self-oriented lifestyle the advertising industry would have us live, and the 'joy through surrender' spirit of following Jesus. The message the world sends us through globalised consumer culture is diametrically opposed to the message Jesus sends us in the Gospels.

The world screams 'me first!' Jesus teaches 'me third' – happily situated behind God and others.

The world pursues personal happiness as an end in itself on which every other decision we make should be based. Jesus teaches that happiness is a by-product rather than an end goal, and is a cheap imitation of the joy that emanates from a person who has discovered what it means to serve rather than be served.

The world looks for 'effective solutions' to global issues that don't require anything of those who benefit from the unjust systems that create the issues in the first place. An example of this is a shoe-for-shoe scheme. For every pair of shoes bought, a pair is given to a shoeless child in Africa. It's vaguely innovative. But it only works because it appeals to a consumerist mindset that looks for a loophole from sacrificial giving. (Besides – who honestly thinks shoelessness is two-thirds of the world's most pressing issues?) Jesus invites us, as a response to the mercy we've been shown by God, to address the issues of the world by offering our *very lives* as living sacrifices. He demands nothing less than our entire selves, poured out in extravagant worship. As a friend once put it, the poor don't need shoes; they need a place at our table for the next twenty years. In so doing, he exposes the fallacy that consumer-oriented charitable gestures will amount to anything lasting, and beckons us towards the hallowed ground of invading systems of injustice and unbelief by crawling on to the altar of surrender.

What does it cost?

I love the book of Acts in the Bible because it's a rollercoaster ride of high highs and low lows. I love reading about the explosion of the early church throughout the world – a movement of supernatural healings, signs and wonders, sacrifice and radical community, led by a ragtag bunch of 'unschooled, ordinary' men and women (Acts 4:13). Their only qualification – walking breath-smellingly close to Jesus for three years. When I read of walls shaking in prayer meetings, thousands coming to faith and becoming a meaningful part of a dynamic faith community, para- lytics being healed by a person's shadow and dead people being raised back to life, miraculous prison breaks, Holy Spirit-infused revolution that transforms entire cities – I desperately long to be part of a version of events similar to that today. Who *wouldn't* willingly give their life to that cause? I'm pretty convinced that not one of my not-yet-Christian friends would need to go on an Alpha course if the Church were living the apostolic lifestyle of the early followers of Jesus. But we're often not – so God bless Alpha!

There is, however, a but.

But . . .

. . . what about the low lows? What about the open criticism by the powers that be, what about being hounded out of town and forcibly removed from your home, what about being sent to jail for preaching hard truth and living under the threat of continual plots to kill you, what about being struck dead by the Spirit of God for lying and holding a proportion of your profit back (banking wouldn't be such a popular career choice), what about getting publicly flogged or killed by stoning, what about living under house arrest or being crucified upside down for holding on to your Christian convictions? This was the flipside to the miraculous and radical lives the early apostles lived.

I'm not saying my life is like a chapter from the book of Acts. In fact, I feel a holy discontent whenever I read it, such is the gap between my day-to-day reality and what those early heroines and heroes did. While I have witnessed some glorious miracles, and I love the Holy Spirit, I long for the gulf between my daily reality and that of the early church to grow ever smaller. And frankly, I have no idea what I would do if I was locked up or tortured for my faith.

Doing what, exactly?

After the CBBC job I moved back home to my dad's place in Sevenoaks and began to look ahead to moving to Cape Town. Over the previous year Andy and I had decided we would return together – brothers in Christ, on a journey for the 'more' of God. We planned to live through raising financial support from friends, churches and charitable trusts. It sounded reasonable enough, but neither of us had any experience in fundraising. Provision, or lack of it, became an imminent concern. We needed to raise about £1,000 a month for living expenses, plus airfares and various other bits and pieces such as visa costs and buying a car.

The thing is, there wasn't much of a plan to speak of. All we knew was that we wanted to return to Cape Town and have a go at living with drug addicts and gangsters so that we could tell them about Jesus and help them get free. However, if someone pressed me for more details – How are you going to get people off drugs? Who do you know in the community? What timescale do you foresee this happening in? – I began to get defensive. I had no idea. It really was as simple as that. I'm pretty sure many were imagining God would shut the door ahead of us pretty soon – that wouldn't have been unreasonable. But, ridiculous as it sounds, that didn't really concern us; we just figured we were stepping out of our comfort zone and that that was a good thing to do. We were so naive. But there was a kind of purity, an innocence, to the whole thing.

22.10.08

Our SA bank account has £450 in it. That's about half what I was conservatively expecting. Andy and I had a long chat about how we're both feeling – weak in faith, drained and anxious. BUT it's these spiritual valleys that make the mountain tops. It's in these valleys that the real preparation is being done – strengthening us, but, critically, not beyond what we can bear (1 Cor. 10:13). Faith is like a muscle, right? Exercising it makes it grow. And like a muscle

*fibre has to rip and weaken in order to form again stronger, so it
seems to be with faith. We are currently at the multiple reps bit
– feeling tired and strained. There's a sign on my bedroom door
quoting Hudson Taylor's famous words: 'I have found there are
three stages in every work of God. First it's impossible, then it's
difficult, then it's done.' I can't wait for the next stage!*

Between sporadic late-night bouts of learning Afrikaans from a
'teach yourself' CD set, we came up with various ideas for raising
funds for our trip. We set up an unoriginally named website –
projectcapetown.org – to keep friends and family in the loop, and
in a subconscious attempt to garner a shred of credibility from
having an 'online presence'. We even had T-shirts printed, with
our Project Cape Town logo emblazoned across the front. Little
did we know that selling these for £10 a pop (a huge profit,
considering the poor quality of both the T-shirt and the printing)
would backfire the first time anyone washed the thing, whereupon
it shrunk three sizes and the logo faded into illegibility.

We were completely sold out on a vision that seemed clear to
us, but impossible to explain. We had no one overseeing us who
could tell us that buying a house in a township and running it
as an informal drop-in centre was unthought-through and patronising (we hadn't even stopped to ask if anyone in such a
community would welcome such an initiative); nor that our plans
for the two of us to lead all the addicts in the Cape Flats to faith
in Jesus might come across as a little arrogant. I spent evening
after evening writing countless letters to trust funds and founda-
tions requesting financial support, blissfully unaware of the sheer
inaccuracy of the fantasy I was describing to them.

The funny thing is, it genuinely felt to me that this had never
been done before. I felt like a pioneer – the first young Englishman
to set up a website and move abroad to 'save Africa'. I was largely
unaware of the disastrous colonial legacy of my nation, and didn't
stop to consider the potential power dynamics at play in imposing
our plans on the marginalised communities of Cape Town. But

here's the thing: looking back, while I do feel slightly sheepish about how we went about things, the crowning achievement in it all was the simple fact that we did anything at all.

First, India

We were due to leave for Cape Town in January 2009. But before that, the process of refining continued. God had plans to raise my faith for the impossible, and as 2008 drew to a close he sent me to a village called Chiddambarram, in the Tamil Nadu region of India, to do it.

I had recently had an operation on my shoulder and was living on government benefits, at home with my dad, while I recovered. I was awful company to be around and was dealing with bitterness and disappointment, this being my fourth bone graft operation for multiple shoulder dislocations (I stopped counting after dislocation number twenty-eight). I spent days on end doing little else other than watching inane videos on YouTube and going through old 'Battle for the Premiership' football videos, impatiently waiting for the piece of bone that had been screwed on to the front of my shoulder socket to heal.

One afternoon, aimlessly scrolling through my Facebook news-feed (the only time, I think, that spending hours on Facebook has ever paid off), I came across a friend's post about an upcoming mission trip. The blurb promised that this trip to India would be characterised by 'signs and wonders and miraculous healings'. I'd not come across this type of language before – it all sounded vaguely magical. The post went on to say that the intrepid mission team was looking for a cameraman to film the trip and document the miracles that happened.

Beyond a vague interest in India, I don't know what moved me to apply. Practically speaking, I had never been a cameraman, and theologically speaking, I really wasn't used to seeing Jesus physically heal people. I couldn't remember ever hearing it preached about at the churches I'd attended in the UK – and even if I had, I'd never actually seen anyone healed. I'm not even sure I believed in it. Despite these apparent blots on my CV, I made contact with the ministry leader – a tall old Etonian called Dom Muir – and we got on like a house on fire. I managed to get my hands on a Sony PD-170 video camera, cast a cursory glance through the instruction manual, charged the spare batteries, bought some extra mini-DV tapes (this was pre-memory cards), spent my last pay cheque on a flight to Chennai, packed my bag and set off with the rest of the team. I went in faith – that my shoulder would be physically able to carry the camera, that God would heal some sick people, and that my meagre experience at CBBC, assembling giant pogo sticks for kids' game shows, had sufficiently equipped me to make a hard-hitting miracle film.

All means all

Once we arrived in India, there were scheduled teaching and prayer times as a team, where Dom taught on key verses and passages from Scripture, explaining that Jesus heals sick people. One such verse was Psalm 103:3. It states that God 'forgives all your sins'. I've never met a Christian who doesn't believe this statement – and, having come to faith in an ultra-conservative evangelical church, I was personally very convinced of my utter depravity – reminded as I was on a weekly basis that I was a filthy sinner in the hands of an angry God. However, the second half of the verse caused me problems: 'and heals all your diseases'. How had I missed the fact that I'd been brought up to believe the first clause, but completely missed the second? Why was it that I was utterly convinced of my own – and all of humanity's – sinfulness, and told anyone who would listen that God forgives 'all who truly repent', but recoiled at the idea of God healing 'all your diseases'?

Dom went on to point out that we often tend to pick and choose which parts of the Bible to believe – but that in the Gospels Jesus healed every single person with a sickness or physical ailment who came to him. He gave out neither slings nor crutches, nor did he ever counsel anyone with the idea that God had given them this sickness to teach them a lesson in perseverance or humility. In short, Jesus had a zero-tolerance policy on sickness, and because Christians have been given the same Holy Spirit and same commission, so should we. On the cross Jesus died to forgive all our sins *and* to heal all our diseases – as Isaiah 53:5 says, 'by his wounds we are healed'. I understood for the first time that forgiveness and healing are both part of the same deal.[4]

These two verses, along with story after story in the Gospels and the book of Acts, persuaded me that God is not just all for physical healing, but empowers and commissions his followers to release this healing power wherever they go, as a sign of his love for people. But it was only when I began to see some outrageous physical healings with my own eyes that I was truly convinced that these ancient truths were as potent today as ever before.

The mother and the baby

One evening towards the end of our trip, we held an evangelistic meeting on the sports field of a village outside Chiddambarram. During a time of ministry, a young mother brought her baby son to a few of us and asked if we would pray for him. The child looked like he was asleep but his mother explained through an interpreter that he had been born with no eyes. I instantly felt a creeping incredulity flood my body. This was truly being thrown in at the deep end. I began to sweat from fear and panic. She proceeded to tease open the child's eyelids. As she had said, there were indeed no eyes. What on earth did she expect us to do? I looked around to see if there was anyone we could call over; someone I could shift the responsibility on to. But all were busy praying for people. So we did all we knew how to do – we prayed.

As the mother used her thumb and forefinger to keep the baby boy's eyelids open, we placed our hands on her and the baby, and prayed, breaking off curses and commanding eyes to grow. Nothing happened. We continued this for a few minutes. Still nothing. We did this over and over, for what seemed like ages.

And then something remarkable began to unfold.

Dark, round spheres started to form in the baby's eye sockets, slowly growing, gradually getting bigger and bigger until eyeballs were formed. At the time I could hardly believe it, and even now I slightly struggle to believe it, as I write. But my journal entry written that evening is a personal reminder and proof, to me at least, that a miracle took place.

We saw many other healings over the course of the two-week trip. We also saw a woman delivered of multiple demonic spirits. As we commanded the spirits to leave in the name of Jesus, she shouted back in a deep voice, 'We are never going to leave her!' It was an intense experience to say the least, lasting most of the night, but eventually she was freed from demonic oppression. She later told the church leaders how she had been to see twelve different gurus, who had performed various occult rituals on her. That made sense then. The pastor had counted twelve different demons, manifesting in twelve different ways, leave her during the prayer-filled deliverance.

You're making me nervous

Many people I speak to (including a good number of Christians) are nervous about the claim that God heals sick people. The very assertion is assumed to be anti-intellectual and unscientific. I suppose it might seem a bit primitive to a 'post-Christian' culture, yet part of the Lord's Prayer, which many of us will have monotonously recited as children, states, 'your kingdom come, your will be done on earth as it is in heaven'. If heaven exists, and if there is, as one would imagine, no sickness in heaven, then isn't it fairly logical that a sign of God's kingdom coming on earth is that sickness is sometimes healed as we pray?

It is certainly true that the Western Church seems to witness comparatively little supernatural phenomena compared to its counterparts in the developing world. Might this be less due to (as I've heard patronisingly argued) the 'lack of education in those parts of the world', and more down to the fact that, certainly in Britain, the Church has sold out to a prevailing culture of methodological naturalism, while the liberal, 'anything goes' theology that appeases the non-churchgoing public, is slowly killing the convictions of those still in the Church? While pluralists deny the existence of any absolutist truth claims (except that one), fundamentalist atheists critique belief in Jesus as 'blind faith' while not seeing how much more 'blind faith' they require to hold to their own highly culturally conditioned views.

I returned from India full of faith and feeling ready to run a marathon. By Christmas 2008, our plans were gathering momentum to return to Cape Town in the new year. We had even received most of the money we needed for the year ahead. One grey mid-January afternoon, we waved goodbye to our families, who had come to Heathrow airport to see us off – and I couldn't help but notice how faded the Project Cape Town T-shirts my sisters were wearing had already become.

3: Knowing Your Place in Cape Town

Cape Town . . . is a city divided, both socially and spatially.
(Tony Roshan Samara)[1]

Three centuries of colonialism and four decades of apartheid
put in place one of the deepest and most structured
forms of inequality in the world.
(David A. McDonald)[2]

As long as the city is part of a socio-economic system
which reproduces . . . poverty, no amount of policing
will stop the ghetto brotherhoods.
(Don Pinnock)[3]

Moving to another city felt really grown up. We were met at the airport by friends who had recently moved to Cape Town, and spent the next couple of weeks trying to buy a car. Mainly, we lazed around in the sun. Once sunburn levels had hit 'beetroot', we set about looking for something to do, after it transpired that there wasn't a great fit between the organisation with which we'd originally planned to partner and us. Unsure what to do next, I checked my Facebook. A friend back in the UK had heard of an NGO 'doing good work' in various communities around Cape Town, and made an introduction for us. We looked up where The Warehouse was situated – it was a five-minute drive away. So we went to visit. It was as random and accidental as that.

The moment we walked in to The Warehouse[4] it felt like we had found home. It was noticeably racially diverse, unbelievably friendly, and people would drop whatever they were doing to answer any questions we asked. Every conversation we had that morning taught us a little more about the dialectic between the complexity and joy of living and ministering in Cape Town, but it was our final conversation with a guy called Jonathan Jansen, a so-called Cape coloured (a local term for those of mixed racial heritage), about the community he had lived in most of his life called Manenberg, that simultaneously seized our emotions and captured our imaginations. Manenberg was established by the architects of apartheid in the 1960s for the coloured people they had forcibly removed from homes in the newly declared 'whites only' city centre. In that sense, Manenberg's history and current social climate was a carbon copy of Bonteheuwel, where we had stayed while on short-term mission as students. We listened intently as Jonathan told us about the ministry he was involved in, set up by his friend Grant Stewart, befriending and discipling young men they dubbed 'high-risk youth'. The fact that Jonathan is a huge man with forearms the size of hams, and has a few teeth missing, added to the gravitas of what he said.

'The problem with much of the approaches to ministering to gangsters and addicts is that they set people up to fail. They are like factories producing backsliders.'

'What do you mean?' I replied, never having heard the term 'backslider'.

'The relapse rate is so high because we tend to make promises we just can't follow through on. Drug addicts don't need a weekly prayer group, they need someone to be with them twenty-four hours a day, praying, serving and discipling them or they'll slide back into addiction.'

'Mmmm,' I replied, beginning to catch his drift. But Jonathan had left the best line till the end.

'Jesus' disciples spent three years of their lives following him wherever he went, healing the sick and raising the dead – and yet one of them still "relapsed"!' Now I knew he was speaking our language – it was the perfect mic drop moment. Andy and I sat there in silence, taking it all in. We realised enough to know

that the conventional model of commuting into townships and
persuading poor, desperate people to 'raise their hands if they
wanted to follow Jesus' wasn't cutting it – nor was it conducive
to heartfelt faith. In fact, it was plain lazy and only served to
further compound the power dynamic we'd noticed everywhere
we went but which no one seemed to talk about, between rich
white people and poor people of colour. But while these entry-
level realisations were instructive up to a point, they generated
more questions in us – questions to which we didn't have any
answers beyond our rudimentary grasp of Cape Town's complex
social dynamics. We were hungry to learn more about Cape Town
and South Africa's segregated past, about the poverty and
inequality everywhere we looked, and about the resulting violent
crime pandemic. So we arranged a time to accompany Jonathan
to Manenberg, a place that up to then we had only ever been
warned against visiting.

'Wat Maak Jy Hieso?'

The day came to go to Manenberg, and we piled into The
Warehouse's beaten-up yellow Fiat Uno with Jonathan behind the
wheel. I had no idea how long it would take to get there, and
was surprised when we arrived in no time at all – it was only
7 kilometres down the road. As we drove through the streets and
along the narrow alleys of Manenberg I sensed something slightly
peculiar going on inside me – what I can only describe as a shift
in my internal consciousness. I began to feel a battle between
intense hope and extreme hopelessness welling up inside me in
equal measure. It was like I was coming alive with excitement
and dying of despair in the same breath. I simultaneously felt
elated and depressed. So conflicted and puzzling was this experience that it was as if my heart was beating alternately 'hope' then
'hopeless', 'hope', 'hopeless', 'hope', 'hopeless', over and over.

Rubbish was strewn everywhere we looked, blowing in the
wind and flapping against the galvanised steel fences running

along the perimeter of the soccer field. The walls had graffiti emblazoned across them, but it was too early for me to recognise the distinguishing features of different gang tags. There seemed a disproportionate amount of people walking the streets mid-afternoon during the week (I would later learn of the unemployment statistics), each street seemed to lead to a different gang's territory (which Jonathan pointed out as we went) and everyone we spoke to was friendly and welcoming, if a little surprised to see us. I don't know how I didn't think that the sight of two white guys cruising around with their heads hanging out of the car window smiling at everyone they saw and giving them a thumbs-up, might have looked a bit strange. The fact is, white South Africans tend not to go to Manenberg. But then, equally, we had no idea that a thumbs-up was the sign for a notorious prison gang called the 26s. I'm sure that was one of many cringey social clangers we made that afternoon.

Visiting Manenberg hit me hard. So hard, in fact, that when I got home I just cried, like a toddler experiencing a new emotion for the first time. I knew I was feeling something fairly over-whelming, but didn't have the language to process or communicate beyond silent sobs. What I did recognise, however, was the vague feeling of familiarity, that I'd experienced this same thing a couple of years before in Bonteheuwel. And I felt that same passion for the forgotten communities of Cape Town's margins begin to rise up in me.

Most people we'd met on the streets of Manenberg that day had asked, *'Wat maak jy hieso?'*, 'What are you doing here?' While I couldn't say for sure, various answers to that question were now starting to form in my mind.

Here's the thing

When I think back to that first afternoon in Manenberg, there are a whole lot of local social dynamics I wish I had known more about. And so, as a context for the stories in the following chapters, I've included some history that goes some way to explaining why Cape Town today is as it is. To better understand the mindset of the marginalised in Cape Town, in particular gangsters and drug addicts (something surprisingly few Capetonians seem prepared to do), one needs to grapple with the various factors that led to the city looking like it does today. It is imperative that the 'haves' change the lens through which we look, in order to see things through the lens of the 'have nots'.

Those of us who enjoy the benefits of an unequal society – whether in Cape Town, London, Rio de Janeiro, Hong Kong or anywhere else – need to wake up to the awkwardness of some of the numbers. In Cape Town, the fifteen police stations with the lowest number of reported murders have on average 1 police officer for every 232 people, compared to the fifteen stations with the highest number of murders averaging 1 police officer for every 1,153 people.[5] South Africa's Gini coefficient, a measure of economic inequality, is consistently over 0.6 – among the highest in the world. The injustice of these inequalities serves to engrain anger in the 'have nots', which creates fear in the 'haves', and thus cycles of racism and violent crime are perpetuated.

Such statistics *should* cause us to feel incredibly uncomfortable. As Bob Ekblad puts it so wisely,

> If we are to see God's kingdom come and will be done, on earth as it is in heaven, we must first recognise that what we mostly experience here on earth is not heaven, and may actually feel closer to hell for some. This recognition is more difficult for those vested with the benefits of this world: credit, capital, economic and social success, acceptance, family support, racial profile, and citizenship that offer special entitlements or any sort of privileged status.[6]

The stark dividing lines that continue to segregate Capetonians from each other did not arise by accident, but through centuries of colonialist-led white supremacy and decades of state-ordained apartheid. *Apartheid* is Afrikaans for 'separateness' – and while the law of apartheid was dismantled in 1994, the spirit behind it lives on as strong as ever in Cape Town today.

District Six

Place of origin – home – has become an essential element of self-definition for Coloured people . . . if there has been any place, any space that Coloured people have looked upon as 'our territory', it is – or was – District Six. (John Western)[7]

Marc Augé, a French anthropologist known for his work on place and 'non-place', lists some foundational characteristics of place. Place, he suggests, is a particular locale marked by fondness and familiarity, and is significant in that it engages with our identity, our relationships and our history. On the other hand, 'non-place' is marked by transition, liminality and lack of meaning. The basic difference between the two is that 'place' is cohesive and has a soul, whereas 'non-place' has neither. One of the most famous examples of destruction wreaked by the apartheid regime, and a callous destruction of a particular community, was the forced removal of those living in an area called District Six. Located at the foot of Table Mountain, and established in the early nineteenth century, District Six was a racially diverse community comprising former slaves, merchants, European artisans and Malays brought to South Africa by the Dutch East India Company. Despite basic housing conditions and overcrowding, life was vibrant and exciting. As one journalist wrote in 1966,

There are tailors by the score, herbalists, butchers, grocers, tattoo-artists, cinemas, bars, hotels, a public bath-house, rows of quaint little houses with names like 'Buzz Off' and 'Wy Wurry' and there is a magnificent range of spice smells from the curry shops. The vitality and variety in the place seem endless and the good-humour

of the people inexhaustible. Anything could happen and everyone
in the end would laugh about it.[8]

The narrow racism of the South African apartheid state could not
comprehend this *joie de vivre* and cultural diversity, and so in
1966 it was announced that District Six would be demolished.
Between 1968 and 1982, as the Group Areas Act was enforced,
over 60,000 people of colour witnessed the bulldozing of their
homes and businesses as the land was declared a 'whites only'
area.

In the public transcript used to justify racial domination, the
apartheid regime cast the vision for segregation as far back as
1938: 'It is possible to achieve this radical reorganisation by drastic
methods only, by a fresh start on cleared ground . . . Through
surgery we must create order, through organisation we must make
manifest the spirit of a new age.'[9]

A number of reasons were given for the demolition of District
Six. It was described as an area of urban decay, the demolishing
of which would bring forth a new start for working-class coloured
people. Criminal activity allegedly stemming from the interaction
of different races was also used as rationale to justify the establishing of mono-racial Cape Flats townships. It was decided that
segregation, rather than better policing, was a more effective way
of keeping the peace. Yet it is now widely agreed that apartheid-era
government projections of life in District Six were wildly inaccurate, motivated as they were by the prospect of grabbing valuable
land at the foot of Table Mountain, close to the city centre.

Matchbox conglomerates

The nostalgic reconstruction of District Six by past residents
contrasts sharply with official statements. Stories of neighbours
sharing food, taking in the vulnerable and raising each other's
children epitomise the neighbourliness and unguarded familiarity
that encapsulated, in many ways, an alternative society at odds

with the rest of apartheid South Africa. Richard Rive, a coloured author and resident of District Six, compared the soul of the community to the 'matchbox' existence of the Cape Flats, and in so doing highlighted the journey from place to 'non-place' that many were made to embark on. They were

> . . . forced to move to small matchbox houses in large matchbox townships which with brutal and tactless irony were given names by the authorities such as Hanover Park and Lavender Hill to remind us of the past they had taken away from us. There was one essential difference between the old places and the new ones. District Six had a soul . . . The new matchbox conglomerates on the desolate Cape Flats had no soul.[10]

Past trauma, on a community-wide scale, plays out in contemporary social dysfunction. Such calculated dismantling of a people's corporate identity was always going to have disastrous knock-on effects. Individual families were removed one by one and deliberately placed in different communities to their neighbours – some might be relocated to Bonteheuwel, others to Manenberg, for example – so that the social web of District Six was methodically and systematically broken down. Powerlessness and panic prevailed in these new 'matchbox conglomerates', where a sense of community, solidarity, safety, collective protection of children, friendships and local traditions had been comprehensively ripped apart. Close-knit neighbourliness was replaced by isolation, as individual families stayed inside their preassigned two-bed units no longer able to call on networks of friends in the wider community.

Fear of the unknown swept over people and was a major factor contributing to 'psychological difficulties and skewed "coping" behaviour'.[11] The fallout of this was increased divorce rates and family breakdown. At the same time, a coloured 'baby boom' occurred between 1961 and 1965 ('the relation between crisis and a high level of childbirth is well-known'): it has been argued that this increase in young people, who by 1980 had reached the ages of fifteen to nineteen, 'the core age of street gangs', and were being raised in a context of social dislocation, contributed significantly to the growth of criminal activity in the Cape Flats.[12]

In depressingly inevitable opposition to the loss of place experienced through forced removals, gangs sprung up all over the coloured Cape Flats, establishing and guarding their 'turf'. The older generation had been bulldozed and relocated, and it was the young gangsters' felt responsibility to reclaim ownership of the land – through aggressively claiming territory as their own. And so we see 'it is through staking out a geographical area that a gang becomes . . . rooted in the community. In this "magical" way the brotherhoods [gangs] of Cape Town express a territorial ownership lost by the relocated parent culture – retrieving thereby the solidarities of the traditional neighbourhood destroyed by Group Areas.'[13] When you dig just a little into the history of Cape Town's coloured ghettoes, located today all around the outskirts of Cape Town, it's not hard to see that the emergence of violent gangs was really quite predictable. Yet, far from addressing the issue, Cape Town's current political and economic systems continue to recreate it.

Dividing them from us: neoliberalism and globalism

A significant driver in these inequality-exacerbating systems is the notion of the 'world city'. The term became popular in the 1980s as technology advanced and communication and travel became easier. External links *between* cities were seen to be as crucial as internal dynamics *within* a city itself. Post 1994, when South Africa transitioned out of apartheid and into Nelson Mandela's rainbow nation democracy, this put pressure on Cape Town to make a name for itself internationally to fuel economic growth. In order to become more prosperous, the decision was made to focus on money-oriented networks abroad (foreign investment, the tourism industry, corporate deals etc.), rather than try and help out of poverty those who had been excluded by apartheid. The consequence is an 'urban capitalist crisis . . . [as a result of] serving the interests of a transnational elite'.[14] The words of the prophet Ezekiel are an equally ominous commentary: 'Now this was the sin of your sister Sodom: She and her daughters were arrogant, overfed and unconcerned; they did not help the poor and needy' (16:49).

And so today, power is fuelled by the pursuit of economic gain rather than (as it was during apartheid) racial discrimination. Globalism sacrifices a sense of local community, place and belonging on the altar of connection, reach and economic development. This feeds the growing inequality between rich and poor that characterises Cape Town. And it thus contributes to the perpetuation of segregation and isolation between races and socio-economic groups – aping the very effects of apartheid. The irony of this whole state of affairs is heartbreaking.

Should this really surprise us? It's a fairly obvious point that if those in power choose financial prosperity at the expense of the poor, the result will be high crime, deeply engrained anger and glaring inequality. As long as those who live in townships and apartheid-spawned ghettoes are seen as the problems of the present, rather than the victims of the past, Cape Town's social schizophrenia will only increase.

A whole list of historical factors – colonialism, apartheid, forced removals, the construction of ghettoes miles out of town, the deliberate decimation of local neighbourliness, a history of violent and unaccountable policing, marginalisation of people of colour – combine with present-day systems that proliferate inequality and racism. This rotten picture has provided, and continues to provide, a fertile environment for the cultivation of gang life and drug addiction throughout the forgotten communities of the Cape Flats. One of the results of this is that Cape Town regularly features in the top ten of the world's most dangerous cities, with a murder rate of over sixty per 100,000. This was a near certainty to happen. As Kofi Annan said prophetically back in 2003, 'we should have

learned by now that a world of glaring inequality . . . where
millions of people endure brutal oppression and extreme misery
– is never going to be a fully safe world, even for its most privileged inhabitants'.[15]

'Ons loop en bid'

None of this was even remotely on our radar when Andy and I
were deciding to join Jonathan and Grant in their work in
Manenberg. Beyond filling up on local knowledge about Cape
Town, our hearts' desire hadn't changed. In fact, more than ever
now, we wanted to be part of a ministry that reached out to
gangsters and drug addicts and led them to freedom and faith in
Jesus.

That first year in Cape Town flew by. We spent most of it
prayer walking around Manenberg, and Jonathan taught us a
standard reply to the question 'Wat maak jy hieso?' It was simply,
'Ons loop en bid' – we're walking and praying. Twice a week from
April to December we joined with Jonathan, Grant and sometimes
visitors, in walking the streets and *gangetjies* of our new chosen
place. In that first year alone it's likely we spent well over a
hundred hours praying in and around Manenberg.

There are plenty of reasons for praying with your eyes open
and legs moving – some of these are specific to context, but you'll
get the point. Prayer walking enables you to pray in response to
what you see in front of you, and prophetically imagine how it
could look if your prayer were answered; gather prayer requests
from people you meet and talk to along the way, and check in
with them the next time you go by; deliberately walk along the
edge of contested gang territories carrying the presence of the
Prince of Peace; pray for those who come up to you then and
there, heal the sick and proclaim the gospel to whoever is looking
on (we once saw Jesus heal a man on crutches who then made a
faith commitment right there, through tears); observe and learn
local rhythms and ways of life – get to know the different school

uniforms and where they're located, bin day on a Thursday, the Muslim call to prayer on a Friday, and so on; make prophetic declarations as you go; bless local business (one lady who joined us weekly would often buy entire boxes of *naartjies* from the fruit seller and hand them out to children as we went); try praying in Afrikaans as you hear words being shouted across the street; subtly lean on walls of gang leaders' houses and pray for them to meet Jesus; the list goes on!

Prayer walking for nine months enabled us to learn the personality of a community that would otherwise have remained hostile and inaccessible to us. It was also helpful in that people now recognised us. Sure, we may have still been called 'whitey and whitey' (to our faces – I have no idea what we were called behind our backs!), but we felt a sense of belonging and mutual acceptance. Time flew by, and before we knew it, big changes were on the cards.

4: A New Home

Manenberg?! No man, those people aren't right.
(Middle-class coloured friend)

*Listen, what you're trying to do is noble, but those people
will never change, they'll just take advantage of you. Look,
you don't understand them like we do. There's a reason
people don't go into those areas.*
(White Capetonian I met through a friend)

You mustn't go there – it's too dangerous, the people are evil.
(Black lady I met in a taxi)

When Andy told me he was going to leave South Africa at the
end of 2009 and return to Scotland to marry Debbie, his fiancée,
I wasn't completely surprised. True love got the better of him,
and off he went. I was left with the question of what to do now
my wingman had left. I began to imagine what it would be like
to move in to Manenberg, having put in the legwork around the
community and now gripped by the vision of my now good friends
Grant and Jonathan – of sparking a redemptive brotherhood as a
generative contradiction to gangsterism. Grant first had the idea
of a residential intervention for high-risk youth in Manenberg
back in 2004 while the ministry, called Fusion, was in its early
days. He would pray at the Salvation Army base, looking out on
the streets of Hard Livings' gang territory. He had been reading
Pete Greig's *Red Moon Rising* and stories coming from the 24–7
Prayer movement, largely based around the transformative presence of worship and intercession in specific places. As he looked
out across Manenberg, he saw many church buildings, but few

alive, vibrant, thriving prayer communities that were outward in focus and inclusive in culture. And this led him to dream of the emergence of a 'new monasticism' within a prophetic community of brothers and sisters whose lives had previously been spent in the drug dens, gang headquarters and backyard shacks, and on street corners. This community would be a visible, tangible redemption of the gangs. Rites of passage would be observed, breakthroughs would be celebrated, intercession would be offered unceasingly and, as in Acts 2:47, 'the Lord [would add] to their number daily those who were being saved'.

I imagined being based in a house in the centre of Manenberg, full to the brim with gangsters and drug addicts encountering Jesus, being filled with the Holy Spirit, getting delivered of addiction, publicly severing allegiance to the gang, sharing testimonies with all their old gang friends and establishing a culture of discipleship. Nothing excited me more than that vision, it totally consumed my imagination day after day and it seemed so perfectly reasonable in my mind.

Things had been developing promisingly. By the end of 2009, we had seen four young men come out of drugs, gangs, violence and crime. Each had encountered Jesus and made a commitment to follow him. One, previously a Muslim, changed his name to a Christian name. Through prayer and daily support, he gave up his R2,000-a-week drug habit and walked away from the Americans gang for whom he had been a 'gunman' (a designated assassin). Another, after being baptised in the Spirit, gave up heroin painlessly – confirming our conviction that addiction, at its root, is more of a spiritual issue than a biological one, and so needs a spiritual solution that medication can't provide. State-sponsored methadone clinics aimed to keep addicts addicted in a way that doesn't harm society are more about crime reduction than recovery from addiction. The reason for this, as Theodore Dalrymple rightly points out, is that it's easier 'to give people a dose of medicine than to give them a reason for living'.[1] Tobias Jones describes recovery from addiction as the repairing of one's spirit: 'It's not

just about repairing a brain, or a vein, but about repairing relationships and the spirit . . . there's no textbook about how to
repair the spirit.'² Another dramatically received the gift of
speaking in tongues in the midday heat of a Cape Town summer.
As we stood around him in a shack that used to be a drug den,
praying and dripping with sweat, he suddenly crumpled to the
floor and began crying and sobbing in a heavenly language. For
at least six months after that he could not pray in tongues without
weeping uncontrollably – an ongoing deliverance, I wonder, of
some of the intense trauma he had witnessed growing up without
a father, and in a house of abusive alcoholics.

But then as time went on we began to feel the pressure of
looking after these newborn babies with little to offer them but
friendship and prayer. And they began to fall away one by one.

It was witnessing this and subsequent part breakthroughs and
relapses, in the middle of much conversation with Grant and
Jonathan, that showed me how desperately unlikely it would be
to see the community-level transformation we were believing for,
without somehow becoming the answers to our own prayers and
giving our *whole* lives to serving these broken young people. A
daily 9-to-5 schedule of activities and prayer would go so far, but
as time went on we continued to hit the same ceiling over and
over again. It was while attending a conference at St Stephen's
Society, Jackie Pullinger's ministry in Hong Kong, that God began
to speak to us about drug addicts' need for 're-parenting', and we
saw that what was most needed was a home in which to base
the growing family.

Searching for a home

A year of living in South Africa had made me increasingly aware
of the sheer number of foreigners volunteering for NGOs – as I
was. While not necessarily a bad thing, it did strike me as strange
that everyone I met who had 'a heart for . . . . . (insert as appropriate) street kids, the poor, AIDS orphans, Muslims, gangsters,

the homeless, drug addicts', et cetera, or who wanted to work in the townships, was doing so as a commuter from the affluent suburbs. This jarred with me. It seemed that to try to engage in this type of work long term, at arm's length, would be to affirm the single-story narrative of apartheid in addition to perpetuating cycles of dependency, and would somehow imply that Manenberg was too toxic an environment for good Christians to live in. As far as I was concerned, it was 'all in or nothing' – move into Manenberg or go back to England. I was a well-meaning, naive British do-gooder with next to no knowledge of Afrikaans, an ignorant, rose-tinted view of what went on in Manenberg behind closed doors or after dark, embarrassingly neocolonial views, patronisingly paternalistic, subconsciously racist, and with only a handful of friends in the community. That said, I did know enough to realise that blogging about my office hours experience in Manenberg from the comfort of a suburban living room wasn't going to serve anyone other than myself. The quickest way I could change this was to move in, deepen friendships and learn the language. Had I known a fraction of how hard it would be, I would never have done it. Thankfully, I was only partially aware of my naivety. Once I'd made up my mind, there was no going back.

I had met Deon and Shamiela through church circles and prayer walking. They had heard of a house that had just been put on the market, perfectly located in the middle of Hard Livings' gang territory, opposite a prolific and surprisingly friendly heroin dealer. The one condition I gave God when I decided to move in was that I didn't want to be on the peripheries of the community, but in the thick of the gangs, violence and drugs, to pre-emptively avoid being accused of not living in the 'real' Manenberg. I started praying for the house, and made an offer the moment it went on the market, having received a thumbs-up from Jonathan and Grant, my 'overseers' for all things Manenberg.

I was immediately out of my depth.

The bank asked if I required a mortgage – I hadn't thought

about that, but said no, I would buy it in cash. Sensing what must have been a distinct lack of conviction in my voice, the person on the other end of the phone asked if I actually had any money. I said I didn't, but that God had spoken clearly to me about buying that specific house, so there was no need to worry. The voice told me banks don't work like that. I told them I understood.

So I went back to God. Foolish as it may sound, I sensed him say that he had already given the house to me, and that I should stop praying for it and start claiming it through prayer. Suspicious of what seemed to be a divine endorsement of 'name it and claim it' prosperity theology, but devoid of any better ideas, I proceeded to claim the house as my own, and was stunned when the bank let me make an offer. There was one condition: that I pay the full amount within thirty days from the time the executor agreed on the offer. I needed R200,000 (at the time, roughly £20,000), and had £0, but offered what I figured was the most logical amount, the price listed on the website. Then three higher offers came in. Rather than praying against them, I asked God to give them better houses for their money. To this day, I'm not sure what happened, but each of the other offers was eventually withdrawn. Then a truly remarkable thing happened.

Money began to come in.

I had sent one email, to everyone in my email address list, explaining that I planned to buy a house in Manenberg, and presumptuously putting some bank details at the bottom. Money was given by an assorted bunch of wonderful people, some of whom I know, some of whom I'd never met. One friend of a friend (whom I'd never met) gave a generous donation, having read my email and sensed God say she should give the money she had been saving up for a knee operation to the buying of the house in Manenberg. I couldn't believe it – my offer was accepted. Initial excitement was followed by deep fear as I still hadn't got the full amount, and I now only had thirty days. I began to entertain the thought that I'd heard God wrong. I prayed from doubt and fear, and petulantly told God that if the remainder hadn't come in by the next Monday afternoon, I'd assume I had acted impulsively and it wasn't what he wanted.

Monday came. I only got one email that day.

A friend emailed to offer a substantial amount of money that took me R200 (just under £20 at the time) above the house value and the attorney's fees. That was that, then – now I had to do it.

So in July 2009 I sensed a call towards moving into one of Cape Town's most violent communities (it seems God is less interested in our comfort than we are), and I said yes. In the ten months that followed he provided R208,200 in answer to a prayer I'd prayed for provision to buy a house I had my eye on. With a fluctuating exchange rate plus a couple of bank charges, it would have been humanly impossible to have landed so accurately. I forgot about the R200. But on the day of transfer, when I moved in, I turned on the lights and . . . nothing happened. I discovered the copper wiring had been stripped by addicts to sell for scrap. A few hours later, Jonathan turned up at the house. Now Jonathan is your quintessential jack of all trades – there's no DIY or computer maintenance, no car repairs or anything-to-do-with-your-hands job that he cannot do. So when he saw my predicament, he shrugged and said, 'Just give me R200 to buy some wiring and I'll rewire your house for you.' The next evening, sitting in my house with the lights on, the penny finally dropped. I realised that God had provided exactly the amount I needed to buy a house, have it transferred to my name, *and* rewire the electrics – R208,200. It was at that moment that I gave up my right to ever doubt his supernatural provision again. It was utterly humbling to believe that the creator of the universe had a vested interest, nay fascination with my life – to the extent that he was more committed to my plans for living in Manenberg than I was.

I learnt many lessons that day. Possibly the most significant was the realisation that when God calls you to step out in faith, he allows for a period of trial and testing (there was an eight-month wait, after telling the bank I wanted to buy but had no money), to give you the tools and develop in you the very character you will need once his promise comes to fruition.

Process precedes the promise.

Developing a heart of thankfulness and perseverance as you navigate this process is the very thing that brings you into the reality of the promise. '[Fix] [y]our eyes on Jesus, the pioneer and perfecter of our faith. For the joy that was set before him he endured the cross' (Hebrews 12:2). If we know God's goodness, we will anticipate good things. Proverbs 10:28 says, 'The prospect of the righteous is joy'. This joy generates a power to endure whatever comes our way in the meantime.

Despite this wonderful miracle, moving in was not without its complications. One afternoon, a week before I was to take occupancy, I received a phone call from a neighbour whom I'd only recently met. She told me someone had started a fire in my house the night before and I should come quickly. When I arrived, there was a group of concerned neighbours outside, all offering different theories on what had happened. I managed to get in and scanned the ground floor, but could see nothing resembling fire damage. Upstairs, it was immediately obvious where the fire had been. One of the bedroom doors had been badly charred from the inside. Someone had obviously broken into the house through the bedroom window only to find we'd locked all the bedroom doors, so proceeded to try and burn the door down. They must have either given up or got disturbed midway through – the door was only half burnt through. Either way, it wasn't the most encouraging sign, so early on.

The next week, 2 May 2010, I moved in. Despite the previous week's incident, I was feeling upbeat and cheerful. I was finally doing what I'd caught a vision for back in Bonteheuwel three years before, and it felt exhilarating. Moving furniture in, introducing myself to the neighbours, shaking people's hands, waving at bemused onlookers, laughing with the children – it was a busy afternoon. Yet from the start, I clocked the feel-good vibes generated by being the 'only whitey in the village'. There seemed to be preferential treatment shown to me because of my colour. Honestly, it felt great. And while the majority of those I met in the first few weeks were genuinely welcoming and friendly, it gradually emerged that something else seemed to be going on. I had never been treated with such unreasonable respect. It began to dawn on me that it stemmed from a distressingly ingrained mindset in Manenberg, passed down from the days of apartheid, that white people were to be held in higher esteem merely due to the colour of their skin. I had done absolutely nothing to warrant it, no one really knew me, but it manifested in multiple ways.

I started noticing that whenever anyone in Manenberg began a sentence with 'We coloured people . . .', the following statement would always be negative or condemnatory. I was informed by various neighbours and new acquaintances that 'we coloured people' don't look after other people's possessions, love to gossip and get drunk, have loose sexual morals, brought the gang situation upon themselves, have a confused racial identity, are inherently violent, unintelligent, crafty and dishonest. But at least 'we coloured people' weren't black – 'those people' were the worst. Where did such patently untrue generalisations come from?

History repeated

Caricatures of coloured people abound in South Africa. One of the fundamental factors contributing to this is that they have often been defined negatively – by that which they are *not*. During apartheid, coloured people were seen as '*not only* not white, but *less than white*; *not only* not black, but *better than black* . . . One often feels one has to choose between blackness and whiteness, which means the denial of some part of oneself.'[3] The issue with apartheid racial classification, and attempts to pin down what 'coloured' meant, is that it was always done by those in power. White people held the power of definition for most of the twentieth century in South Africa, and to be classified as 'coloured'

meant a double negative – not white enough, not black enough
– a unique disempowerment. The Wilcocks Commission of
Inquiry into the Cape Coloured people, established in 1937, found
great difficulty in categorising coloured people, and so divided
them into three classes: 'farmworkers/household servants, the
relatively well-to-do and educated, and the "skolly boys" (often
habitually armed with knives or razor blades)'. The word *skollie*
has been suggested to come from an Old Dutch term *scholtje*,
referring to seagulls that scavenged waste from ships. It could be
argued that this ugly apartheid term has become internalised
particularly by young men in coloured townships, who feel the
social isolation of being seen as an urban menace.

During the apartheid years many coloured people feared being
relegated to the same category as black people, and this acted as
due incentive to conform to the status quo. However, conformity
was a double-edged sword, as 'the claim to kinship with whites . . .
also meant accepting racial hybridity as an integral part of their
being'.[4] This is encapsulated by the poetry of James Matthews, a
coloured author who wrote during apartheid as part of the Black
Consciousness movement. His statement, 'our pain has linked us
from Manenberg to Soweto',[5] emphasises a unity of purpose and
identity across racial lines between Manenberg, a coloured ghetto,
and Soweto, a black township. There are layers of complexity that
come out in other statements he made, testifying to the unique
coloured experience: 'I can't truthfully say that my soul is one
with that of Africa. There is a gulf between me and the [African] . . .
Culturally my outlook is most certainly European . . . Racially,
it's the African who pushes me aside, labeling me as Ama-Bushman.'[6]
Further adding to the difficulty of the coloured experience during
apartheid is the fact that many lighter-skinned coloured people
applied to be reclassified as white (termed 'pass-whites'), as white
people were afforded greater employment opportunities and
salary.

It is not at all straightforward, and I have no insight beyond
the generally agreed upon discourse that during apartheid the

white supremacists favoured coloured people above black people, creating a widespread sense of superiority in coloured communities towards their black counterparts. This meant the coloured experience was simultaneously shaped both by oppression and by complicity with this oppression in aligning with apartheid categories that put black Africans at the bottom of the pile. It is hardly surprising that today there is a prevailing self-condemnation within poorer coloured communities. It represents a collective agreement with the legacy of a white supremacist hangover, and continues to keep whole swathes of Cape Town bound.

5: Early Impressions

---

*Do not despise these small beginnings, for the LORD rejoices
to see the work begin.*
(Zechariah 4:10, NLT)

*The situation in which young people find themselves in many areas of
the Cape Flats is – by any gauge of human rights – intolerable.*
(Don Pinnock)[1]

Life is not easy for children growing up in Manenberg. Beyond
the more 'normal' aspects of a community struggling with poverty
– such as the continual battle of parents to put food on the table
and money in the electricity meter – there are the additional factors
of a widespread gang presence and the availability of all sorts of
hard drugs. Positive role models are a rarity, and there is a pandemic
of fatherlessness. Combined with the fact that the Western Cape
has some of the highest levels of foetal alcohol syndrome in the
world, there's simply no escaping that the odds are stacked against
a child in Manenberg finishing school and finding employment.

Dowayne grew up in a particularly intense corner of Manenberg,
in the middle of Hard Livings' gang turf. However, a family
member had been involved with another gang – so while the
majority of Dowayne's neighbours were affiliated with the Hard
Livings, he was expected to carry on the generational ties to the
rival gang. It could be said, to borrow the phrase from Isaiah,
that from birth Dowayne was 'doomed to misfortune' (Is. 65:23).

As a teenager seeking an identity and a place in the world but
with no one to guide him, Dowayne began to skip school and fall
in with the wrong crowd. Smoking marijuana was followed by
dabbling with Mandrax (a tranquiliser with psychotic side effects)

and then, at age thirteen, *tik* (crystal meth). *Tik* is a vicious master, and it's impossible to stay away for long – it can be made easily at home, and costs as little as R20 (between £1 and £2) a hit. Soon his dabbling became a fully fledged addiction, and he would stay up all night gambling and stealing to fuel his habit. His addiction developed to such an extent that he had to smoke increasing amounts of *tik* just to reach anywhere near the high he'd enjoyed when he'd started. The fact was, a few years later, *tik* no longer offered him the euphoric high it had at first. So, aged seventeen, Dowayne graduated to *unga* – street heroin. And that was when the wheels really came off.

Regular signs of functionality such as maintaining personal hygiene or going to school became an irrelevance in the daily grind of *skarrelling*, stealing and stabbing for the next fix. Dowayne's mother, weary from his incessant lying, locked him out of the house to protect the few possessions she had left from being stolen and sold for drugs – the sad irony that the very substance destroying her son was being sold outside her front door seemed lost on her. His entire family ostracised him, and any last semblance of a functional life was handed over to the demon of *unga*.

I first met Dowayne a couple of weeks after my initial visit to Manenberg. He was nineteen. His eyes were dull and lifeless, his body gaunt, his clothes filthy. The only topic of conversation that brought any animation from him was football and in particular, Manchester United. We happened to have a couple of football magazines in our car, so I got one out and gave it to him. For a fleeting moment his eyes lit up. But we both knew that no amount of football magazines or conversations about Ryan Giggs (his favourite player at the time) would give him a roof over his head.

Dowayne began to open up and share more of his story as Jonathan met with him daily to chat and pray. There was always (such is the life of an addict) a new issue to be worked through – the latest restraining order his mother had taken out against him, the conundrum he was in, having smoked all the drugs he was meant to be selling for the Hard Livings, the late-night knife fight he'd got into, the hammer blow he had received to the face after an argument with a fellow addict, the police raiding his mum's house and beating her up, the night he had spent in police cells after he was picked up for gambling on the street, his near-death experience having overdosed on heroin – the list seemed never-ending. And, of course, none of it was ever his fault. He would always maintain he had been in the wrong place at the wrong time, or that someone had an unfair grudge against him because he won so often in the gambling games (he had built a shack in his mum's backyard, which he called his casino – his home life now consisted of playing dice and smoking copious amounts of heroin, all day every day), or that his mum just didn't love him enough.

The muddled, manipulative mind of an addict is able to twist any scenario into a simple case of victimisation. But we began to learn that God delights in breaking into such conspicuous brokenness. As the months went by, Dowayne slowly began to change. He was open to the suggestion that he wasn't born an addict, that Jesus' plans for his life didn't involve gangs and drugs, and he was keen to learn more. He was hungry to hear about heaven as he was living a version of hell every day. And when we took him to church he would lift his hands, close his eyes and sing in a monotonal voice to the God he was beginning to trust in. That August he prayed a prayer of surrender to Jesus, asking for forgiveness for all he had done wrong and for strength to live a life free from the oppression of violence and addiction. Jonathan and I then took it in turns to sleep in the 24–7 prayer room in The Warehouse, next to him night after night, as he detoxed off heroin. Whenever he woke up in pain from the withdrawal we would pray together and encourage him to speak in tongues, and as he did the pain would subside and he would fall back to sleep. It was exhausting but utterly beautiful to witness.

When the time came for me to move into Manenberg, I couldn't think of a better house-mate than Dowayne. We had rapidly become good friends, he was a new believer, newly off heroin, would be able to instruct me in cultural and linguistic nuances, and was just incredibly kind and helpful.

My first evening living in Manenberg, some friends from church came round for dinner. The electrical wiring hadn't been fixed yet, so we sat around some candles and ate and prayed together. I was buzzing for most of the day, embarking on this brand-new chapter of my life. But I realised the insecurity I was feeling around this new move out of my comfort zone when the time came for my friends to leave, as I was suddenly struck with a deep sense of loneliness and fear. This wasn't necessarily without reason. Dowayne had walked to his mother's house for reasons I couldn't quite work out, and that night I sat alone writing my diary with a couple of candles for company:

2.5.10

Dowayne said he saw some guys standing outside the house with crowbars and other housebreaking tools this afternoon. What on earth am I meant to do? I could literally do nothing if people decided to break in. I'm sitting here on my own in one of South Africa's most dangerous communities, completely alone right now. What do I think I'm doing? It seems so futile on one level – the deep-set crime, addiction and poverty have been here since Manenberg came to exist: why do I think that living here is such a great idea? What difference can one person make? (And one rather sad, lonely person at that!) Yet here's the thing – do I focus on lack and loneliness or on joy and Jesus? Friends have offered their old fridge and a stove this last week, along with a church in the UK giving £500 towards doing up the house. God is totally looking after me. Totally. Did I ever imagine this would be easy? And is that even what I want – ease? And what of this whole 'one person' thing, as if I am the pivotal factor here? God calls a man and 'bidst him come and die'. All of this feels like more and more selfishness, self-reliance, arrogance and knowing-it-all is being gently and lovingly squeezed out of me.

A question at the forefront of my mind was how I should decorate and furnish the house – what would be appropriate, considering the widespread poverty in Manenberg? I later learnt that one of the kids on my road had told all his friends that 'everything in the whitey's house is made of gold' – I'm not sure what he had seen that made him say that! And it was a particularly unhelpful rumour to have circulated in a community with high levels of house-breaking, and where the perception is, rightly or wrongly, that if you're white you're automatically rich. The young boy's rumour triggered my deep-set white guilt, and I would only allow myself to furnish my new home with donated, second-hand or obviously damaged items. I didn't have much of an eye for interior design, nor functionality, so I ended up with a pretty sparse living room, a kitchen with a stove that continually tripped the electrics, and a tired fridge/freezer that leaked water all over the floor. The exception was a donated top-of-the-range memory foam bed.

I made endless trips to hardware stores to buy various tins of paint, varnish, bags and bags of screws, rolls of sandpaper and countless padlocks. I had no idea what I was doing. I also quickly came to realise that my elitist British education hadn't prepared me to carry out even the most rudimentary DIY tasks – I couldn't wire a plug, hang a door, paint walls well, sand and varnish a table, or even put up curtain rails. I was embarrassingly (or gloriously) dependent on the help of drug addicts, and began to recognise the irony – that in order to decorate and move into a house in Manenberg for me to 'help drug addicts', I first needed drug addicts to help *me*. This irony has matured into a natural relational reciprocity in various forms – because as we continue to befriend and disciple addicted and broken young people in Manenberg, they continue to teach us as much as we could ever teach them, just in very different ways. As their brokenness and pain rises to the surface in anger or manipulation, we have a choice to react in anger or to examine our own hearts and seek to respond with love. It is a lesson that revisits us over and over – the paradoxical beauty of losing your life in order to find it.

Regular routine was hard to find as I essentially reacted to whatever was going on around me. Daily, different scenarios would play out as people approached me with various needs or requesting intervention. One particular morning I was praying with Dowayne and a couple of other young guys we were trying to help kick drugs, when there was a knock at the door. I walked over and opened up. In front of me was a concerned-looking middle-aged man, hopping from foot to foot, eager to explain what he was doing.

'I'm sorry to bother you, but may I ask what you are doing in your front room?'

'We're actually praying – would you be able to come back later maybe?'

'Umm, well, please could I come in?'

'Err, why . . . ? Is there anything we can help you with?'

'As I was walking past your house I felt a strong urge to knock on your door. I just heard a voice tell me I need to speak to someone in here about asking to receive Jesus as my Saviour.'

I was completely taken aback – this had never happened to me before. A random stranger just knocking on the door asking to receive Jesus into his life. Of course, we gathered round Clint, led him in a prayer of salvation and prophesied over him. He left beaming, and we sat there stunned with how easy evangelism is when the Holy Spirit has your address and sends people to you. I had also just heard from Jonathan that evening that a lady called Fadwah had made a commitment to follow Jesus. Good news indeed, but all the more remarkable considering her past life. She had grown up as a Muslim, been affiliated with the Hard Livings and, being rather large of frame, used to attend gang-related court hearings as she was able to smuggle guns into the courtroom under her ample bosom without setting off the metal detectors, in case rival gangs were also there and anything kicked off. As I lay in bed that evening replaying the events of the day, I remember thinking *Man, this is too easy!* I was right. It was. And it would get a whole lot harder.

But during those blissful early days as a new homeowner in Manenberg, life was just great. I would spend the winter evenings walking the streets around my house, obliviously crossing gang territories during gang fights and greeting all with whom I came into contact. On colder nights, I'd head to Uncle Patrick's front yard along the road from me, where people gathered round an open fire to keep warm. I was something of a novelty coming from abroad, and as aeroplanes flew overhead I would be asked over and over, 'So what is it like that side?' Local Manenberg ways of explaining the whereabouts of places baffled me – phrases such as 'there by Coke' (next to the Coca-Cola factory on the edge of Primrose Park), '*daar* by *die darkies*' (in Gugulethu), 'at the back' (the opposite location to where you are now) – it all took a bit of getting used to. I realised 'that side' was England. So I would explain how much more I preferred Manenberg, and people couldn't believe it. They couldn't believe that Londoners could have a world-leading public transport system and free National Health Service, both available twenty-four hours a day, but still complain about both. They couldn't believe, in a country where so many have such relative material wealth, that the majority would ignore God, from whom all these blessings come. To most South Africans I've met, the UK seems like the promised land, a hallowed utopia where crime is non-existent, politicians aren't corrupt, and where all races and nationalities get on unreservedly. I did my best to burst that bubble, but nothing seemed to change people's minds.

Life was beginning to take shape. From watching the sun set in the distance over Table Mountain, to hugging talkative and tipsy aunties, to learning DIY skills and dreaming of what a life spent in this community could look like, I was content. The only real concern I had was that most mornings I would discover a fresh human turd in the carport, meaning that someone was using our outbuilding for a midnight poo each night. I couldn't work out how they got in, and didn't really want to know.

6: Tea with the Gang Leader and Other Stories

The life of each neighbourhood is to a major extent shaped by forces that far transcend the local scene . . . it should, thus, always be remembered that many apparently local problems are in reality malignant microcosms of vast conflicts, pressure, stresses and strains of the entire social order.

(Saul Alinsky)[1]

Humanity's broken relationship with God is the ultimate cause of all other brokenness . . . Creation is bound together by relationship with our creator since it is Creator God's love that binds us together. To break one tie is to break them all.

(Lisa Sharon Harper)[2]

When praying alone one day, God spoke to me through a vision. In it I saw the local leader of the Hard Livings gang running towards me, shouting desperately that he needed this Jesus he had heard about. It wasn't dissimilar to Paul's dream in Acts 16:9–10, of a Macedonian man begging for help. It was obvious what I had to do – so I arranged to meet up with him.[3] I'd been wanting to meet with him for some time, determined to make an effort to get to know him and learn a bit about what made him tick. I had heard so many stories about him – like that he was one of the main accomplices in the break-in at a local police armoury, when a whole cache of guns was stolen and then distributed throughout the Cape Flats. People spoke about him in extremes. Either he was described as a violent money launderer, or spoken about with a kind of holy reverence. I wanted to know what was folklore and what was true. And I thought if I met him

I might be able to sense a bit of Jesus' heart for a man who, one way or the other, had a lot of blood on his hands.

So after weeks of driving past and stopping to ask if he was home, the old gnarly gangsters who sat watch outside his house (veterans of the gang scene who were so addicted and slow that they weren't much use any more, but who remained fiercely loyal to the cause) finally helped me arrange a time to meet with their boss. It was a peculiar couple of hours. We spoke about Manenberg, about plans and visions for the community, and about his life. He beamed like a child at crèche showing off a painting they'd done, as he flicked proudly through a special notebook he'd written in during his time in prison, containing the blueprint he'd penned for the future of South Africa, 'just like Mandela did'. He was hospitable and friendly, and as he showed me round his house, MTV *Cribs* style, he pointed out various mundane design features he had chosen – a well-placed light switch here, a space-saving cupboard there. We slowed down as we got to a room with a huge flat-screen TV on the wall and he stood in the doorway, admiring it.

'Guess how big?'

'Well, I, ummm . . .'

'Fifty inches. I bought it for my children.' And on he walked, self-justified in his love for his children, but unwilling to recognise his insidious complicity in destroying the lives of thousands of others through his gang activities, the profits from which probably bought this TV.

As we walked I felt a barrage of conflicting thoughts fill my mind. In some ways he came across as a sort of endearing, self-made guy, who'd somehow managed to stay clean of drugs, even back in the day when he was committing armed robbery and house-breaking at 'sorry for this, white people's houses' (as if I would be less offended if he had broken into black people's houses). Yet mainly I was struck by his endless insistence on being the 'good guy' – how he got all his money (to pay for his brand new sports cars and boat parked outside his front door on a trailer) from legitimate business, and how he is such a positive influence on the community. His persistence didn't sit well with me – because to all intents and purposes he was the exact person-ification of all the forces coming together to create the malignant microcosm of wrongs in Manenberg.

His rationale for setting up a local soccer club? 'To give children a chance at the big time.' In reality, it was just another arm to his empire, rumoured to be built on the foundation of money earned from gang activities. The club fast became one of the best teams in Manenberg, with many pro-players allegedly lured in by the money he could afford to pay. Again, as with his children's TV, the word on the street was that the poorest, and most desperate in Manenberg, are the ones who would ultimately fund his soccer team's success.

The tragic truth is, children growing up in Manenberg look up to gang leaders like him – the money, the house, the TV, the cars, the soccer clubs – and aspire to the same things. This innocent aspiration leads to them joining his gang and doing whatever they are told by their seniors, which means dealing drugs and shooting guns, which leads to using drugs to anaesthetise against the horror of their new reality, which leads to violence and crim-inal behaviour, which leads to jail. And so another young life is sacrificed to generate a little more cash for the gang bosses and their cronies. The fact so many of them present themselves as benevolent philanthropists just adds to the evil allure of this lifestyle. It is nothing short of demonic.

We returned downstairs to the kitchen. 'Tea?' he asked.

'Yes, please.'

What unfolded next was as surprising as it was funny. He didn't seem to know how to make a cup of tea. He put a teabag in a cup sitting on the counter in front of us, then looked in most of the cupboards for sugar, eventually finding it on the counter next to the cup. Then he took milk out of the fridge and placed it next to the sugar. Then he began to drum his fingers on the counter top, lost in thought.

'What else . . . ?'

'Water?'

'Ah yes!'

He waddled over to the kettle (one of the results of a lifestyle of plenty), filled it to the top, and switched it on. As we waited for the kettle to boil, it emerged we had both run out of things to talk about. He had given up on telling me more lies, and I had given up asking questions to which I knew I wouldn't get a straight answer.

Finally, kettle in one hand, he poured four spoons of sugar into the cup closely followed by the water.

'Sugar?'

'No thanks.'

'Oh. Sorry.'

He put the full kettle down too quickly, splashed his hand with hot water and, muttering under his breath, ran around looking for another cup, searching up and down throughout the kitchen. He couldn't find one. Keen to put an end to what felt like a scene from a pantomime, I agreed to drink the first cup. Mercifully, he let me pour the milk. As I took a first sugary sip, I reminded myself I was looking at one of Manenberg's most notorious gang leaders, and let out a snort.

'What?' he asked.

'Oh, nothing.'

The fact is, however much I struggled to like this man, I drove home needing to remind myself that he is also made in the image of God, created with a purpose, looking for meaning and belonging. Jesus died for him as much as he died for me. It's an uncomfortable truth – and the great leveller of the gospel – that God has infinite grace for those for whom we may have none. I could understand this in relation to addicts and low-rank gangsters, pawns in the leaders' plots and schemes, but I found it much harder to extend such love to the ones at the top of the pile.

A gun and a golf club

Personal encounters with gangsters weren't always as cordial, however. I had been living with Dowayne for a couple of months by the time Sepp Blatter and his travelling circus called FIFA arrived in South Africa for the 2010 Soccer World Cup. My friend Barry (a British architect who, with his wife and children, gave up climbing the corporate London ladder and moved to Cape Town to devise incremental building solutions for the poorest of the poor) had heard a rumour that the England football team were staying at the Vineyard Hotel, in the heart of Cape Town's southern suburbs. So, naturally, we went for a drink in the hope of meeting a couple of footballers. We didn't see anyone famous, but ended up having a great conversation that lasted for hours. I got home to Manenberg at about 12.30 a.m. Dowayne was asleep. So I did the normal routine of putting the car into the carport (a precarious homemade corrugated iron and wood structure erected by the previous owners, and described by an estate agent as an 'illegal fire risk that adds nothing to the value of your property'). This involved parking outside the gates, getting out of the car, locking it, walking round to the front of the house, unlocking the burglar bar gate and front door, locking them again behind me, unlocking the back door and burglar bar gate, walking into the carport, wrestling with the two padlocks, opening the gates, unlocking the car and driving it into the carport, then wrestling with the two padlocks again to get the gates shut.

However, that evening, as I was getting into the car to drive it in, a group of three men walked towards me asking for a cigarette. I told them I didn't have any, but offered them what I did have – *naartjies* – I had a bag of them in my car. A fruity dose of vitamin C was obviously not the nicotine hit they'd hoped for, and they politely declined. As they stood there, I began to sense something wasn't quite right. My fears were confirmed as one of them asked for my wallet and phone. I naively said no. One of them grabbed me as another put his hands in my pockets, taking out whatever he could find. I began to struggle, and was put in a headlock. I managed to get out of it, but as I looked up a gun was pointed in my face. There were no words said, no 'start cooperating or I'll shoot' – none were needed, it was a fairly unambiguous message.

I handed them my phone, a tired Nokia taped up to keep the battery in, and my wallet, which had R40 (£2–£3) in it. As I did this, I had a flashback to a rather surreal conversation I'd had with someone shortly after I arrived in South Africa where they'd said *if ever you get mugged, ask for the sim card to your phone – it's totally normal here for your muggers to give it to you, and it's got all your numbers on it and is of no use to them.* I thought I'd put this counsel to the test and asked my assailants if they would mind taking out my sim card. Seemingly well versed in South African mugging etiquette, they kindly agreed. As one of them was untaping my phone to get the sim card out, I noticed another one rifling through my wallet. It occurred to me that, apart from the R40, most of the cards in there (such as my UK National Insurance card or my driver's licence) were useless to them but a complete pain for me to lose. So I asked if I could have them back. Again, they kindly obliged. I was on a roll – so I asked them for my bank cards too.

They chatted among themselves in Afrikaans, and then declined my request, potentially imagining the bags of cash sitting in my account. I said I would have the cards cancelled immediately. That felt good – asserting my consumer right to cancel my card – no amount of late-night headlocks could take that away. And as I began to surf on the wave of consumer confidence, I told them a white lie. I said that once I notified my UK bank I'd been robbed in South Africa, if anyone then tried to use my bank cards they would be arrested immediately by the UK secret service. This was met by another more animated Afrikaans discussion, after which they begrudgingly returned both my bank cards.

By now, my blood was pumping and I could feel the adrenaline kicking in. My attackers left with R40 and a simless phone that belonged in a museum, and I ran upstairs to tell Dowayne what had just happened. I woke him up and relayed the entire story. He reached for a golf club under his bed, and suggested we take a drive around Manenberg and ask if anyone had seen my four new acquaintances. The golf club seemed ominous, but I wasn't thinking straight and went along with his suggestion. After getting the car out of the carport again and locking up the house, we drove to Peta Court and picked up some of Dowayne's friends (only later did I discover they had been drinking all night and were up for a fight). I wasn't consciously on the war path or looking for revenge, but wanted to make sure my assailants knew we knew who they were so they wouldn't do it again. A naive thought, perhaps.

By this time, it was past 1 a.m. and the streets were deserted. As we turned into Pecos Walk (one of Manenberg's more notorious roads, affectionately known by locals as *Tik Straat* – Crystal Meth Street) we stopped, as a police vehicle was parked in the middle of the road. I turned around to ask Dowayne and his friends whether I should go and report my mugging, only to see that the three young guys we had picked up were all now lying down in the back, on top of each other, in an attempt not to be seen by the police. '*Jarre my broe*, we've got cases against us, they mustn't see us!' I was suddenly aware how this late-night drive could be perceived; a clueless whitey driving down *Tik Straat* at 1 a.m. with three drunk guys hiding in the back, all wanted by the police, and one passenger in the front holding a golf club. *What should I do? Should I get out? Should I stay in the car? Should I reverse and drive off? Which option would look least dodgy?*

In the end, inexplicably, I chose to flash the police van with my brights a couple of times, got out of the car and made my way towards them slowly. I got to the passenger window. A policewoman was sitting in the passenger seat, her gun cocked and pointing at me through the closed window. I put my hands up, explained what had happened, and asked if they could help us. 'Could you identify any of your attackers in a police line-up?' asked the policewoman.

'No, because they were wearing caps and balaclavas and it was dark,' I replied. 'Then there's nothing we can do.' Keen to get home and go to bed, I returned to the car and dropped off Dowayne's friends. Back home, I could hear the next-door neighbours arguing. I laid my hands on the wall and prayed a prayer declaring peace over their household. Then I put my earphones in and turned my iPod on, playing very peaceful music very loudly in my ears to drown out the sounds coming through the wall.

Moeneer, the miraculous Muslim

That evening was the beginning of a series of experiences that would start sending me over the edge. I began to get used to the feeling of hope draining out of me as more and more people offloaded their stories of abuse and trauma. The only way to describe it is like my batteries didn't charge to capacity, as they did at first. 'Fullness' was an ever-diminishing state. Meeting Moeneer, a friend of Dowayne's we had round for dinner one evening, didn't do much for the encouragement levels.

22.6.10

I've been chatting to Moeneer all evening about his life. It's literally the saddest thing I've ever heard. As a boy he was badly treated by a family member, whom he lived with after his dad got sent to jail for murder. Moeneer turned to drugs after joining the Junky Funkys aged just 14. He said he joined the gang because he was so angry – he first went to jail aged 20 for firing a shotgun at rival gangsters in a shootout. In prison on his 21st birthday he was given the only birthday cake he's ever received – made of slices of white bread squashed together. Once out of prison he then got stabbed so badly he almost died. He's currently on heroin, tik and Mandrax, and is a part of the Jester Kids, having defected from the Junky Funkys. He turned 27 this year and yet has experienced more trauma in those years than I could ever imagine. WHERE DO YOU BEGIN WITH SOMEONE LIKE THAT?

The following week I asked Moeneer to come and stay with me. Dowayne was going to be away helping on a youth camp (where I later learned he stole all the leaders' mobile phones), and I wanted to make more friends and get to know Moeneer better, so it seemed like a good opportunity. It was a mixed week of ups and downs, as Moeneer offloaded more and more 'war stories' from past gang fights. He reminisced over the time the Hard Livings broke into a local police base and stole a whole host of weapons. He laughed as if telling a hilarious joke, describing how he ran after a rival gangster, across the greens (the local soccer field), holding a grenade and threatening to blow them up. Or the time when he opened fire with a semi-automatic rifle during a gang fight in the street. I was genuinely shocked by these tales – which were confirmed by others – as, to me, Moeneer seemed such a lovely guy.

Each day we would follow the same morning routine I'd established with Dowayne: up at 6.45 a.m., wash, get dressed, make coffee, and then an hour of prayer and reading Scripture together. Moeneer was a Muslim (albeit in the loosest sense of the word), and had very little knowledge of the Bible. So we started with the main event, Jesus' death and resurrection, and then began to look at some of the parables in the Gospels. One morning we read the Parable of the Sower. Simply put, it's a story of a farmer sowing seed, which lands in four different places – a path, rocky ground, thorny ground, and good soil. The seed, representing the Word of God, only grows and bears fruit in good soil – leaving you with the question, 'Which soil are you?' Moeneer wasn't sure which type of soil he was, except that he was pretty sure he wasn't the good soil. When I asked him if he would like the seed of God's Word to grow in his heart, he replied that he would – but that he wasn't able to follow Jesus. I asked him why not.

'Two things are stopping me. I'm a prison gangster and a Muslim, and both of those are lifelong commitments. I can't follow Jesus, because I can't leave Islam or the gang.'

I figured that these were legitimate concerns, and didn't try and convince him he was wrong. Instead, I had a brainwave – or maybe the Holy Spirit spoke to me. 'Why don't we pray to Jesus that he would show you that each of these obstacles to following him needn't hold you back? Why don't we ask him for a sign that you should let go of Islam and your prison gang identity?'

He agreed, and we prayed that the true God, the one who could truly offer Moeneer forgiveness for his wayward past, would reveal himself over the next couple of days.

Later on in the week, Moeneer sauntered into the house and started making a cup of tea. Stirring in half a jar of sugar, he began to tell me about a strange encounter he'd had with a group of men on the corner of Manenberg Avenue.

'Yesterday a group of five men came up to me and asked if they could have a word with me. We started talking, and I became a bit confused. They introduced themselves to me, and they all had Muslim names – Achmat, Sulaiman, Mogamat, Ibrahim and Igshaan – and each of them had tattoos on their arms and faces showing they were part of The Number. But they were holding Bibles and speaking like *kerk broes*. It didn't make any sense.'

'Sounds interesting! What did they say to you?'

'They said they all used to be Muslims and prison gangsters, but had met Jesus, received forgiveness for their past and now they follow him. They also said God had sent them to me to tell me he was opening a door in front of me and I should walk through it. Then they prayed for me and walked off.'

I stood there in front of him, lost for words. Eventually I managed to ask him, 'So do you think God answered your prayer, then?' To which he replied he wasn't sure – but either way he didn't feel ready to follow Jesus.

I've subsequently lost touch with Moeneer. I hear about him here and there and sometimes see him pushing a trolley of scrap metal. Little seems to have changed. He is still a gangster and still heavily on drugs. The only thing that has changed is he is now father to two children. And I'm left reflecting on how, despite one of the most miraculous occurrences I've ever witnessed, of

God breaking into someone's life and pretty much handing them revelation on a plate, you can still miss out on what's put in front of you. I believe Moeneer's story is still unfinished. Jesus continues to knock at the door, seeking a relationship with him. But if it teaches me anything, it's that while God longs for every individual to know him intimately, he will never ever invade our free will.

At the end of the week Moeneer went back home to his self-made shack. Dowayne returned from camp, positive and buoyed by stories of new friendships and expanded horizons. In the days that followed, however, I became progressively more on edge. The shooting outside my house had become so heavy we had to move the sofa to the opposite corner of the living room. 'People sometimes die from a stray bullet coming through the window, you know.' I didn't know. It had never occurred to me. And I resented having to talk about it. But I wasn't particularly keen on testing Dowayne's statement.

As the gang fighting continued, armoured cars from the Wynberg military base patrolled the street day and night. Again, I felt a resentment towards such measures, as it seemed such a violation of community life. How could this represent normality? On the one hand, it struck me as rather an extreme reaction to trouble – what kind of illegal activity could possibly merit sending in such obtrusive urban tractors, emblematic of violence and oppression? The futile myth of redemptive violence came to mind: *Let's intimidate and shoot people in order to show that intimidating and shooting people is wrong.*

Panic.

Yet on the other hand, every conversation I had had with local friends served to dictate that when serious trouble does brew in Manenberg, it's more than likely to end in death, often of innocent civilians. To allow bloodshed to ravage unchecked through a community is negligent in the extreme – so send in the armoured vehicles.

Peace.

I found myself strangely drawn to the sight of these camouflage monoliths, spewing out black smoke behind them as they grunted and growled their way along the uneven Manenberg roads.

One evening, as I was peering out of the window, I noticed a *bakkie* pull up to the house opposite and load three beds on to the roof rack.

'What's going on over there?' I asked Dowayne.

'That house is a heroin den. Those people are selling things to buy drugs. Beds are always the last thing you sell.'

'Oh, right. I guess that makes sense.' I went upstairs and got ready to go to sleep. As I lay on my bed, I couldn't get my neighbours out of my head, imagining the children sleeping on the floor. I started thinking about who I could ask to donate towards buying new beds for them. By now, though, I was struggling to keep up with the intense emotions generated by so many new scenarios. I simply didn't have the energy to take on another desperate situation. And if they had just sold their old beds for drugs, wouldn't they just do the same with new beds? I drifted off to sleep devoid of any answers.

Isolation and burnout

Nothing manifests our motive better than poor results. (Jason Upton)[4]

Above all the other conspicuous needs in the community, it was the continuous petty squabbles among the young men I was discipling that drained me most. It felt like, just under the paper-thin surface of visibility, there was a brokenness and internal agony carried by all the young men I met. I later learned that the anger and rage that so regularly surfaced and led to such disastrous results was only a secondary manifestation of primary feelings of fear and rejection – as author Caitlin Moran points out, 'anger is just fear brought to the boil'.[5] This wasn't simply PTSD. It wasn't just a reaction to a once-off memory buried deep in the recesses of the soul – though often such memories were significant drivers in behaviour.

I didn't know it then, but what I was seeing in these young men was a state of *continuous trauma*. The impulsive unpredictability and violent outbursts were a result of living as 'marked men' in a community perpetually on the brink of civil war. They were suspicious and unsure of who to trust, regularly losing friends in the fight, constantly exposed to violence, not knowing where the next plate of food was going to come from, and with no one to look out for them. Their issues were complex and entangled – and, pivotally, had little prospect of relenting.

One evening Dowayne and I took a walk. Embarrassingly, my voyeuristic instincts had got the better of me and I told him I was curious to see what a drug den was like, having lived in Manenberg for a few months but never set foot in one. It was still so early in my time in Manenberg that I hadn't experienced sufficient trauma to rid me of the enigmatic exoticism attached to the mention of illicit gang-related goings-on. We didn't have to walk far; there was one at the end of our road, down an alleyway. This was where a lot of Hard Livings went to use heroin, and was so well known that I remember being puzzled as to how the police hadn't shut it down. (As I say, it was early days, and I had yet to learn of the bribes and tip-offs that went on as a matter of course.) Dowayne knocked three times, very quietly in quick succession. Almost immediately the door was opened and a head peeped round.

Wies jy? Waat maak jy? Who are you? What are you up to?

Nee man, ek wil net my vriend die plek wys. No man, I just wanted to show my friend this place.

I have no idea why they let us in, but they opened the door – maybe their curiosity about me matched mine about them. Bodies were lying everywhere, sprawled on old moth-eaten couches, legs straight out in front, heads slumped forwards and chins resting on chests. They looked like puppets whose strings had been cut, collapsed onto themselves, unable to move. No one spoke. Some sat on old beer crates, others on upturned paint pots, but really it was pretty underwhelming. Apart from a pair of older men in the corner lighting up, the room was completely still. It was only once we had left that the reality of the situation hit me. Countless people came here, day and night. *Unga* was rapidly taking over from *tik* as the drug of choice on the Hard Livings side of Manenberg (the Americans seemed less interested in dealing it), and many of the people we saw slumped in on themselves were fathers and mothers of children who would be in danger of choosing the same path. These were meant to be responsible adults, but so deep was their pain that this was their lot. Gone was my curiosity-fuelled voyeurism. Gone was the sense of mystery and intrigue; what I had seen was chronic, sad and actually quite unexceptional – just another manifestation of the banality of evil.

The Deep River

The depressing nature of some of what I was experiencing in Manenberg for the first time was quite bizarrely juxtaposed with something rather different. A particularly exciting development at the time was the Deep River, a monthly revival meeting I accidentally found myself co-leading alongside my friend Alan, a pastor in the Southern Suburbs, about half an hour from Manenberg. We had invited another friend, Dom (the same friend who had led the trip to India I'd been part of two years earlier, and who ran Now Believe, an evangelism ministry in London), to run a 'Growing in the Supernatural' conference at Alan's church. The first night was electric, with hundreds of people packing the small Anglican church to the rafters. No sooner had Dom laid hands on the worship team than it all kicked off. People dropped like flies. There were bodies everywhere, lying on top of each other, slumped in pews, eyes closed. Not entirely dissimilar to the heroin den in Manenberg – but with rather a different feel, and a completely different source. Some people were sobbing, others laughing hysterically, and there was a vague farmyard atmosphere, with moos and clucks coming from all corners. The presence of God manifested in physical healings and deliverances like I'd never seen before, and have rarely seen since. Alan and I decided that whatever this was, we should probably keep it going until God decided to put an end to it, so we announced this was now a 'thing', and we would see everyone next month.

Each month more people kept coming. I got into the habit of driving a lap of Manenberg before heading to the Deep River, to take whoever wanted to come along. One evening I ended up with Dowayne and Reswell in the car. The meeting that evening turned out to be particularly dramatic. A couple of people came to the front and shared how they had arrived that evening sceptical about what was going on, but then God had healed some physical pain or sickness, and now they were in tears giving him praise in front of everyone. The man responsible for making the projector work, who wore glasses for short-sightedness, was sitting at the sound desk at the back of the church and found he couldn't see the words on the screen clearly. So he took off his glasses – and to his amazement he could see perfectly well. He had muttered a prayer at the beginning of the meeting asking for a sign this was all of God, and now he seemed to have been given 20/20 vision!

As we drove back to Manenberg, Dowayne and Reswell were singing worship at the top of their lungs, full of joy from all they had seen Jesus do in and around them that evening. When we got home, a thought came to me.

'Hey, why don't we take some of this joy to people around Manenberg?'

Dowayne and Reswell looked at each other, unsure.

'What? Now?!' they asked. It was a fair enough question. It had just gone midnight.

'May as well! Go on, what's stopping us?' So with that, we began to walk the streets together, singing a Sunday School song in Afrikaans about the story of Zaccheus climbing the fig tree.

We got to the other side of Manenberg, the Americans' gang turf, and decided to drop in on a guy I'd met previously, known as Aggies. If there was anyone I knew who needed the hope of the gospel that evening, it was Aggies. We knocked and walked in. He was there, sitting on a crate, dirty and gaunt, smoking crystal meth alone. Reswell launched into his testimony and excitedly told him some of the amazing things we had seen earlier that evening. But Aggies was high and wasn't really listening. We prayed for him and walked on. We walked past Reswell's mum's house on our way home. He asked if Dowayne could sleep over, and in the morning they could tell Reswell's family all about our evening. Encouraged by the thought of them getting on so well, I didn't think twice – it was kind of sweet, two young guys having sleepovers for Jesus. They walked me home and then returned to Reswell's house.

I didn't see Dowayne or Reswell for the next two days. And when I did, it was evident what had happened during their sleepover. As they were walking home they passed a drug merchant's house. One of them had money on them. They went back and forth over whether or not to buy drugs – surely just one hit between brothers wouldn't be so bad? In the end, they stayed up all night bingeing on heroin together, their innocent-minded sleepover hijacked by cravings for drugs. I was devastated. Finding out that news was one of the most depressing things I've ever heard, and I suddenly felt completely alone.

I was completely out of my depth. It felt like I was trying to scale an unclimbable mountain. On the phone to my mum one evening, as I was verbally processing some of my disillusionment, she likened my life to that of Sisyphus, the Greek god who was condemned to a perpetual existence pushing a rock up a hill every day only to see it roll down again each time. It is a picture of such extreme futility that it inspired French existentialist Albert Camus to write a book on the philosophy of the absurd. I was mortified that what was meant to be an exciting journey of pioneering mission work was viewed rather differently by someone so close to me, but if I was completely honest, my mum only verbalised feelings I recognised within myself but had been too scared to admit. She saw right through my external appearances and it hurt like hell.

My journal became my only place of refuge. Night after night I would find myself writing for hours on end. I would try to 'talk myself happy' on paper – stating all the (mostly negative) facts of the reality in which I was living, and then attempting to reframe them in light of whatever understanding of Scripture I could infer.

5.7.10

A desperately hard day. I am beginning to totally lose hope, and today may have been the day I did lose hope in the vision that I believe God has given me for seeing guys come out of gangs and off drugs. I'm not sure how much more I can take. So far the list of stuff stolen from the house amounts to:

iPod, digital camera, basin, clothes vouchers, bolt cutters, toaster, hammer, saw, copper wiring and water pipes, electric drill, beef mince from freezer, toilet duck and half tube of toothpaste. (!)

Add to that the killing of 3 gang members on Friday, meaning shootings on most days recently, and armoured cars from the army base patrolling the streets at night – there was even a shooting down my street, and I was mugged by three guys with a gun as I got out of the car a couple of weeks ago.

Not a pretty picture. I'm feeling worn out and cynical. I'm meant to be trying to think about God's strength in my weakness (for a talk in the UK) – and maybe this is it – that I'm sitting writing this on my bed, not crying and not scared because I believe that 'everyone who wants to live a godly life in Christ Jesus will be persecuted'.

And that's it – if we really grasp the fact that opposition will always come, but ultimately God works for the good of those who love him – if we really get that, we are basically invincible to anything Satan can throw at us, because God will redeem everything.

Physical opposition always starts as spiritual opposition. Which means Satan's not happy. Which means we're doing something

right, which means God is with us. Which means weakness is just
fine because it leaves a whole lot more scope for HIM to do what
WE never could.

I had got to the end of myself.

And as Dowayne was beginning to show the recognisable behavioural patterns of an addict in full flow, and starting to brazenly
take whatever he could find, the next battle I found myself facing
was internal.

7: You'll Die Alone

---

*Life is difficult. This is a great truth . . . because once we see
this truth, we transcend it. Once we truly know that life is difficult
– once we truly understand and accept it – then life is no longer
difficult. Because once it's accepted, the fact that life is
difficult no longer matters.*
(M. Scott Peck)[1]

*When life is tough they tell you to be strong. Don't be strong.
Be weak. Unclench your fists. Dare to be vulnerable. Honest weakness
takes courage. It affirms our common humanity,
deepens friendship and elicits grace.*
(Pete Greig)[2]

Our Father really is perfect Goodness.
(Bill Johnson)[3]

If I had let any friends into my state of mind at the time, I'm
pretty sure I would have soon realised how badly I was doing.
No matter the lengths I would go to in my journal to convince
myself I was living out God's will for my life, and that therefore
everything would be OK in the end, there was no escaping the
fact I was a mess. The issue with burnout is that it stops you
seeing what would normally be blindingly obvious. Five months
after moving to Manenberg, I was spiritually and emotionally
spent. If I needed any persuading that my mental state was not
as it should have been, I could have just looked at my kitchen
habits. Around this time, I began to find myself cooking what
might be loosely described as Italian recipes. Each afternoon I
would head to the shops to buy whatever ingredients I needed.

Every recipe I made up seemed to 'require' a 'splash' of wine. So I would dutifully add this, only to sink most of the rest of the bottle. Most nights. Alone.

Of all the negative thoughts I was weighed down by, one of the most cynical and close to home was the inner voice that told me I would die single if I fully committed to living in Manenberg long term. I had, as someone once remarked, become like a single parent to a drug addict, living alone in a township. Who would be mad enough to join me, with my drug-addicted house-mate and my alcohol-soaked Italian comfort food? I needed a slot on *The Jerry Springer Show* more than I needed a wife. Although I was only twenty-four at the time, a large, lonely part of me was genuinely scared that I would be single for ever.

By September 2010 the wheels had really come off. Our morning routine had become one of drudgery, as the effect of drugs began to show on Dowayne's mood and actions. It began to take longer and longer to wake him up for our hour of morning prayers, during which he was less and less engaged. Things that had previously taken him a day to do – fixing something in the house, or writing out reflections from a chapter in the Gospels – wouldn't get done for weeks. He had become adept at playing the part he knew I expected him to play, and started pushing me to my absolute limit. He had relapsed hard back on to heroin – and subsequently admitted he had never been completely clean since we had moved in together. And while I began to be able to see through the act, I ignored it because I didn't want him to move out. I loved him and utterly resented him in about equal measure – we were a picture of co-dependency.

Desperate measures

On 17 September 2010 I told God that I would be willing to give my life to living and working in Manenberg on one condition: that he give me a beautiful, radical wife to do this with. I then packed a bag for the weekend and drove to a friend's birthday party in town.

That night I met Sarah.

Sarah raises the bar on both beautiful and radical.

The party had been going on for a couple of hours – drinks, music, mingling, that sort of thing. It struck me afresh, as I ordered a drink from the neon-lit bar, passed a couple of sharply dressed guests and headed outside, how different this world was, in the heart of Cape Town just 20 kilometres from Manenberg. It was a strange sensation, but one that I would become more and more familiar with as I navigated the contrasting realities of a divided city. Some friends from church were there, so I knew a handful of people, and I went to join them sitting on the restaurant's front veranda. As I drew closer, I saw Sarah. She was surrounded by people, engaged in conversation, so it took me a while to ~~unashamedly throw~~ subtly nudge others out of the way and sit next to her.

And then we got chatting.

We chatted and chatted and chatted. Not once did we have to rely on small talk, and not once did one of us say something the other strongly disagreed with, had no interest in, or knew nothing about. The coltan crisis in the Congo, Sarah's time studying in Paris, shared feelings of frustration with Cape Town's white suburban church population, xenophobia, racism, Jesus, whether it's OK for Christians to smoke, dreams for the future, child soldiers, Manenberg's gangsters and the Middle East conflict.

Looking back, I can still feel God's smile over the whole evening. I remember feeling a mixture of completely overwhelmed with excitement and a little scared that this whole thing might be a dream – it felt like God had made these two people just for each other, and as we discovered more of the other we became, silently, subconsciously, convinced that the person sitting in front of us might be 'the one', desperately hoping the other felt the same. I can just imagine the angels in heaven looking on and cheering – this semi-depressed, trauma-laden, would-be evangelist, having packed a bag for the weekend and run away from his train-smash of a life, meeting a fascinating young woman whose beauty and poise were way beyond his wildest dreams.

The evening came to an end, and my mate Jake drove me back to his place. Before leaving, I managed to skilfully procure Sarah's number (she remembers this detail rather differently). As Jake and I drove home, there was one CD in his old Toyota Corolla's sound system – Damian Rice's album *O*. So I played 'Cannonball' over and over, wailing along to the lyrics and repeatedly asking Jake if Sarah had said anything to him about me.

Thankfully, the feelings seemed to be mutual, as we had our first official date a couple of weeks later.

It didn't quite go to plan.

I'd booked a table at a place I knew Sarah liked and, feeling the nerves, arrived there a little early. Five minutes before we'd arranged to meet, my phone started ringing.

Unknown number.

Figuring it was probably Sarah letting me know she'd be late, I picked up. It wasn't Sarah. It was Dowayne.

'Pete?'

'Hey dude what's up?'

'Pete, you need to come home. I need you to come home.'

'It's not a great time Dowayne, what's the matter . . .?'

'I'm *smaaking* my *broe*, feeling heroin cravings really bad, I'm desperate to go use, I need you here to talk sense into me. I don't want to relapse again. I can't go back to that. I'm so desperate, I need help. Please come home.'

As we're chatting, I see Sarah's car pull up and park across the road.

'Dowayne, give me five minutes and I'll call you back on this number, OK?'

'OK.'

And just like that, my first date with Sarah became a joint intervention to help Dowayne stay clean. We dropped Sarah's car at a petrol station in town, and drove to Manenberg in my Toyota Tazz. Dowayne was at home, crying. We put on some worship music and prayed. Dowayne lightened up after whispering in tongues for a bit. Not sure what else to do, I suggested the three of us go for a walk. It was only much later on that Sarah confessed to being terrified, walking around Manenberg at 10 p.m. But that walk wasn't in vain. As well as Dowayne staying clean that night, God began to develop in Sarah an affection towards a community she had only ever feared – and that would prove more lasting than a cosy dinner date in town.

Despite this Saturday night intervention, things did not miraculously improve in Dowayne's life. He was using more and more heroin every day and was in freefall towards rock bottom. I couldn't see a solution and was devoid of any hope for his future. Multiple times a day there would be another disaster.

6.10.10

Dowayne's mum threw boiling water over him this evening. He demanded money for chips, she wouldn't give it to him, so he stole her cigarettes. Thankfully, Grant went and got Jonathan, who then took Dowayne to the day hospital where he got treated. I'm seeing more and more how ridiculous my life has become – I have got to the end of being able to deal with the pressure of raising a dysfunctional, addicted and traumatised man-child. This is not the vision, but even more than that, this is not life-giving to anyone. Boy do I need a break. Dowayne just doesn't seem to care any more. I'm beginning not to care either. Why should I bother? Who the hell does he think he is? Of course in some ways this is par for the course, though I never quite realised or contemplated the extent of the problems in a drug addict's life.

He can't seem to make any kind of simple, logical link in his head that to get to a certain place there are specific small steps he needs to take. We talk about it every day, I've got him to write down his goals for the future, we've prayed our socks off, been working through the same issues for 18 months – but still, he gets in fights over drugs and then throws bricks and swears at his 'mates'. Still, he goes round to his mum's and slags her off and steals her stuff until she, not knowing how to interact with him, throws boiling water over him. It's the saddest, most ridiculous situation I've ever witnessed.

Do we have what it takes to work with individuals and their families such as this, and even worse? I saw Tasreeq the other evening [another one of the addicted young men we had been working with], *and he is deep deep into Sexy Boys' gang life. Bereaved and then brainwashed as a teenager – now he's 26, with no critical faculty in his head to see that he is being used to murder. He steals off drug merchants for goodness sake! They won't touch him because **** [the then local leader of the Americans gang] *is coming out of prison in just over a month, and Tasreeq is his personal hitman. So when he's ordered to shoot someone, he doesn't get a choice. Yet, as compensation for denigrating himself, while simultaneously ruining the lives of countless others, Tasreeq might get given a pair of trainers or some cash. I mean who wouldn't commit multiple murder for a pair of shoes and a golden handshake?! It's desperate. Life here can be so demonic.*

Within this maelstrom of trauma and hopelessness, God kept me going through reading about the faith and perseverance of others. Books gave me the encouragement I needed to contend for the vision we held of seeing gangsters come out of lifestyles of violence and addiction through coming to faith within a family of believers centred on prayer, mission and justice.

19.10.10

I've been reading Red Moon Rising *today – Pete Greig's book chronicling the birth of the 24–7 Prayer movement. I reached a point of such intense emotion with how so much of the book hits a chord with where God is taking us that I broke down crying at Vida e Caffè on Kloof Street this morning. This quote in particular, blessed me – written by someone at 24–7 Prayer who was struggling with their prayer room at a Mexican festival not coming together in the timing they had expected:*

'God has been so faithful, but has taught us a huge lesson to do with patience and perseverance. I really want people with a heart to do prayer rooms in specific locations to be encouraged and

challenged that when God clearly speaks about his heart for prayer in that location he means it. We need to take God at his word and persevere in prayer until it happens.' (Emily Moore)

What timely advice, thank you Lord, keep our fire of intercession and crying out to you burning!

Whose need are we meeting?

Looking back at the difficulties of that season living with Dowayne, it strikes me that there's a delicate tension for Christ followers who carry a big vision for a place or a people. It must never be doubted that God will back up vision with provision. To quote a well-worn Christian phrase, 'God doesn't order what he can't pay for.' If he inspires in us world-changing dreams, if he breaks our heart for a particular demographic, if he moves us to pray in faith, hours on end, for seemingly hopeless situations, then we have to believe he will give us all we need to keep going when opposition comes. Whether or not the dreams and visions he's given us become the reality for which we had hoped – for we may never see the full fruit of our endeavours – if it's truly inspired by God, it's God's vision and God's ministry, which means he's infinitely more invested in it than we are. The recognition that we are but a small part of an infinitely larger unfolding story, and that others may reap the benefits of what we sowed, just many chapters later, is a deeply liberating truth as it takes from us the burden of false responsibility or the saviour mentality we may possess, and places our whole life and every endeavour in God's more than capable hands.

There are two potential errors we could make here, on opposite ends of the spectrum. The first is to imagine that because God has spoken to us about something, we are guaranteed and entitled to see the entirety of that promise fulfilled before our eyes. This turns the entire focus from God to 'me and my dream', and undermines the witness of, for example, the persecuted church, where scores of faithful believers have died without seeing the liberating

God free them from torture and oppression. The second error we could make is of reducing God's goodness and provision to the level we've experienced, as a justification for not believing impossible things can happen through yielded hearts. This turns the focus from God to 'me and my disappointment', and undermines any reliance on the supernatural power of our Father. Either way, both extremes crumble and fall on the basis that they make *us* the main character in the story. Heartbreak is real, but the key is yieldedness to, and confidence in, the goodness of God. Shane Claiborne puts it well when he says, 'rather than asking what God's will is for my life, I find it helpful instead to ask what God's will is and how my life might fit into that. Maybe that's what it means to seek first the kingdom of God – the world does not revolve around us, but rather we are revolving around God.'[4] If we can hold on to that, it should spur us on to step out in faith, focused fully on him, over past setbacks or reasonable-sounding advice coming from well-meaning cynics standing on the sidelines.

The tension was this. I believed wholeheartedly that Christians are called to be world-changers – but I believed it so strongly that it blinkered my awareness of my own need for community, fellowship, accountability, emotional support, rest, holiday or even sleep. I subconsciously judged anyone not in 'ministry' (or at least, my definition of it), and simply couldn't see the importance of cultivating friendships with anyone other than gangsters or drug addicts. In my dogmatic narrow-mindedness, it simply never occurred to me that others may have had that same vision, or may be doing something similar. I had no friends, just acquaintances whom I was trying to convert as they were trying to steal from me. This was true of my relationship with Dowayne. Ultimately, my big-vision saviour mentality set Dowayne up to fail. He needed me – to steal from me to buy drugs, and for me to keep standing up for him when he got in fights. And yet I needed him even more – because he legitimised my life, ministry and reason for being in Manenberg. I got jealous when anyone else helped him, and I found my validation in what I was doing.

Though it became blatantly obvious, to admit *he* had a deep-set problem would be to admit *I* had a deep-set problem. I wasn't willing to admit the latter, so I ignored the former.

Eventually we both admitted we couldn't go on. We were both finished – he was done pretending to be in recovery from addiction, and I was done pretending I hadn't noticed he was stealing from me to fund his habit. It was a sad but strangely liberating moment when we both acknowledged our little experiment had failed. It had lasted just six months, and we were both worse off than before. Mercifully, I had found a Christian rehab out of Manenberg that had agreed to take Dowayne in. He would go there, and I would move to a friend's house in the southern suburbs – neither of us were sure how long we would last in this new set-up, or even if we would ever see each other again.

Beginning to realise we had little to offer

I had become the very thing I loathed.

Having moved out of Manenberg, I was now an NGO worker commuting to a township from the safety and comfort of the suburbs. I tried not to think about it, as it embarrassed me and sent me into a spiral of self-condemnation. Time was divided between establishing new relationships with angry, addicted young men on the streets of Manenberg and chasing Dowayne back to rehab.

In August 2011 I went to London for my sister's wedding. It was a beautiful wedding and a much-needed time away, connecting with old friends and trying (I fear in vain) to explain again to certain family members what exactly I was doing in Manenberg and why I was choosing to live there. I returned to Manenberg to hear of an incident that disturbed me deeply.

Earlier that year, my house had been broken into by a guy called Harley, a Hard Livings gangster who smoked heroin in the drug den opposite. He broke in through the carport and back-door window, and stole a lot of stuff belonging to Leon, a friend who was living there at the time. Having been told by the community that there was no use in going to the police because 'they are corrupt', we then went around asking people what they knew, and in the space of a couple of days and after some fairly awkward conversations with a couple of well-known housebreakers we got all of the goods back. Harley was subsequently caught and went to jail.

Justice was done, it seemed, and we hadn't even involved the gangs despite claims that they would be able to procure the stolen goods for us much quicker than we could. They had even offered to beat up the offenders in front of us to show how deeply ingrained their moral compass was. We turned down the offer, not least because we didn't want to legitimise their illegitimate authority in Manenberg.

Harley came out of prison the day before I left for the wedding in England. I wanted to chat to him before I left – to let him know that we loved him, wanted God's best for his life, and forgave him as Jesus had forgiven us. Yet in my disorganisation I forgot to find him before heading to the airport. It was only sitting at the departure gate that I remembered, but figured I'd just see him when I returned.

I got back three weeks later to find out that Harley had been shot dead. He was part of a group of Hard Livings gambling late one night when two masked gunmen opened fire on them.

It was a huge wake-up call for me.

Life is balanced so delicately. Harley died possibly never having had anyone share the love of Jesus with him. Seven years later God in his vast kindness introduced us to Harley's younger brother Kevin. We would only later realise the significance of the connection. But for now I resolved to learn from Harley's story that I would follow the promptings of my spirit with a renewed zeal. One such prompting happened sooner than I may have imagined.

On a prayer walk the next week we bumped into Reswell. He was on his way home from Nyanga Junction where he and a friend had sold his mum's iron for R25 for their next *unga* hit.

I spoke to Reswell and said I knew where he was off to and what he was off to do, and he could give the money to his friend and then come walk with us. His eyes were sunken and colourless, and he was twitchy. He was completely unable to make any decision that didn't revolve around his next hit. Even just stopping and talking to us was causing him physical pain as his body had begun to go into withdrawal (they say the rat poison mixed in with the heroin in *unga* is the thing that causes stomach pains – and the only way to numb the pain is with another hit; heroin is, basically a painkiller). His bones and muscles were crying out for heroin's warm, fuzzy satiation.

So he left – but before we let him go, I prayed for him, my hand on his heart, that God would supernaturally change the longings of his soul and deal with his cravings and addiction. We kept walking. On the way back, I was reminded of a picture God had given us back at the beginning of the year, during a time of prayer, of dragging Reswell out of drug dens. Initially I was irritated to be reminded of this as it meant I couldn't just settle for praying with him, but now had to act. So we went to the road where he lived. Almost immediately he walked past us without seeing us and went into his friend's shack. We gave it a couple of minutes and then followed him in. His co-conspirator was making up the heroin as we walked in, delicately pouring the brown powder on to the tinfoil that he would then heat from below using a candle or lighter. When he saw us he quickly swept it away and put the foil in his pocket. After initially refusing, Reswell eventually agreed not to use, but to come with us. It was an encouraging intervention in and of itself, but soon the body pains would become even stronger and he would need to go and find another way to use. And again I realised we had nothing beyond prayer and friendship to offer this desperate addict to whom God had directed us.

Blinky

A couple of months after Harley had been shot dead, we were praying for people on the streets of Manenberg. Up walked Blinky, a Jester Kid who lived down the road. He knew who we were because we regularly prayer-walked down his street. Normally he avoided us, but today he wanted to talk. He began to tell us about his *tik* addiction, and how desperate he was to kick his habit. It's not unusual to hear this – I've never once met a drug-addicted gangster who, when out of earshot of his fellow gang members, hasn't admitted how desperately depressed and lonely his lifestyle has made him. There is no such thing as a happy gangster. Despite public displays of bravado, these violent young men often admit to crying themselves to sleep, alone, in a shack in the back of their mother's yard.

Blinky asked if we would pray for him to stop smoking *tik*. We agreed, and added that if he was serious about finding freedom then he would need deep inner strength beyond what he was physically capable of, and might he consider praying a prayer of surrender to Jesus? He agreed that that sounded like a good idea. We prayed, he prayed and shed a couple of tears (usually a good sign), and that was that. Off he walked.

I never saw Blinky again.

Not long after that encounter on the street, he too was shot dead – killed by a rival gang. It emerged he had never been able to leave drugs behind and died as an active gang member. His death, and life, had been marked by tragedy. Yet, somewhere in the midst of this depressing picture of addiction and hopelessness, was a hunger for freedom that had led Blinky to tears as he ever so briefly encountered the love of Jesus.

One of the main sources of inspiration for us to keep going even when things are tough is the sheer conviction that the vast majority of Manenberg's most dangerous demographic are desperate to be shown a viable way out of gangs and drugs. It's an extreme, tangible example of what Paul writes about in

Romans 8 – that gangsters are waiting 'in eager expectation for the children of God to be revealed . . . [so that they too] will be liberated from bondage to decay and brought into the freedom and glory of the children of God'. The world (whether it knows it or not) is groaning for those who know and follow Jesus to show that another way is possible.

I found Blinky's story both encouraging and distressing. I was encouraged by his encounter with Jesus, but distressed that, at the time, we had nothing physical we could offer to assist him. A gangster had voluntarily walked up to us in public and asked for a way out, and all we could offer him was a short prayer. Some would say that was enough, because in the eternal scheme of things Blinky has gone to a better place.

I believe that is true, and that Blinky's spirit is alive and loving it there, where there is 'no more death or mourning or crying or pain' (Rev. 21:4).

And yet there has to be more to it than that. Randomly, I remembered a well-known strapline used by Christian Aid that I had first seen on a poster when I was at school. There was a photo of a smiling African woman selling vegetables at a market. Bold font at the top of the photo declared, 'We Believe in Life Before Death'. This woman may or may not have known Jesus – but here she was selling fruit and vegetables, empowered to run a small business and (one presumes) lift herself and her family out of grinding poverty. As the explanation of the slogan on the Christian Aid website explains, 'when we only believe in life *after* death, we defer hope to the beyond – to the far future and leave the present in despair'.[5] Christianity is so much more than a free ticket to heaven when you die. It brings a life of fullness and purpose here on earth whatever the struggles. We resolved to work towards physical, sustainable solutions to the despair that epitomised the life of those in gangs and drugs. We resolved to pour our lives into seeing life before death spring up all around us in Manenberg.

Shihaam

It wasn't long before we saw this unfold before our eyes. By now
our team had grown to five – Jonathan, myself, Sarah, Clare (from
Belfast, who was overseeing the work with women) and Patrick
(Manenberg born and bred and establishing a local coffee shop).
One morning, just after we'd finished our daily time of prayer
together as a team, there was a quiet knock at the door of our
new office – we had recently located to a community centre in
the heart of Manenberg. So quiet was the knock, that you immediately knew the person the other side of the door was already
having second thoughts. Clare opened the door, and Shihaam
stood there nervously. Sensing an opportunity to love someone
God had brought to our door, Clare introduced herself, took
Shihaam into a side office and closed the door. They remained
in there for a couple of hours, as Shihaam poured out her heart
and Clare prayed for her.

We were all due to go to a mission conference in Franschoek,
about two hours' drive from Cape Town, the very next day. Our
past experience with addicts had taught us the importance of
striking while the iron's hot – if someone manages to walk to
your office and bare their soul to you as a cry for help, you want
to keep them close before the cravings, lies and internal accusation
set in. It was obvious to us that God had brought Shihaam to us
and that she should come to Franschoek, despite being Muslim
and on drugs. Quite apart from enabling us to get to know her
more, Jackie Pullinger was going to be speaking and would no
doubt touch Shihaam deeply with stories of Jesus healing and
saving addicts and triad gangsters in Hong Kong. Shihaam, hungry
for whatever hope was being offered, agreed to come along.

We arrived at our hostel in the early evening, checked in and
began to prepare dinner – hotdogs, rolls and salad. As we served
each other it dawned on us that we had forgotten to consider our
newest friend's dietary requirements. Shihaam only ate halal.
So one of us rushed to the kitchen and made her some cheese

sandwiches, apologising profusely, as we wanted her to feel at home with us.

It soon emerged that the conference was pitched rather higher that we had thought. Complex strategies for church planting and methods of evangelism were way beyond most of our group's comprehension. Sensing this, Clare decided to take Shihaam for a coffee during one of the sessions, and they went and sat under a tree on a grassy patch along the main road. As they spoke and Clare shared the simple message of the gospel – that Jesus made Shihaam, loved her, died for her so she could be free from sin and addiction, and had destined great things for her life – she began to cry, received his forgiveness, and spontaneously broke out speaking in tongues.

We got back to the hostel that evening and immediately heard Shihaam's news. We were, of course, overjoyed. As we began to prepare a final dinner before leaving Franschoek the next morning, we realised we'd bought way too many hotdogs – we still had a lot left over from the first evening. It turned out not to be a problem as, freshly baptised in the Holy Spirit, Shihaam tucked in and helped us finish every last one. She had come to Franschoek as a Muslim, obeying the religious rules she had been brought up to follow, but now – two days later – she was a spirit-filled, born-again believer exercising her new-found freedom in any way she could imagine!

Having returned to Manenberg, Shihaam proceeded to pray for everything that moved. A sick family member, random people on the street, her children – everyone received faith-filled prayer from this fired-up new believer.

8: Asking, Seeking, Knocking

---

*When a vision is born in the pride of a prayer-less imagination, it is
nothing more than a projection of the self – what Freud called the
Ego . . . But when a vision comes to us not as human aspiration, but
as divine revelation – then the whole equation changes. God's
commission always comes with his provision: He promises to supply
our needs, to sustain us, to renew our strength, to redeem our
mistakes, to use our weaknesses, and – best of all – to journey with us.
He uses the weak and foolish to confound the wise, ordinary people to
do extraordinary things for His glory. With God, there is no 'just me'.
Our protestations of stupidity simply fall on the deaf ears of grace.*
(Pete Greig)[1]

It was now almost two years after I had moved out of Manenberg.
A lot had changed. Sarah and I had got married and moved into
a home in the suburbs. Friends Leon and Vincynthia were now
staying in my house in Manenberg with their children, Dowayne
was in and out of various rehabs as he continued to struggle
staying off heroin, Shihaam joined the team to assist Patrick with
the coffee shop, and we began to look for a home to accommodate
recovering addicts. This time, I wouldn't be doing it alone – we
would run the place under the ministry – at the time called Fusion
– volunteers would assist us, and we would learn from my disastrous solo attempt with Dowayne.

None of us had any idea where to start in finding a suitable
property, but I had just got hold of a book about prophetic 'treasure
hunting'. In brief, treasure hunting, in this sense, consists of
praying for prophetic clues to help you find the treasure, with
the end goal being that you are able to share Jesus with those
you meet. You write down your treasure list – things you sense

God saying or bringing to mind (for example, a person's name, an item of clothing, a location or building, maybe a physical ailment, and an additional random item), compare notes, and set off looking for the clues. It's a fairly risk-oriented approach to evangelism as you can sometimes end up completely deflated if you don't find any of the clues. But we were keen to step out in faith and had adopted this approach for our regular prayer walks around Manenberg. Most of the time the results had been really encouraging.

20.06.12

God revealed to me a picture of crutches, and that we'd meet a man with a name beginning with the letters RE. As we were about to walk past the Americans' gang headquarters, we spotted a bloke hobbling on crutches. We ran up to him, and slightly shocked him I think, because he kept asking 'Who are you, what are you doing?' I explained we were looking for treasure and sensed that maybe he was it, and I showed him the treasure list with 'crutches' written on it. He then calmed down and said yes of course we could pray for his leg – he had a blood clot behind his right knee. I asked him his name – it was REggie! This raised my faith to pray healing for him, knowing God had made our paths cross. I got him to walk and tell me if there was any pain – he said there wasn't. I asked him if he wanted to receive Jesus, the healer, in his life. He said no, 'because I sometimes smoke tik, and if I become a Christian I can't smoke tik any more'. An honest answer if ever there was one! I told him Jesus can heal his addiction as well as his leg, but by this time he didn't seem to care. God pursued Reggie, sent us to him, and took away the pain in his leg. He hasn't given up pursuing him. But every human can choose to say no, as Moeneer did previously, and Reggie did today. God, in his deep value for human life, will not invade our free will.

Meanwhile, as I was talking to Reggie, Patrick was asked by a lady to come upstairs and pray for her 14-year-old son. Three other clues God had given us before we went out were a picture of a

hanging basket, a boy's face with a scar on it, and the word 'shame'.
We walked upstairs to find the lady's son sitting next to a hanging
basket, with a scar on his face. It emerged as we prayed for him
that he is deeply ashamed of himself for dropping out of school at
the age of 12. We prayed new hope into him, and encouraged him
to re-enrol at school. What an opportunity to bless that family!

If nothing else, treasure hunting gave us the opportunity to meet
those who spent most of their lives on the streets of Manenberg.

07.07.2012

Yesterday, we walked around Jester Kid territory. We didn't find
any of the specific clues we thought we'd been given, but did come
across Bobby and Marco. I met Bobby over a year ago when he
came to my house while Dom was staying. We spent a long time
praying for him that night, and he had a real encounter with the
love of the Father – he then came back the next night saying, 'Where
is your friend, I need some more of that prayer!' Yesterday he told
me that he didn't smoke unga for over three months after that. But
then when he had a bust-up with his wife, he relapsed. It epitomises
the power of anointed prayer to break addiction in an instant, but
also the need for follow-up and a protective environment for those
struggling with addiction. We, as a ministry, have the first, and are
making plans for the second. The sad bit of the story is Marco. He
is 26 years old, and has been on unga for 11 years. He told me he
spends R140 a day on his habit (A LOT in Manenberg, where you
can get a hit for R20), which equates to R980 a week, which is
R50,960 a year, which over a decade comes to R509,600. You can
buy a house for that! Marco has children – I have no idea how he
supports them, with such an expensive habit and no job. Man, Marco
needs help.

After these profound experiences on the streets, I thought we
could try treasure hunting as a way to find a house. A few days
later we met and prayed, and asked God to give us clues about

the house we could buy and renovate to provide the residential intervention the likes of Bobby and Marco so desperately needed.

The clues we felt God gave were:

- A bent STOP traffic sign on the side of the road
- The colour yellow
- The initials S and H

We hopped in the car, drove along Manenberg Avenue and right there was a yellow car parked on the left of the road, next to which was a man sitting on yellow crates. So we turned left. As we drove along the next road, we passed a bent STOP sign and reached a cul-de-sac. As we drove to the end of the road, we saw a dilapidated house. The gates had been stolen, there was rubbish strewn everywhere, holes had been made in the roof, the inside was stripped and littered with faeces, the walls were peppered with gang tags and graffiti. And we immediately knew this would be perfect. When the neighbour came round to see who this random bunch was, we asked her if she knew the name of the owner. She had their details, and went inside to find them. To our astonishment, the owner's first name and surname began with the letters S and H!

Soon after, however, we were at the property auction where this rundown old shell of a building was up for sale, and stood and watched as it was bought by a local property developer who, when he heard we were interested in the property, tried to fleece us, forging the auction documents and inflating the sum he had paid. After consulting structural engineers and estate agents, all of whom warned us against buying, we walked away, confused as to why God would lead us along the proverbial garden path to a dead end.

Strike one.

The very next day, a British social entrepreneur emailed me, excited about our vision, which he had heard about from a friend in London. He offered to help design and construct a brand new modular building that would be manufactured in the UK, shipped over to South Africa and assembled in Manenberg. We scrambled a design team together, and asked Clare's husband Lloyd, a recent architecture graduate, to design a dream house with a bakery, prayer room and rooftop vegetable garden. Around the same time, a charity in London had emailed to offer to help us furnish the house once it was finished. We sensed a growing momentum, and told ourselves that this was the more that God gives when one plan falls away. We all got very excited. This line of dialogue became increasingly serious. We had numerous Skype meetings and were sent concept papers and all sorts of elaborate modular designs until, by the end of the year, the social entrepreneur called to say both the building company and his own private equity company had gone bust in the double-dip recession in the UK.

Strike two.

Disappointed though undeterred, we kept asking and knocking. Rather than buying a house, we decided to look for somewhere to rent for a year, and pilot the discipleship house concept. (In hindsight, this wasn't the voice of wisdom we thought it was at the time. It was fear. We'd just become scared of getting disappointed again, and so lowered our sights and reduced the risk factor.) After sticking up around eighty adverts across Manenberg, a homeowner got back to us and said she would rent out her house to us. The house seemed suitable for what we needed, and we drew up a lease commencing two months later. We spoke to two young men we were working with at the time who needed to get out of their homes in order to get clean from drugs and out of the gang – they were keen to be the first intake.

During this period of house hunting we had been throwing around ideas and compiling a daily schedule for the house that blended all the best parts of material Sarah had gleaned, and research she had carried out, from rehab centres and communities throughout the Western Cape. We had never got this far before and really felt, despite previous setbacks, that this was going to happen – that the original dreams were coming to fruition.

However, the day before both parties were due to sign, we visited the property only to be told the landlady had gone back on her word and decided to lease the house to a Somali family, who would pay her higher rent to run a tuck shop from the living room.

Strike three.

Although this was difficult news to receive at first, and we were absolutely gutted, I remember summoning up the faith to text Jonathan the following: *this is such bad news, humanly speaking, that God must be up to something far bigger than we'd imagined, and is protecting us from small visions.* Had we known at that point all that was in store in the next couple of years, we would probably have run a mile. Thankfully, God knew better than to tell us. We hadn't found anywhere suitable in months of searching, and so for now the plans for a home for addicts were put on hold. It was a classic example of the 'now and not yet' of the kingdom. We felt pretty certain of the next stage – a home for addicts. And though we were sure God was speaking, for whatever reason he also seemed to be delaying the process. Why? We didn't know. But it would be a question we would find the answer to later down the line.

A new friend

I had begun getting to know Neville, a young man who had approached me asking for help finding something more constructive to do than beating people up and dealing drugs. He was a Ghetto Kid, addicted to *tik* and Mandrax, and remarkably open to meeting up and talking about life. His life was intense to say the least. There were two warrants of arrest out against him for beating a guy with a baseball bat. The shifty eyes, and worried look on his twitching face suggested he was guilty – along with the fact that in a perverse way he didn't have a huge amount of choice in the matter. He was the Ghetto Kids' delegated representative in that particular area of Manenberg, and in order to maintain order it was his job to dole out 'justice' to those who were caught housebreaking. He was on a suspended sentence, meaning were he to be caught engaging in any criminal activity in the next fifteen months he would go to jail for ten years. And with the police searching his house every other day to find him, he was sleeping in a truck in a back yard, vulnerable to being shot by rival gangs as he slept. He wasn't sleeping a whole lot anyway, because aside from dodging the police, he was fairly consistently *skarrelling* for *tik* to keep him awake in this fugitive lifestyle. The day we first met, the truck had just been sold, so he had nowhere to go.

One of the things Neville told me the first time we hung out was that he was interested in getting to know Jesus. But something was weighing heavy on him. He had no issues with the reliability of the Bible, no questions of whether science may have disproved religion or if post-modernism rendered the absolutist truth claims of Christianity obsolete. His one concern was that he knew if he followed Jesus he would need to leave the gang, and so his question was whether God would protect him from getting shot by rival gangs. It was a vulnerable question and I honestly didn't know what to say. A part of me wanted to reply, flashing a saccharine evangelical smile, and giving him a knowing pat on the back, '*Of course* God will protect you – once you know Jesus you'll be just fine! Now repeat these words after me: Dear Lord Jesus, I invite you into my life . . .' But while I do believe in the protection of God over his children, if I told Neville God would definitely protect him from all harm once he made a commitment to follow Jesus, then why had Blinky been killed after making that same commitment the previous year? It would have been easy to get him to make a verbal commitment of faith then and there (which seemed to be what he was expecting), but I couldn't bring myself to do that. Did he even know what he would be getting himself into? Had he honestly counted the cost of leaving behind the sense of belonging and protection from being a gangster, not to mention the money coming from a fairly successful drug business? Maybe he had, and my own lack of faith robbed him of making a life-changing decision. It's possible. But if he hadn't, what value would a thirty-second prayer have had? Either way, it seemed better to encourage him to hold off making promises he couldn't keep, and for us to simply begin to pray together and explore who Jesus really is.

I often wonder if we Christians get people to make hasty confessions of faith without them really knowing what's going on, just to make *us* feel better, consciously or not. In the Gospels, when Jesus called each of the disciples to follow him, it was a personal invitation to a life spent learning how to believe as he believed, to be able to love like he loved, in order to do what he did. Nowhere in Scripture is there a flat-pack, one-size-fits-all 'sinner's prayer'. In fact, even while following Jesus the lives of the disciples were often characterised by doubt, jostling for status, getting the wrong end of the stick and lack of faith. But, pivotally, there was a spiritual hunger in each of them to discover the things of faith to which Jesus alluded and to walk in the love and power which he displayed. I left the meeting with Neville encouraged and excited to continue walking alongside him.

And then a week later, a Manenberg-wide gang fight broke out. On a sunny afternoon in May I was at a friend's house in a leafy suburb, watching the last day of the English football season. My phone buzzed. It was a text message from Jonathan: *Gang fight in Manenberg. Pls pray one dead one possible dead not yet sure.* It's quite a jarring text in any context, but it jarred with me that I was watching football in a comfortable, safe, alarmed house in a peaceful neighbourhood. My mind immediately began imagining how Neville was coping in Manenberg. I suddenly just wanted to be there in the thick of it, not in a cosseted bubble. But the gang fight meant Neville became 'too busy' to meet up with me, and also made it nearly impossible for me to find him.

The next day, during the weekly team meeting, we heard some gun shots quite near by. Then more – closer. Then some more – this time right outside our building. We looked out of the window and saw a couple of groups of three or four young gangsters.

These are not the expensive logo-wearing, confident-in-what-they're-doing gangsters of hip-hop videos or Hollywood movies. Without exception they were all in old, dirty tracksuit pants, beanies and hoodies. Had they not been shooting guns at each other it would have been almost comical to watch them crouching, hiding, jumping out from behind walls, desperately trying to look like they knew what they were doing. It was shocking to see how utterly clueless they were – like little boys wearing plastic sheriffs' badges and cowboy hats, riding around on tricycles in a desperate attempt to assert authority.

Suddenly, one started shooting like a man possessed, all over the place, quite possibly in a *tik*-induced haze. This fusillade of shots was followed by screams from the Erica Court area. Then, a load of shots back. This continued for the best part of forty-five minutes, right in front of our office. We kept trying to resume our meeting but couldn't. As the shooting became more erratic, we moved away from the window and began to pray, sitting on the floor out of harm's way – not long previously a bullet had come through the office window and lodged in the wall. It was crazy how traumatic it felt as we watched these poor, addicted, confused, angry *children* shooting at anything that moved. Running around feeling like hardened champions but looking more like headless chickens, groups of terrified people ran a gauntlet through the streets to get away. We would later learn about how to process the effects of trauma. At the time, apart from doing a couple of star jumps to release the tension, we had no idea how to cope.

A change of direction

Since before we were married, Sarah and I had dreamt of moving to London for a year to study masters degrees. She was still fascinated by development in war zones and the reintegration of child soldiers back into society; I was keen to relate personal faith to societal issues in a Cape Town context. We had been accepted for courses at King's College addressing our areas of interest, and Sarah had even received a full scholarship for her fees and expenses. The rest of the team, which by now had become more of a tiny church family, agreed that this was the right time for us to go and so we began to prepare ourselves for leaving Cape Town. It was a disorientating time. Having spent the last three years immersed in the intense complexities of Manenberg, I was now preparing to return to what felt like the staid familiarity of England.

My chief concern was what would happen to Dowayne. He had been in and out of the rehab we had initially sent him to, but ran away whenever an issue surfaced. For the last couple of months we'd dreaded any knock on the office door as we knew it was likely to be Dowayne having checked out of rehab again and wanting us to listen to his meandering, emotionally charged story justifying why, this time, he wasn't in the wrong. One way or the other, it had become clear this rehab wasn't working – which, in retrospect, shouldn't have surprised us as we later learnt that residents were forced to write Bible verses out hundreds of times as punishment for breaking the rules. The problem was, we didn't have any better ideas. But God did, and he provided a miracle that would set Dowayne up for the year.

As we had prayed for a way forward from this impasse, we dreamt of sending Dowayne to a house of healing that we had heard about, and that had great results with those in addiction. The only problem was that it cost thousands of rand a month. The more we prayed, the more we began to see this problem transform into an opportunity – and so we decided to send Dowayne to Beth Rapha without knowing how we were going to pay. We felt God encouraging us to trust his provision as we stepped out in faith. So that's what we did – and through two strands of God's sovereign tapestry entwining, this time around Dowayne stayed in rehab.

The first strand materialised the third week he was at Beth Rapha, when I received an email from someone with whom I had not been in contact for a considerable time. A year before, I'd applied to the trust this person ran, for a donation to an emergency intervention fund we were establishing. The idea behind this was that there was so much need around us that we couldn't possibly budget for, but that one-off donations could help with. Out of the blue, eighteen months after my last email had been unanswered, he replied apologising profusely for having forgotten about my proposition, and committing to giving an amount that (he had no idea) would cover exactly a year's rehab fees for Dowayne.

I only found out about the second strand much later on, when Dowayne was months into his recovery. Sarah and I had him to stay one weekend and he told us the story. About a week into Dowayne's time at Beth Rapha, the old familiar lies began to assail him. *You're not going to make it, what's the point pretending? You don't belong here. Go back to Manenberg and the gangs, that's where you belong – you'll never get free from drugs.* He was on the verge of packing his bags and running away after fighting with someone in his dorm. But something reminded him of a CD of worship music I'd made for him. He dug through his bag and played the CD. The first track was a song called 'Keep Believing'.

> I saw the light, a gentle light, dawning brightly in
>   your eyes.
> I saw a hope; I saw the million years of stone wash
>   away.
> I saw the cast of your past quietly leave the room.
> The power their voices held within was conquered
>   silent, gone from you.
>
> Keep believing,
> Your eyes hold faith,
> Keep believing,
> Your heart has been changed,
> Your redeemer lives today.
>
> You've seen the land you understand, you have the
>   power to roam there.
> Opportunity is written on the trees and in the air.

I saw the joy, the pure joy seeing your father's eyes
So though the storm may batter on, I know this love
   is so much stronger.

Keep believing.

The song was by a British friend of ours called Cate, who had written it after watching a film we had made about Dowayne's life. She describes the effect watching Dowayne's story had had on her: 'His eyes were truly bright. I so longed for him to never give up this fight.' So she wrote a song. And just as he *was* about to give up the fight, he listened to it on repeat and decided, against all the odds, to follow its advice and keep believing.

Words carry power. We should never underestimate the effect our encouragement can have on others. The eternal truths we declare over people and their circumstances trump the temporal reality they may currently be experiencing. In Romans 4:17 it is written of God that he 'calls into being things that were not'. In the beginning, light was created by God speaking to the darkness. We can continue this prophetic creativity by speaking hope into hopelessness, truth into lies, love into despair, and by so doing create a reality on earth that resonates a little more in sync with heaven. The effect is cumulative and exponential. Dowayne's story so encouraged Cate that she wrote a song, which in turn encouraged Dowayne to stay in rehab. He is now, at the time of writing, six years clean. Cate has moved to Manenberg with husband Nick and their three young children, and they have opened a pre-school and a media company – offering their lives as part of the emerging story.

London

Student life was a far cry from dodging bullets in Manenberg. Most of the decisions Sarah and I found ourselves needing to make revolved around which modules to study, which library to sit in, and which combination of the lunch 'meal deal' to opt for.

We were able to rest and grow, and were stimulated by a world of books, lectures and online articles that had been inaccessible to us in Manenberg. Up to that point, I had found working in Manenberg so arduous and all-encompassing, continuously trying to meet the needs of others, doing my utmost just to keep my head above the water, always seeming to fall two steps back after any forward movement, living to merely avert disaster and hold on to hope, that it simply hadn't seemed possible to study as well. (It's no coincidence that the number of high school students in Manenberg entering tertiary education is shockingly low – beyond a failing local education system, life can be so intense that there is little capacity for anything much beyond survival.)

We spent our time processing what we had learned in South Africa, and applying it to academic study. I found the combination of theory and praxis a thrilling mix – each informing the other in cyclical and reciprocal ways. But we were well aware of the immense privilege it was for us to study for a masters when so many of our friends in Manenberg would never have such an opportunity. The tension of living such a privileged life in London while staying connected and committed to the community in Manenberg wasn't straightforward.

Use your brain

Some Christians can be dismissive of academic study, as if the process of learning is somehow threatening to faith. For me, it was quite the opposite – buried in books, I experienced a kind of awakening. The more I read, the more I realised how blinkered and culturally conditioned my faith was. It was the perfect counter-point to the education I had received on the streets of Manenberg, and no less hard-hitting in very different ways.

As I read Latin American liberation theology, I became aware of my unthinking alignment to, for example, capitalism and globalism. Living in Manenberg had shown me both the struggle and value of living on the margins of society with those excluded by the 'system' – but actually studying the theology gave me words to express my undeveloped convictions. Up to that point, I had been wrestling with what it meant for someone to 'convert' to Christianity – to become born again and be adopted into the family of God. The writing of the Peruvian theologian Gustavo Gutiérrez was instructive to say the least. His definition of conversion is particularly exciting: 'A conversion is the starting point of every spiritual journey. It involves a break with the life lived up to that point; it is a prerequisite for entering the kingdom.'[2] That much I knew. But he continues, 'insofar . . . as a conversion is a break with sin it will have to have both a personal and a social dimension'. Put slightly differently, it simply isn't enough for an individual to come to faith in Jesus and live a life unconcerned by the issues all around us. Gutiérrez pushes further, saying conversion 'also has consequences for the web of social relationships of which the individual is a part'. In other words, Christians need to break out of the safety of friendships that merely affirm our worldview or socio-economic standing. Beyond the social relationships we are part of, 'the conversion required will have to be radical enough to bring us into a different world, the world of the poor'. For Gutiérrez, there is simply no separating conversion to faith in Jesus with a life lived among the poor. This was deeply comforting to read, as I had begun to think my chosen path in Manenberg was an extreme or fringe response to the call of Jesus. What Gutiérrez taught me was that it was perfectly reasonable, and to be expected, of someone who had started their spiritual journey following Jesus.

Another academic awakening I had was related to race and white privilege. I came to see that so much of the Christianity preached and circulated among churches in the West, as well as in Manenberg, was rooted in racist assumptions stemming from a blind following of the pattern of white-dominated culture. As James Cone explains, 'biblical thinking is liberated thought, i.e., thinking that is not entrapped by social categories of the dominant culture'.[3] Throughout more recent Western history white culture has dominated black culture – sometimes in a premeditated way, at other times obliviously. Reading black theology as a school of thought was a gift to me because it helped me view Jesus not simply as a forgiver of individual sins but as a liberator from systemic oppression and the misuse of power. I thought of the gospel I had heard preached in so many churches in Manenberg that failed to address the widespread agony felt by the community, a direct result of systemic sin by apartheid policy makers, but only focused on individual piety. It didn't surprise me that not much was changing.

My relationship with Jesus grew closer as I realised he was as invested in delivering people from economic, social and political oppression as he was in defeating emotional, spiritual and moral oppression – and so I learnt that one of the biggest lies peddled by the evangelical church is that the message of the gospel is apolitical. In fact, Jesus' life and teaching was fused with political connotation. Cone explains that 'to be oppressed is to be defined, located or set aside according to another's perspective'.[4] Because black people have historically been the victims, not the benefi-ciaries, of systems, black theology centres not on systematic logic but on storytelling – 'the theological expression of a people who lack social and political power'. It is a theology of survival, constructing a way of living for those whose lives are devalued by existing power structures. The irony is, of course, that those who will not listen to the story are the ones who need to hear it the loudest. It is by definition impossible for the plight of the oppressed to be understood by those aligned to a life of privilege.

Our year at King's messed me up. Quite beautifully. It meant I could no longer go along with the standard 'Christian' way of things. It generated real excitement in me as I anticipated putting all I had learnt into practice once we had returned to Manenberg. Meanwhile, back in Cape Town, Dowayne was going through his own process of awakening. He had now been in rehab for eighteen months, was doing better and better, and was being exposed to a different way of life outside of Manenberg.

9: Placed with the Displaced

Christianity is an invitation to be part of an alien people who make
a difference because they see something that cannot otherwise be
seen without Christ. Right living is more the challenge than right
thinking . . . That which makes the church 'radical' and forever 'new'
is not that the church tends to lean toward the left on most social
issues, but rather that the church knows Jesus whereas the world does
not. In the church's view, the political left is not noticeably more
interesting than the political right; both sides tend towards solutions
that act as if the world has not ended and begun in Jesus. These
'solutions' are only mirror images of the status quo.
(Stanley Hauerwas and William H. Willimon)[1]

The world as we have created it is a process of our thinking.
It cannot be changed without changing our thinking.
(Albert Einstein)[2]

After a year of studies we returned to Cape Town more convinced
than ever that there are simply no economic or political solutions
to the problems the world faces and itself generates. If the assertion is true that God (and not free-market capitalists or Islamic
terrorists) rules the world, then it logically follows that only
through learning to live out Jesus' sacrificial love will the transformation of communities, societies and nations be possible. As
we weighed up various possibilities of what the next stage of
Cape Town life could look like, we couldn't let go of the deep-set
feeling that commuting from the suburbs to Manenberg each day
would just perpetuate the unhealthy prevailing narrative of white
people going to do things for those living in townships.

The fact is, 'being with' is a lot more meaningful and generative than 'doing for'. Put slightly differently: when you are neighbours with someone, you develop an equal relationship based on familiarity and friendship; when you visit somewhere to 'help', 'minister' or 'serve', you can develop a skewed relationship based on providing something. As such, you create a power-laden transaction rather than a reciprocal relationship. So much Christian ministry that goes on in the world is based upon transactional service provision over relationship building. And we honestly wonder why things don't change.

Where would Jesus live?

If Jesus was living on earth today and moved to Cape Town, I genuinely believe he would live in Manenberg, or somewhere like it. And if the Christian life is about trying to follow Jesus, and be like him in everything, it seems quite clear that more of those who claim to follow our penniless Messiah should be living among the poor, traumatised, disempowered and addicted. Jesus came from an accursed and belittled place. ('Nazareth! Can anything good come from there?' was asked of Jesus, at the beginning of his ministry – John 1:46.) He was financially poor (Luke 2:24 – his parents offered two doves rather than a lamb – a sign of their financial poverty). He seemed to spend more time among the poor and marginalised than among the influential ('While Jesus was having dinner at Levi's house, many tax collectors and sinners were eating with him and his disciples, for there were many who followed him' – Mark 2:15) and was criticised for doing so ('Here is a glutton and a drunkard, a friend of tax collectors and sinners' – Matt. 11:19). Might Manenberg be a contemporary equivalent of Nazareth – accursed and marginalised, feared and misunderstood, a community from which 'nothing good' can come? It would seem so, based on newspaper headlines I've read and conversations I've had. If Christians are to walk as Jesus walked, might this mean exposing the Western world myths of 'quality of life', 'security' and 'comfort', based, as they are, on idols? What about the apartheid mindset of fear and division?

As Sarah and I followed this line of reasoning towards its logical end, we reaffirmed in ourselves that to move back to Manenberg continued to make more sense than not. If the reading of the Gospels leaves us with the question 'How then shall we live?', reorienting our lives in this way was the most politically and theologically congruent response we could come up with. This conviction, along with the inheritance Sarah had received from her mother, who had passed away before we'd moved to the UK, enabled us to combine two dreams – a home for Sarah and me (the previous house had now become home to a dear friend and his family), and a home for addicts wanting to get clean. We could all live together. We began house-hunting right away.

Let's try again

Do not stop short of your destiny. Do not stop short of his glory . . .
You are not big enough, strong enough, prepared enough or spiritual
enough to do the work that God wants you to do. But he is. God is
more than big enough. He will complete the work he has set out to do
in and through you. (Heidi Baker)[3]

If you were to draw a simplified outline of Manenberg, you would basically draw a rectangle with the long sides running vertically. The majority of Manenberg's more explicit and visible criminal activity and gang violence happens in the central third of the rectangle, which is sandwiched between two areas at the top left (Primrose Park) and bottom right (Sherwood Park). We would later learn that the open secret in both of these gang-neutral, more well-to-do areas was widespread heroin addiction, and that while there was less gang activity, the atmosphere was anything but neutral. Be that as it was, we were motivated solely by the need for a home in a gang-neutral area, for us to be able to accommodate young men affiliated with different gangs. As we began to look for houses, our vision was to find a place that would enable us to welcome any young man from any gang, regardless of which gangs were fighting each other at the time. The idea was that their very coexistence in the house, sharing life together united in a common fight (against addiction and brokenness) and fuelled by a common purpose (discovering true identity in Jesus) would become a microcosm of the community-level reconciliation we envisaged. I would sometimes find myself daydreaming about the prospect of angry fatherless young men, brainwashed by gangs, addled by drugs, convinced they should be enemies, becoming lifelong friends. This is, I believe, what Manenberg needs more than anything.

Initially we couldn't find anything suitable. There were simply no houses on the market. The three false starts from before our time in the UK came back to me, and I began to feel hopeless about ever finding the right place. Then, one evening while having dinner with Clare and Lloyd, I was moaning about how slowly things seemed to be going. Clare randomly piped up, 'You know what, I think you're going to find your house this week.'

I let out a cynical snort and asked, 'Is that prophetic?!'

'Sure, why not,' she replied, rather unconvincingly.

It was the most understated prophetic word I've ever been given. Sure enough, that week we came across a plot for sale with two adjacent cottages and a good-sized garden. It would mean Sarah and I could live in the back, with the boys' house at the front, with a shared wall connecting the two. It was ideal.

A couple of months later, having made various offers and going back and forth with the estate agent over the price, I was again feeling disheartened.

'I just don't think they're going to accept our offer – I'm not even convinced they're serious about selling.'

'Nah – I think you'll get it by Christmas. In fact, I can see it wrapped up under a Christmas tree, like a special gift to you guys from God.'

'Clare, are you prophesying again?'

'Maybe . . . yeah I think so.'

Sure enough, at 7.30 p.m. on Christmas Eve we signed the official offer to purchase. We were learning yet again that when God's in something, whatever setbacks present themselves, it all comes together in ways we could never ourselves engineer.

Biting off more than you can chew

Although we couldn't have been happier to be finally moving into the house that was the answer to our prayers of the last five years, it didn't come without its ups and downs. We had spent all the money we had on purchasing the house *voetstoets* – 'as is' – and were becoming increasingly aware of the scope of the renovation work that was needed. The roof needed sealing, the plumbing and electrics required a complete overhaul, internal walls had to be altered, ceilings were caving in, the guttering and fascias were mostly broken, the external cavity wall at the back was unfinished and exposed, and there was widespread rising damp due to most of the window frames having been left unsealed and packed with loose bricks and newspaper. The closest to a guarantee the structural engineer would give us was that he didn't think the house was going to fall down.

One evening during a 24–7 prayer week, I was expressing to God how overwhelmed and fearful I was feeling. We were going out on a limb, I reminded him, and what had begun as a big adventure wasn't feeling particularly adventurous any more. In fact, during my less-than-full-of-faith days it seemed kind of reckless – and there were various people waiting in the wings to give us a patronising pat on the shoulder and a sanctimonious 'I told you so' as and when our plans, or new home, collapsed – whichever came first. As I was ~~complaining~~ praying, a random thought came to mind.

Crowdfunding.

I vaguely remembered seeing a crowdfunding campaign a

friend had shared on Facebook. Nervously, I opened my laptop
and logged into my account – aware that this was the last thing
I should be doing in my late-night prayer slot. But, as I stalked
this friend's Facebook page in the middle of the night, I came
across the page I'd remembered. Sure enough, a substantial
amount of money had been raised for an exciting initiative somewhere in the US, all in less than two months. I closed my laptop
and breathed out a confused two-word half-prayer: 'Really, Lord?'
Really. And it was at that moment that he reminded me of a word
he'd given Sarah and me as we were going back and forth on
offers to purchase the house: *If you give me everything you've got,
I'll give you everything you need to turn this house into a home
and habitation for my Spirit.*

Provision is nothing new

I'd recently been finding encouragement from two seemingly
random stories in the Old Testament, both of which I drew upon
as I considered what I felt God was saying to me. The stories
were of Elijah being fed by ravens in 1 Kings 17, and the widow's
oil in 2 Kings 4. In the first story, Elijah follows the direct
command of God to 'leave here, turn eastward and hide in the
Kerith Ravine, east of the Jordan'. He was to survive by drinking
water from the river, and wasn't to worry about food, as God
assured him 'I have instructed the ravens to feed you there' (vv.
3–4). Elijah is obedient to God's direction and sure enough the
ravens do their job. He eats and is sustained and all is well.
However, this arrangement changes when 'some time later the
brook dried up because there had been no rain in the land' (v. 7)
– a direct consequence of the prophetic decree Elijah had himself
announced in verse 1.

At this point it would have been completely understandable
for Elijah to be a little confused as to the mixed messages he'd
been getting from God. He may even have begun to second guess
whether he'd even heard correctly. He was to announce that there

would be no rain in the land – widespread drought – until he gave the word for rain, but then he was to survive on water from the river that dried up in accordance with that very word.

How often do we see that happen in our own lives? Maybe we haven't felt moved to declare nationwide environmental disasters, but we may well have felt we heard God clearly say something that we then followed, only to end up in a pickle somewhere down the line. In such cases, it would be a fairly natural instinct to pray something like, 'Umm, God, what are you up to? I'm trying to follow your plan!' And if nothing particularly shifted, we might then give up on listening to God's voice because we'd tried that once and it didn't work out so well.

In the very next verse after the river drying up, we read 'Then the word of the Lord came to him' (v. 8). There's a new word to follow. 'Go at once to Zarephath in the region of Sidon and stay there. I have instructed a widow there to supply you with food' (v. 9). It wasn't that God had deliberately led Elijah into disaster, nor that God was unaware of the drought. But the grace on that season by the river was over, and it was time for Elijah to move on – move on to the next assignment God had for him, where there would be provision.

Elijah could have stayed around the river, waiting for water. Had he done so, he'd have been acting in obedience with what God had said. But he didn't. Instead of holding on to what God *had said*, he sensed a shift in his assignment (through discerning what was going on in front of him – the river drying up), and began to focus on what God *was saying*. The grace for the previous word had literally dried up, and that was the very thing that led him to seek the voice of God for the next season.

The story continues in a similarly confusing vein. It turns out the widow Elijah is sent to doesn't actually have much food (just 'a handful of flour in a jar and a little olive oil in a jug') and seems to be suicidal. It takes a pretty direct command from Elijah – that she is to make him food first, and then watch as her food supplies replenish supernaturally – to unlock the provision she needs. But, again, every need is supplied as God had said it would be – and all is well.

In 2 Kings 4 there is another story of a widow receiving the supernatural provision of God. So desperate was her situation that the creditor was on his way to 'take my two boys as his slaves' (v. 1). This time, it's Elisha not Elijah being used to do the miracles, and he simply asks the widow what she's got to work with – what can she contribute to the situation to bring about a breakthrough? Her response is interesting. At first she replies in despair – 'nothing . . . at all'. But then, overcoming the shame of her poverty, she adds, 'except a small jar of olive oil' (v. 2). And it's as if the miracle was released then and there. She is told to fetch as many jars as she can, and pour the little oil she has into them, which she does. Somehow, the oil fills so many jars that no more jars are left – and she is able to sell the supernaturally multiplied oil to not only pay her debt but live on the remainder of the profit.

There are a whole lot of lessons we can learn from this story. First, that desperation and an inability to help oneself out of a conundrum is the perfect prerequisite for a miracle. (This shouldn't surprise us, as Jesus did say that the poor in spirit are blessed.) Equally, it was as the woman broke out of her poverty mindset, saw that she had something to offer and began collecting jars that the miracle came – in other words, it required more than just sitting around praying in passivity or self-pity to 'unlock' the miracle. And finally, both the stories are a clear reminder that each end of the theological spectrum (on the one end, supernaturally minded Christians with little concern for the poor; on the other end, social justice-oriented Christians with little concern for the supernatural) needs the other. In other words, situations of desperate poverty and fraught hopelessness need to be seen and heard by followers of Jesus living in proximity to the vulnerable and marginalised. And where human solutions simply don't cut it, we need to minister in the supernatural anointing of the Holy Spirit.

We had spent the entirety of Sarah's inheritance on what could have euphemistically been called 'a renovator's dream', and were now feeling a bit like Elijah at the dried-up river – 'Uhm, OK, Lord, now what?' Thankfully, rather than sending us to a mouthy, despondent widow he prodded us in the direction of crowd-funding. We set up an online campaign, and over the course of the next month and a half, as all the money we needed to reno-vate the house came in through the generosity of 229 different people from around the world, we stood, open-mouthed, in amaze-ment. And we began to realise, as I imagine both Elijah and Elisha and their widow friends did, that because God wants to change the world through us, he's not at all concerned by what we don't have. Whatever we have, however small, if we give it all to him, he'll make sure there's more than enough for our need.

So, what do you have? These things, if fully given to God, can be multiplied to propel you into the next assignment God has for you. Faith is the highway along which all provision from God comes. Everything you give to God, he will multiply. It really does seem to be as hilariously simple as that.

Moving in

Sarah and I moved in to our house in a gang-neutral corner of Manenberg on our second wedding anniversary. The previous year, while living in London, we'd saved up some money to go backpacking in Morocco. This year, our celebration involved a McDonald's lunch. That deteriorated quickly, then – though we did get free chicken nuggets due to an administrative error, so, every cloud . . .

I tried to make conversation with whoever I met on our street. I was, I suppose, overcompensating for the anxiety we had been feeling from the crowdfunding campaign. While it had been a great success in terms of raising the funds needed to renovate the house, it hadn't come without controversy. In my mid-campaign excitement, I had agreed to an interview with a local tabloid newspaper that was interested in the story. I made the mistake of going in totally unguarded in how much of the vision to share, even mentioning the likelihood of us building a Christian prayer room on site. The resulting article, quite apart from being desperately inaccurate, used the details to construct an utterly sensationalist scenario. '*Portaal lei na genesing*' screamed the head-line – '*Paartjie uit Londen wil gangsters, junkies help*'. 'Portal leading to healing. Couple from London wants to help gangster junkies'. I received threatening emails and Facebook messages, and an anonymous letter was posted in the mosque about the danger we posed to the community. The contradictory message being spread by people was that we were simultaneously opening a 24–7 'prayer centre' and a Hard Livings drug den. It was so obviously not true that in other circumstances we would have laughed it off. But we knew it was imperative we developed good relationships with the neighbours, so we did as we were asked and visited the local imam to show him Sarah's signature on the house purchase agreement – it had been rumoured that Rashied Staggie himself had bought the house, and was paying us to run it for him.

While most were generally very welcoming and friendly towards us, what struck me was the number of people in Sherwood Park who warned me about those *skelms* from 'the other side'. Some actually used the term Upper Manenberg, to emphasise distance from gang activity. Gang membership, drug addiction, a life of prostitution – none of these are anyone's plan A. Those who have landed up in, or chosen, this way of life (for whatever reason, and there are many) are not morally inferior to anyone else. Putting people into categories that distance *them* from *us* based on the specks in *their* eyes is inevitably futile when one has a plank in one's own. The curses of those in Sherwood Park directed towards those in the gang-ridden blocks of slightly more central Manenberg become a self-fulfilling prophecy of doom. The obvious irony is that the very people who are worried about gangsters breaking into their houses are in some way exacerbating the problem by refusing to see any potential or hope of redemption in them. It gradually dawned on me that behind the judgment was deep-set fear – hence the extremity of the rumours that had been spread about us. Once, while I was chatting to an elderly neighbour, she warned me against spending time with those in gangs. 'After all,' she said, *'meng jou met die semels dan vreet die varke jou op.'* 'If you mix with the pig food the pigs will eat you.'

We were due to take ownership, swap keys and bid farewell to the previous owners at 2 p.m. on the Monday. Legally speaking, the house became ours on the Thursday before, but we gave the two families an extra weekend to pack their things up. They had lived there for decades, had never moved house and simply seemed to have underestimated what was involved. The numerous shacks in the backyard (whose demolition was written into the offer to purchase) were still standing at 1.15 p.m. – four months after signing the contract. Sarah's uncle Simon came with us to the house, having lent us his *bakkie* to transport some boxes. As he watched the chaos, three white horses galloped past us along the street in front of the house. Christians love prophetic signs, right? Well I have no idea what that one meant.

When we did eventually get in – at about 6 p.m. – we found most of the light bulbs had been taken, as well as the external gates. I had needed to explain to one of the aunties that stripping the burglar gates off the front door to take them with her wasn't part of the deal. One of the brothers of the previous owners took me aside to say he would leave some old guttering for me 'as a gift'. We had no need for guttering, as we had been donated brand new stuff, but I decided against rejecting this philanthropic gesture. It was only after having personally paid for three truck-loads of rubble to be removed (which I understood to be the sellers' responsibility) that the removal men explained that the old broken guttering at the back was a serious health hazard as it was asbestos! Whether the brother knew this or not, I have no idea.

Now gateless, we borrowed one of Jonathan's German shepherds as an interim security measure. Stacey, affable but infuriating, treated our wet cement like the Hollywood Walk of Fame, and put her paw prints in each new section. She also monitored the painter's workmanship by jumping all over the newly painted window frames and walls. However, she did seem to embrace faith – wailing along with the Muslim call to prayer five times a day.

Just a thirty-second walk from our front door, the friendly shop owners at our local corner shop, Big D's, seemed to be running some kind of informal sweepstake on what was going on behind our gate. Did we drink? Was the building work still happening? When were we next going to England? Who were the white people at our house the other day? Beyond the friendly and relational aspect, Big D's attracts human traffic most of the day and night – an effective security measure from housebreakers. Not only that, but Shiraaz and Naeema's gatsby stall (a gatsby is a foot-long sub roll filled with meat, chips and salad – 'traditional coloured food', I'm often told) wafts the delicious scent of tikka chicken over our wall most weekends – we miss them in Ramadan.

Building work started right away, with a hopelessly misjudged deadline of three months to have everything finished.

Gangs, bangs and guilt pangs

Anyone who has ever done up a house knows the sheer number of tiny decisions needing to be made each day. From trying to agree on paint colours and plug socket placements to water-proofing rising damp and discussing appropriate security measures that were sufficient but not over the top, we were beginning to feel pretty overwhelmed. One of the fairly disappointing discoveries I made was that I was a distinctly amateur project manager, prone to miscommunication and impulse decision making when things got difficult.

One morning, as I was in a haze of building contractor-related confusion, a mysterious *bakkie* drove into our driveway laden with bags of food.

'Good morning! Are Igshaan or Mansoor in?' chirped the driver.

'Umm, no – sorry. They've moved. Can I help?'

'Do you know their new address? I've got a delivery from PAGAD – because of their son, you know?'

'I'm sorry, you'll have to ask someone else, they didn't give me their new address. All I know is it's somewhere in Grabouw.'

The man drove off, and I stood there contemplating our brief encounter. Why were PAGAD bringing bags of food to the previous owners, and what did he mean about their son?

I knew a little about PAGAD: similar to the gang bosses, they are revered or hated depending on who you ask. People Against Gangs and Drugs was established in the mid-1990s in reaction to widespread drug dealing and gang activity in the Cape Flats. Initially multi-religious, they rapidly became associated with radical Islam and militant terrorism due to explicit religious motivation and violent methods. In 1996, PAGAD made headlines for the killing of Hard Livings gang leader, Rashaad Staggie, twin of Rashied. The extreme manner in which Staggie was executed – shot, beaten and set on fire – was caught on camera by the national media, sending shockwaves throughout South Africa.

Anything established on a negative, or formed in opposition to something, is unlikely to offer much in creative ideas. So with PAGAD. Shameless propagation of the myth of redemptive violence – in this case, shooting and killing people in order to show that shooting and killing people is wrong – is not only morally nihilistic but fundamentally flawed. It was therefore rather unnerving to hear that the food deliveries were by way of compensation from PAGAD to the previous owners for the dedication their son had made. In a brief chat with the neighbours, I discovered that one of the previous owners' sons appeared in court for his part in the construction of cellphone-activated pipe bombs, likely put together in what was now our living room.

Legacy

Inbred in me and all humans is an inescapable feeling that what comes after us matters; that legacy matters, that what we do, what we build, how we live our lives and what we leave behind, is important to us. (Matthew Parris)[4]

Investing in individuals and *really* discipling them in faith can change the course of history. Floyd McClung tells the story of a man called Edward Kimball, a Sunday school teacher in the 1880s.

Kimball began to strike up a friendship with a few young men in his Sunday school class. Kimball was particularly committed to a fellow classmate fresh from the farmlands who had begun working in a nearby shoe shop. One day Kimball decided to visit his new friend at work. He entered the shop, found him in the backroom, and struck up a conversation. Later he led his friend to a personal relationship with Jesus. When describing this young man years later, Kimball said, 'I have met few friends whose minds were spiritually darker, or who seemed more unlikely ever to become a Christian.' But Kimball's faith in his new friend, and his investment of time and personal mentoring, made a huge impact. His new friend was D. L. Moody, who went on to become an evangelist who led tens of thousands to faith in Jesus. Eventually Moody invested in the life of a man he met in England, called F. B. Meyer. Meyer was a pastor who resisted Moody's evangelistic zeal and fiery preaching style, but responded when Moody invited him to the States to spend time together. Meyer was more impacted by Moody's personal life than by his preaching.

Meyer in turn influenced a man named J. Wilber Chapman, who decided as a result of his friendship with Meyer to go into full-time evangelistic ministry. One of Chapman's disciples was a man named Billy Sunday. Sunday in turn spent time discipling a group of businessmen in North Carolina. After years of praying together, these men were prompted by God to invite an evangelist named Mordecai Ham to speak to a citywide gathering in Charlotte, North Carolina. During one of the meetings conducted by Ham, a young teenager came forward and gave his life to the Lord. His name was Billy Graham.[5]

It should be the desire of each follower of Jesus to leave the world a better place – to leave behind a legacy of faith and a bunch of people who you led to faith in Jesus. The fact is, you don't get Billys without Edwards. It could reasonably be said that Edward Kimball's tenacious pursuit of one single convert influenced millions upon millions of people to come to faith in Jesus. Two people I met who seemed to understand this concept of legacy were a local entrepreneur called James Thomas, and Sarah's mum Diana.

James was full of bright ideas. He was always scheming some kind of plan to improve people's lives or make the world a better place. Among other ideas, he devised a board game to train young African entrepreneurs in starting small businesses, and generally gave his life to serving Jesus with compassionate, creative flair. When Jonathan and Grant were trying to come up with local business ideas that could be established in Manenberg, back in the early days of the ministry, James was an obvious guy to rope in. His idea of a Manenberg-based bakery and coffee shop was met with enthusiasm, and the name he suggested calling it was received with hearty laughs. Based on the notion that we were trying to cultivate a community of faith in direct contrast to the 'brotherhoods' of the gangs, and that the language of the street needed to be 'made new', James proposed the coffee shop be called *Jou Ma Se Kombuis*, 'Your Mum's Kitchen'. Yet James never lived to see the fulfilment of this dream. In September 2013 he was killed by Al-Shabbab terrorists in the Westgate Mall attack in Nairobi – senselessly gunned down while visiting Kenya to train up more nation-changing entrepreneurs.

Sarah's mum, Diana, was someone who understood the idea of

legacy and lived her life accordingly. Coming to faith in the 1970s at a Benny Hinn crusade, she lived a life of uncompromising kindness. She'd brought up Sarah and her brother James as a single parent, and instilled in them a deep sense of right and wrong. Sarah can't remember a time when, as a child, she didn't know Jesus. When, in 2010, Diana discovered she had stage 4 bone cancer and was given a few short months to live, such was her faith in the power and goodness of God that her first reaction to the news was what a perfect set-up this was for a powerful healing testimony. And so she took a voice recorder to her doctor's appointments so that once she had been healed there would be audio proof the cancer ever existed!

The sad fact is that Diana wasn't healed of cancer. She died less than a year after her diagnosis. Her final months were spent travelling with Sarah to the US, Mexico and Costa Rica, in search of a healing that never came. Diana's life had an impact on many others. But she also left Sarah an inheritance. Sarah was left with memories of a mum full of faith right till the end, stories of people healed through her prayers, and the experience of being discipled from such a young age.

The point is, death doesn't get to have the final say. Neither the destruction wreaked by Islamic terrorism nor stage 4 bone cancer can vanquish God's work through a person fully yielded to his purposes – even after their physical body is no more. The far-reaching legacy left by James Thomas lives on – in the continent of Africa where local entrepreneurs he trained up are transforming communities – and lives on in Manenberg through the memory of a jauntily named coffee shop. In the same way, the impact Diana Dixon made in the world lives on. The prayers she prayed for her daughter have grown hands and feet – in Sarah living her life for and among the marginalised. And the money she left Sarah was what enabled us to buy our house and open it up to addicted gangsters. We call it Cru62 (more on that later). Diana's legacy is every life that experiences acceptance in the family of God through Cru62.

Each one of us who know and follow Jesus have this same privilege of continuing the advance of his kingdom on earth. Physical embodiment, or air in lungs, is non-compulsory. As we dream of what Manenberg could look like in the future, we're aware we may not see all that we hold out hope for. In the humdrum of day-to-day ministry, we are determined to keep our focus looking forward with our hearts set on leaving a community in a better state than we found it. One of the ways we aim to do this is by raising up transformed local young men previously living lives of destruction, and equipping them with all they need to pour hope into others. Legacy is the key motivation behind Cru62.

10: Cru62

God takes a long time to act suddenly. Between the time that God gives us a promise and the time that we actually see the fulfilment of that promise there is often times a process, and that process is actually what we need to come into the promise.
(Kris Vallotton)[1]

If you give God the right to yourself, he will make a holy experiment out of you. God's experiments always succeed.
(Oswald Chambers)[2]

I think my dad might be more prophetic than he thinks. He had come over to Cape Town for a holiday – so we did what all good tourists do and took a day trip to Franschoek for a spot of wine tasting. *Franschoek* is an Afrikaans name, meaning 'French corner'. The town was established by French Huguenot refugees who settled there in 1688 and began planting vines right away. Today it is widely considered to be one of South Africa's most picturesque places to visit and produces internationally acclaimed wine.

As we sat in the warmth of the afternoon sun, looking over the valley, we were given a description of the wine-making process, including various details concerning types of grapes, optimal climate, north-facing terroir, and other slightly pretentious-sounding wine-related trivia. The piece of information that stuck with me most was how difficult it is to grow pinot noir grapes. It seemed a bit random, but I remember the sommelier going on about the particularly thin skin of the grapes. Or something. He seemed to make a real thing of it, and emphasised how little wine the pinot grapes had produced, but that the quality was exquisite.

It made me value the glass I was holding all the more, knowing it had been a real labour of love.

A couple of days before this sun-hazed viticulture lesson, I had had a frustrating meeting with a representative from a charity who had come to Manenberg to see whether their organisation might financially support our work. It gradually emerged that they only funded a specific type of project, and were obsessed with numbers. Their idea of effective community transformation seemed to be defined by the number of people churned through a particular programme. If we were willing to run multiple short-term life skills courses for hundreds of unemployed youth in Manenberg, the money would be ours. Ultimately, they wanted to be able to say they had affected the highest number of people for the lowest amount of money. I pointed out that our approach was more of a slow burn, and explained we were currently walking alongside just four young men. I wanted to explain to them why their idea was highly unlikely to have any lasting impact in Manenberg; that we had come across inch-deep, mile-wide, funder-driven strategies before, and that this represented more of an anti-development strategy than anything else. But while their heart was in the right place, it didn't seem worth it. Needless to say, the meeting amounted to nothing.

Having sat through an afternoon of wine-fuelled cantankerous-ness about how hard I was finding it in Manenberg, and the lack of visible breakthrough in the lives of those we were trying to help, aggravated by this silly meeting I'd had, my dad came up with a brilliant line.

'It seems to me that people are expecting you to run a sausage factory when you're trying to run a pinot noir vineyard.'

'You what?'

'The organisation you met with last week say they want to help but they aren't really interested in depth, or quality. They want quantity. They are happy to shove everything into a one-size-fits-all approach, switch on the machine, and watch as a large amount of low-quality "product" is produced. But producing a "crop" in

Manenberg is more like making a vintage of wine. There are a number of different factors to consider – the guys you work with are a difficult demographic, life in Manenberg is intense, you don't have much of a team, you haven't got any money. The odds are stacked against you, a bit like the odds are stacked against the pinot noir wine maker. You need the right environment, suitable terroir and enough labour to grow a crop. The right conditions produce a good crop and a memorable vintage – but it's likely to be small. It's a delicate art, it will likely be frustrating a lot of the time, it may take ages, it's largely out of your hands, and whole harvests might be wiped out by unfavourable conditions. But when you do finally get there, it'll have been worth it because what you will have produced could be beautiful beyond words.'

Here goes

It was with these words of wisdom ringing in our ears that we opened Cru62 on 12 January 2015, nine months after moving into Manenberg, and almost five years after I had lived with Dowayne. He was now three years free from heroin and part of the team, ready to impart all he had received from his own time in rehab. Fusion, the project we had all previously been part of, had now become Tree of Life. We finally admitted we were best described not as colleagues working at an NGO, but as a community of believers – a church – living life together and running ministries to help uplift Manenberg. The reasons behind the name Cru62? *Cru* is a French word referring to a vineyard known for exceptional quality (also, it sounds the same as 'crew'); and 62 is our house number, and also the chapter in Isaiah that we have had prophecies from relating to the house – 'The nations will see your vindication, and all kings your glory; you will be called by a new name that the mouth of the Lord will bestow' (Is. 62:2).

We now had six beds in three bedrooms that we could offer to addicted gangsters. It was, in many ways, beyond our wildest dreams – though I felt it had taken much longer than necessary to get to this point. We would only learn through actually running the house that the process God had us on was absolutely what we had needed prior to opening. Nor did that process stop once we had launched.

It took me twenty-four hours to freak out.

A day after we opened, the implications of what we had started began to sink in. The elation we had felt on getting to the point of opening Cru62 did not last long; we were immediately swamped – and I began to find myself feeling responsible for everything and everyone. One of the young men in the first intake had been so desperate for a place to live that he had come round a couple of times the week before we opened to try and persuade us to let him stay in the meanwhile. He was so badly beaten up that blood was showing through his T-shirt and his face was swollen and bloody. It emerged that some of his family members, at their wits' end due to his compulsive stealing, had run out of non-violent ways to stop him ransacking the family home. Once we opened, he spent his first week processing feelings of deep rejection and intense anger as he lay in bed shivering his way through heroin withdrawal. As we sat with Reswell and prayed, giving him our full attention, Brandon took the opportunity to run away. He jumped the fence and went straight back to the gang. He had lasted just one day of the eighteen-month process. The next morning, already exhausted and with the false burden of three young men's recovery and salvation weighing heavily on my shoulders, I got up early to pray. *Lord, this is ridiculous. What on earth do we think we are doing? How did you let us get to this point? We are one day in, and already I feel like a complete failure.*

I then went round to the boys' house, on the front of our property, to check no one else had done a runner. It seemed calm. Worship music was playing, Dowayne was chatting to Ashton, and Reswell was in bed. I returned to our side of the house and checked my emails. One was a prophetic word from people we have never met, whose prophetic emails Sarah signed up to receive. It spoke right into the process we had been on, and of the weight of false responsibility I was now feeling.

Faith Tabernacle, 13.01.2015

In a vision I saw an old and completely dilapidated house. The foundation was cracked, the exterior siding was rotting, and it needed new windows and roofing. The interior of the house was badly damaged and in need of repair. I watched as the cracks in the foundation were filled in, and the exterior of the house, roof and windows were replaced. In the interior the wiring and plumbing were repaired, the walls were replaced and painted, and the appliances were upgraded. What was once condemned became a beautiful habitation. And the Lord said, 'Behold, my house!'

I read these words over and over again as I let them sink in. I knew God was speaking, an echo of the very words he had spoken to me during that prayer week months previously, about our home becoming a habitation for his Spirit. The lie, that somehow everything depended on me, dissipated in the peace of God's voice. I understood that he was reminding me this house was his idea, it would only succeed to the extent we cultivated an openness to his Spirit, and that the buck stopped with him as none of it ultimately belonged to us, but him. I breathed a sigh of relief and smiled for the first time that day. It wouldn't be the last time my issues with success and failure came up.

Cultivating beauty

Transforming place through cultivating beauty is deeply therapeutic. Doing so with those who have, up to that point, predominantly broken, damaged or destroyed things, brings an additional satisfaction. While we had worked round the clock to renovate and furnish the interior of the boys' house, there was no shortage of external work for us to throw ourselves into once Cru62 opened. Just a couple of inches below the sandy surface of the back yard, rubble and rubbish by the truckful were buried, three foot deep. As the south-easter wind blew, sand would blast the unfinished walls and windows of the house day in, day out. Hardy marijuana plants grew, emerging from cracks and mounds of earth. I quite liked them. They reminded me that nature always finds a way, that life will continue, and that growth even in the harshest of environments is possible. But we thought it wisest to pull them up.

Sarah has an eye for the aesthetic, and began designing a garden layout as soon as we moved in. 'We can put raised vegetable beds here' she said, moving her finger across her drawn-out plan, 'and an indigenous aloes garden at the front. Then there's the grape-vine – you can build a trellis for that, right? It also needs careful pruning. And the granadilla plant is going to grow up by the back there – so you'll need to get digging, to make a flower-bed along the wall.' It was clear who of us was the brains behind this oper-ation and who was the brawn. So the boys and I dug. And dug. And dug. Using the pickaxe, we broke up the patchwork brick areas that had served as a foundation for where the shacks had previously stood. And as one of us sorted through the old bricks, which would prove useful as a base for our water tank, others filled old concrete bags with sand and dirt and carried them on bruised, sunburnt shoulders to a trailer bound for the dump. A few days later, having treated and levelled the soil, we laid a small patch of grass. Ashton puffed out his chest in pride as he announced he had once worked for a turf company. We made a conscious effort to let him show us how he wanted us to do it. In the end there really wasn't much to it; we just laid the turf in lines. The work had been in levelling and treating the soil. But Ashton, usually quiet and withdrawn, revelled in barking out orders as project manager for the afternoon.

The raised beds began to thrive. None of us had grown our own food before, so we Googled which vegetables to put where, and the necessary conditions for each. Soon we had a whole lot of colourful produce. Butternut, aubergine, spinach, kale, cherry tomatoes and potatoes all grew no problem. Most of the carrots came out looking warped and deformed, and our attempt at onions proved particularly unsuccessful. In one sense, it didn't particu-larly matter – the main purpose for the vegetable beds was to help create an environment conducive to recovery from addiction. It offered the opportunity to bond with one another as well as learn to appreciate nature. Writing of his own experience developing a community of the wounded and marginalised in a Somerset wood in England's West Country, Tobias Jones remarks that this type of fellowship

> . . . is vital to recovery . . . Communal living focuses the mind on something outside the self. It can turn people from takers into givers, from users into makers. It's not just contact with others that's important, but also contact with the earth – the origin, after all, of humility. We're by no means the first to discover the irony that getting muddy is an integral part of staying clean.[3]

As well as mid-week gardening with Sarah, we decided that on Fridays the boys would do woodwork with me. Along with devotions, it became part of the week I looked forward to most. Gnarly, reclaimed wood, the sort of thing you find at demolition yards and which used to be beautiful but has been smashed up by life – that's the best stuff. Because once it is sanded down beyond the visible layer of grime and nail marks it can usually be made to look as beautiful as ever. Every Friday we spend hours and hours belt-sanding wood that others had thrown out. We are redeemed people, redeeming wood. Sure, it's a little cheesy, but if you saw the look on someone's face when they've restored an old teak beam to its former glory, you'd see the analogy works. It's cathartic for the boys, and it's therapy for me. In a life of helping people through multiple unresolved issues, harrowing trauma, warped relationships and dampened dreams, to spend a day making something you can see with your eyes and touch with your hands can feel as satisfying and important as that first intake of air when you've been holding your breath under water. Besides, it's discipleship 101, and meets a prevailing need – 'for holistic models of church that integrate job creation with discipleship, drug rehabilitation with Bible teaching, and starting new churches with teaching in life skills'.[4] Who better to learn the basics of regeneration in Christ through restoring old planks than young men who learn through seeing and doing, who have been thrown on the scrap heap of life? If you can see some hope for an ugly old warped floorboard, you can generally muster a little for yourself.

Arm's-length issues

It's easy to become obsessed with 'issues' – from war in the Middle East and the ensuing refugee crisis, to the negative gastro-intestinal effects of gluten on our gut. There is no shortage of issues to address or causes to fight. If I'm honest, I've begun to become just a little sceptical about some of the fads the causes of which churches adopt. (I'm aware that the notion of there even being 'fashionable' causes is pretty grotesque, but it's all around us.) These issues and causes can easily become all-encompassing and all-consuming. Shane Claiborne, a well-known Christian activist, suggests a different starting point. He urges us, 'don't choose issues, choose people . . . Fall in love with a group of people who are marginalised and suffering, and then you won't have to worry about which cause you need to protest. Then the issues will choose you.'[5] It never ceases to amaze me how polarised our advocacy can become. Couldn't we be pro-life *and* pro-choice? What if, sometimes, we don't throw out the baby with the bath water? What if we carefully held the baby and loved it as best we could? And, if we poured the bath water on to a flower-bed or vegetable patch, we could even find generative ways to redemptively use something we'd previously written off as waste.

I didn't expect one of the most upsetting aspects in being friends with young people in gangs and on drugs to be the misunderstanding of others. Namely, the ear-bashing that more polished, less obviously addicted people, enjoying the trappings and conveniences of living in the centre of inequality-exacerbating systems, give me about the moral nihilism of my marginalised friends, whom they have never met. The thinking usually goes something like this: because that person smokes drugs and commits crimes, they must be a bad person. And from that skewed logic, the question becomes, how can you work with *those* people, aren't you scared? Or, even worse is the naive notion that society's problems would all be solved by locking all of *them* up in prison.[6]

The problem is US

One evening Sarah and I took the boys and some visitors to a talk by a well-known journalist and researcher of all things gang-related. He was articulate and insightful as he expounded his ideas based upon four decades of research. While his theories relating epigenetics to a chemical predisposition towards addiction, and his stinging critique of the mayor of Cape Town's shameless neo-liberal agenda were fascinating, by the time he finished his presentation and invited questions from the floor, I found myself bothered by something much simpler and more obvious that had little to do with him. The entire audience, except a group of us from Manenberg in one corner, was white and middle-aged. And while the questions that this demographic posed were worded eloquently, they betrayed an ignorance about or reticence towards two of the most undealt-with issues in Cape Town – race and inequality.

The questions got me thinking about the extent to which society at large could be held responsible for issues of gangsterism, drugs and crime. A lady in one of the front rows asked (somewhat rhetorically) whether Dr Pinnock agreed that the gang problem could be solved by imposing a year of military service on all eighteen-year-olds. He gave a nuanced and rather gracious reply, suggesting this could be a small part of an answer. Another, bespectacled and demure, aired his opinion that better town planning would sort everything out.

There were a few elephants in the room that evening. Yet the biggest elephant was also the least acknowledged. The majority of opinions given by the middle-aged, white audience, aired in the form of questions, all centred around a single narrative. In their eyes, coloured youth that join gangs are an issue to be solved, a threat to suburban security and an embarrassment to an otherwise world-class city. There was no mention of the fact that 95 per cent of people in that room were still, over twenty years into non-racial democracy, surfing the wave of wealth, entitlement and privilege left to white people as an inheritance from apartheid – and that this might just be a significant factor in perpetuating violent crime, anger and hopelessness among vast swathes of young coloured men.

Saul Alinksy, the father of community organising, wrote that 'to unslum the slum . . . [means] battling all of those forces in the city and the nation which converge to create the human junkyard'. In other words, there is 'a dynamic interrelationship between a community and the general social scene'.[7] These words were written in Chicago in 1946 by a Jewish American of Russian descent, and yet they encapsulate the grand narrative that desperately needs addressing in Cape Town today.

Manenberg's gang problem and the rampant racism and economic inequality in Cape Town today are dynamically interrelated. Every time a gangster is shot dead, it's a reflection of the state of Cape Town as a whole. Nothing will change until the violence and drugs and crime in Manenberg affects those in wider Cape Town beyond just motivating people to build higher walls and install more armed response panic buttons. And until the haves stop pointing blame-assigning fingers at the have nots, no amount of expert research and strongly held opinions will count for much. This may sound rather bleak and intense. It is, and there's no escaping it.

Where the rubber hits the road

In a period of three months during the first year of running Cru62, while driving with the boys around various parts of Cape Town,

Sarah and I were stopped and searched by police seven times. Neither of us had ever been stopped and searched previously, except for an occasional police roadblock. One evening when Dowayne was driving the boys to Narcotics Anonymous in the suburb of Observatory, they were stopped and searched and made to lie face down on the road as the police stood on them, interrogated them and checked that the car wasn't stolen. Another time, five of the boys were prohibited by security guards from entering a shopping mall, with no reason given. They had saved up money they'd earnt working at *Jou Ma Se Kombuis* in order to take a trip to the mall to play video games. Their trip was ruined because security didn't like the look of them. At a cinema, a group of white people got up and left when Sarah walked into a movie with the boys with her, and she is regularly followed by shop attendants when food shopping with one of the boys. The insidiousness of the single story is that it manifests in so many different scenarios.

One Saturday evening I went out with the boys to buy gatsbys. We decided to go to a viewing spot about twenty minutes' drive away to watch the sunset over the city. We arrived at the car park to see that the gate was closed, prohibiting cars from entering. I turned the car around, and decided to head home. As we were turning out of the road, a police van pulled up alongside us and two black policemen told us to get out of the car. We complied, though slightly confused as to what we had done wrong. We were made to put our hands on the vehicle as police searched us and then the inside of the car. As they searched, they asked us what we were doing there.

'We've come to watch the sunset and have dinner.'

'Where's your dinner, then?'

'You're sitting on it.'

'Don't be cheeky.'

'I'm not – you are literally sitting on our dinner.'

'Where are you from?'

'We all live in Manenberg.'

'So what are you doing here?'

'We just explained – we've . . .'

'If you're from Manenberg you shouldn't be here. You need to come to the police station with me so I can take your fingerprints.'

Of course, we put up a fuss – why shouldn't we have been there? Especially galling was that the policemen made all four of the boys sit in the back of the police van on the way to the station – as if they were criminals who had been caught breaking the law. Once at the station, fingerprints were taken (though I had to make them take my fingerprints too – I was equally [un] guilty), questions were asked and when, to the policeman's utter disbelief (he was convinced we were dealing drugs), a more thorough search of the car yielded no illicit substances, they had to let us go. One of the policemen picked up a semi-automatic rifle and marched us to the door with the words, 'Now get out of my area.' The single story rearing its ugly head through figures of authority.

You know they are planning to mug you, right?

Three friends from Kansas City were visiting our community in Manenberg for a couple of weeks. On their bucket list was a climb up Lion's Head, an easier climb than Table Mountain and with comparably beautiful views of the city and the Twelve Apostles, rocky outcrops from Camps Bays all the way down the coastline. It is also one of the boys' favourite hikes to do. So they went together. As they reached the top, a concerned-looking young white South African approached Jordan, one of our visitors.

'Hey *broe*, those coloured guys who were chatting to you and followed you up here – you do know they're planning to mug you, don't you? You're welcome to walk down with us if you want – it would be much safer.'

Jordan replied that 'those coloured guys' were actually his friends and they'd walked up together. He called out the young white South African's racism, and said, 'I appreciate you trying to be kind, but actually you're making unhelpful assumptions.'

Not long after this, Sarah sent Frikkie and Maruwaan to a local NGO to see if Cru62 could volunteer with them, or just do anything to help them out. Both of them were quite nervous, and keen to ask what they should say and what to avoid. Sarah prepped them, and off they went. They returned half an hour later looking pretty despondent.

'The people weren't so friendly. They said they had no opportunities for us to help, and then closed the door.'

Sarah's phone beeped. It was a message on the Manenberg Neighbourhood Watch group: *Everyone please be aware, there are two suspicious young men walking around pretending to want to be volunteers. Don't let them in – they're addicts!* Her heart sank as she made the connection. The very people Frikkie and Maruwaan had been offering to serve were so fearful and distrusting that they'd spread false rumours.

Multiple unrelated occasions. Different parts of Cape Town. Police and public, white, black and coloured alike. A single story circulated and recirculated. Fear, distrust, condemnation.

How would you view yourself if everyone else in your city saw you as an urban menace, good for nothing, inherently bad, a social ill to be contained?

If you told someone you knew, every time you saw them, that they stink, they might begin to wash more, though at the same time start resenting you. If you continued to tell them they stink, despite them washing multiple times a day and wearing deodorant and clean clothes, they might begin to believe that they have a fundamental problem, that they really do smell and that there's nothing that can be done about it. And they would probably hold some level of anger towards you for telling them they smell but doing nothing to help them with what *you* perceive to be a problem they have. This isn't dissimilar to the problem faced by young coloured men trying to leave gangs and drugs behind. Systems, authority structures and individuals are all against them, continually telling them they stink (despite the fact that they don't), doing nothing to help them, and refusing to examine prevailing judgmental presuppositions.

The front line

I think I know what people are alluding to when they say that because we live in Manenberg, we are 'ministering on the front line'. I *think* I know what they mean. We have had two bullets fly through our office windows during gang fights, dear friends and family have been killed, our houses have been broken into by those we have been trying to serve, we've seen miraculous financial provision come in as we've prayed for salaries or emergency rehab funds, we've watched friends come painlessly off drugs through the power of the Holy Spirit, and felt the hope drain out of us as others crash and burn for the umpteenth time, and we're all committed to living among the poor and marginalised.

But here's my issue with the F word – isn't this just the normal Christian life? What else do we honestly think following Jesus is about? He did miracles of great power, loved until it hurt, equipped his disciples to cultivate counter-cultural communities of faith, celebrated the outcast, and obediently followed the Father's voice (despite Peter's sensible-sounding but ultimately demonic advice to the contrary) all the way to Calvary. Then he told us to 'go do the same'. I sometimes wonder where the concept of 'front-line' ministry came from. Might it have come out of the boredom of the Christian ghetto – where Jesus' passions have largely been replaced by chatting about church culture or running Christian courses while sipping a cold drip coffee and Instagramming a photo of our home group?

The notion of 'front-line' ministry creates two problems. It disempowers and it dichotomises. Let me explain. You'll rarely hear those who are part of 'front-line' ministry describing their lives that way. It's a term generally used by Western Christians who don't spend their lives, say, preaching on street corners or living among the poor. And it's a concept that automatically disempowers those who subscribe to it – because it implies they aren't 'doing the stuff', 'sold out for Jesus', or 'living a life of sacrifice' (to use the clichéd phrases), and are unable to, living as they do in middle-class suburbia. Is it any less 'front line' to stack supermarket shelves, or buy out bankrupt companies, or sell cars, or arrange flowers, or raise children at home, or make multi-million-pound deals in a boardroom? As Bill Johnson helpfully puts it, 'there is no such thing as secular employment for the believer. Once we are born again, everything about us is redeemed for Kingdom purposes. It is all spiritual. It is either a legitimate Kingdom expression, or we shouldn't be involved at all.'[8] It's got to be true that any *vocatio* can be 'front line' – if we live with the deep-set conviction that we have been placed in a specific sphere of influence to represent Jesus and make him known.

Once during an ugly gang fight in Manenberg I went to buy milk from a local house shop run by a Somali man. This involved running from the door of our office building, looking left and right to make sure no one was about to blow my head off, and nervously jog-walking across the road. The shopkeeper was stood behind a metal grille that was not remotely bullet-proof. He'd been there all morning witnessing the gun battles on the street. I asked him if he was doing OK and how he was dealing with life on the front line. His reply was a belter: 'My friend, I'm from Mogadishu – living in Manenberg is easy! It's pieces of cake!' I wandered back to the office, struck by how relative everything is. I grew up in middle-class Sevenoaks, half an hour south of London, in the county of Kent, aptly named the Garden of England. The only gang I came into contact with, growing up, was a group of prepubescent kids roller-skating on a road up from ours who called me names. And so to me, some of the things that go down in Manenberg are pretty shocking. Yet, had I grown up in war-torn Mogadishu, my perspective of Manenberg would be completely different.

And so I wonder if the 'front line' might be a myth. I wonder if, like the single story, it really exists. Might it be yet more evidence of the unhelpful dichotomy we've established between what is seen as being sacred and what is termed 'secular'. That a dichotomy has been created between the sacred and the secular is no secret. But it's unbiblical. To assert one vocation as being secular and another as front line is theologically wrong. It fails to understand what Richard Foster calls the 'incarnational life' – namely, that Jesus is

> . . . the Lord of all vocations, and he really can teach us how to fulfill our callings. If you are a dentist, Jesus can teach you to do dentistry as he would do it if he were you. The same is true if you are a court stenographer, a computer programmer, a research scientist, a janitor, or the CEO of a multinational corporation. It is just as true if the thing you do to produce good in the world is raise a family or paint pictures or create stained-glass windows or peel potatoes. Whoever, whatever, wherever – he will teach you. Learn from him.[9]

So let me say it again: we are all in front-line ministry if we are doing what God has asked us to do.

It would be infinitely more helpful for each of us to think and live in terms of obedience to God's specific call on our individual lives – living on the front foot, if you like. Then, when we're walking our own narrow path, we'll see it need be neither glamorised nor feared (as our life in Manenberg often is). Rather than evoking militant images of brave souls engaged in *front-line warfare*, we can all just engage in *front-foot living* – passionately pursuing whatever life in its fullness looks like for each of us, whether in Sevenoaks or Somalia, Manenberg or Mogadishu. For me, living on the front foot means loving and living in Manenberg. For someone else, it might look like living in suburbia and raising children. The issue is less about what kind of *job* I do, and more about how I demonstrate Jesus' love to the people around me as I live out my *vocation*, my calling.

11: Young Men Will See Visions

Without miracles there can never be a full revelation of Jesus.
(Bill Johnson)[1]

*God sets the lonely in families, he leads out the
prisoners with singing.*
(Psalm 68:6)

The eagle on the barbed-wire fence

Despite the strength of the prevailing tide against the young men
we were working with, and that many feel those with whom we
share our home really belong in prison, it would seem God has
a different view. Testimonies and miracle stories began to become
quite commonplace in our shared life together, and we began to
see astronomic spiritual growth in certain individuals, as illus-
trated in what happened a year into running Cru62.

It was mid-December and I had planned to take the boys
camping for a week to get them out of the FOMO mindset
they had developed being in the house over the festive season.
There is a breathtakingly beautiful municipal campsite at Kogel
Bay, looking out on the ocean in front and with mountains
behind, about an hour and a half from Cape Town along the
winding coastal road towards Hermanus. At R100 a night per
tent, it was within our 'festive season outing' budget, and it
even had a tidal pool near by for the boys to ~~belly flop~~ dive
into to their hearts' content. I booked our place, and we made
various lists of things to take. (I'm no good at remembering
things, but Sarah is, and she's taught me to make lists – and
besides, I was trying to teach the boys the invaluable life skill

of good holiday planning, as well as use up some time one morning.)

We planned to pack everything in the morning and leave at lunchtime, right after Dowayne and Brandon got back from court for a hearing Brandon was required to attend for an old house-breaking case in which he was implicated. We had been assured by the Legal Aid lawyer that the hearing was a mere formality, as it was Brandon's first offence. And because he was clean from drugs thanks to living at Cru62 for three months, the decision would be to give him either a suspended sentence or a fine. This was reassuring news to us, as the main prison in Cape Town, Pollsmoor, is infamous for being a gang breeding ground and would have been completely detrimental for Brandon's recovery journey. It was good news for Brandon, because Pollsmoor was in the middle of dealing with a rat infestation (it would seem that gangs are not the only thing to breed in jail) and packed out to over double its capacity, meaning it would be highly likely new inmates would be required to share beds with some of the more unsavoury characters, in cells of forty.

As the morning wore on, the other boys and I packed all we could fit into the car. We watered the garden, made sure windows were closed, fed the cats, tidied up, and generally checked everything about three times more than necessary. It began to emerge that something may be wrong – the court hearing was taking ages. Then Dowayne arrived at the gate. He was alone. With a loud groan, our hearts audibly sank – Brandon had obvi-ously been locked up. But Dowayne hurriedly explained he'd just come back to get some cash so he could pay the fine at court and not delay the camping trip any further. Wise decision. We all had a nervous laugh together about how we'd all assumed the worst.

About an hour later Dowayne finally returned. Alone again. We waited patiently for Brandon to jump out from behind a wall, whereupon we would all can it laughing and hop in the car, a relieved and reunited bunch of happy campers on their way to Kogel Bay. Or something.

'They took Brandon,' Dowayne mumbled.

'Whaaaaaat?'

'The judge said he had a particular aversion to housebreakers and that he wanted to make an example out of Brandon even though it's his first case.'

'But Legal Aid said . . .'

'I know. They were just as surprised as we are. There's nothing they can do. He's on his way to Pollsmoor.'

Brandon had made a courageous decision to sever ties with the gang and rejoin Cru62, having run off twenty-four hours into his first attempt. Despite being three months clean and living in Cru62, and despite Dowayne accompanying him to court and vouching for him on our behalf, the defining factor in the judge's verdict was that he 'didn't like' housebreakers. Quite who the judge was trying to make a point to was unclear. It certainly wouldn't matter to Brandon's ex-comrades in the gang – there had been three others with him during the break-in, but when the security guards came they ran off and left him to take the punishment on his own. The judge seemed to have delusions of his own grandeur, which, when combined with a glaring ignorance of the nature of addiction, along with a disconcerting lack of legal accountability, resulted in him giving out the most counter-productive sentence he could have come up with. Brandon was sent to prison on a whim. The saddest part of the story was that this was going to be his first sober Christmas for years – and he would be in jail.

We visited him a couple of times over the festive season, trying to encourage him and giving him some money for *twak*. He also phoned us fairly regularly on a friend's illegal cellphone. But we were unable to talk long or phone him back – unless he paid, the phone would stay firmly in its hiding place – up his friend's backside. The last thing we would have wanted was to phone him back, only for the phone to be on and hidden in its usual place! Each time we went he would tell us proudly that he was still clean from drugs, despite most of his fellow inmates openly using drugs in the cell. We wanted to believe him, but knew that the longer he was in this 'correctional service', the more likely he would be to fall back into old ways.

One Sunday at our church family gathering we felt a corporate need to pray for Brandon – that he would stay strong to his new faith and even be able to have a positive impact on those around him. One of the Cru62 boys saw a picture in his mind while we were praying, of an eagle sitting on a barbed-wire fence and flying off into the distance. It was an intense time of prayer, with many of us weeping over the injustice of such broken systems. A few days later, Sarah and the guys were working in the garden, tending to the vegetables and watering flowers. They heard Brandon's voice, 'Surprise! I'm home!' and looked up from what they were doing. There he stood in front of them, grinning. This was, of course, met with joy-filled pandemonium as the mental link was made between their prayers on the Sunday and the miracle standing in front of them. Once the screaming and jumping around had died down, Brandon explained what had happened. Without any prior indication, the prison authorities released him just one month into his four-month sentence. A prison van dropped him off in Mitchells Plain, and he caught a train to Manenberg and walked to the Cru62 house. The final crowning detail of the story was that because no one could hear him shouting to open the gate, he decided to jump over. We later worked out that this all happened exactly a year and a day after he had first jumped over the gate the other way. The first time he was jumping the gate to run away and relapse, just twenty-four hours into his recovery. This time, he jumped the gate to come home, having stayed clean in prison. The whole situation encouraged us no end – specifically that when we 'proclaim freedom for the captives and release from darkness for the prisoners' (Is. 61:1), God listens!

The length to which an addict will go

As the months went on, we would hear some of the myriad ways in which members of Cru62 had procured drugs. Reswell would tell me stories of the fascinating yet heartbreaking ways he managed to buy heroin. He would travel out of Manenberg day by day having been thrown out of the house for stealing something for his first fix of the day. But when he got thrown off the train for not having a valid ticket, he'd then just spend the day *skarrelling* – walking to see what he could find. One day when he got thrown off the train at Plumstead, he walked from the station to Constantia Village, an upmarket shopping centre, having had nothing to eat all day. He went into Pick n Pay, grabbed a trolley, and wheeled it round the supermarket filling it with readily edible things, filling his stomach as he walked. Then, when full, he stole a couple of large boxes of headache pills, putting them under his clothes as he walked out – laden with about R100 worth of swag he could sell at Nyanga Junction for heroin money.

Other times, he would make it all the way to Simons Town by train (the southernmost end of the line, towards Cape Point), get high and then miss the last train back and be stranded there for the night. On one occasion he walked from Simons Town to St James – a distance of about 12 kilometres – in the middle of the night. He had managed to procure a couple of fish heads from fishermen gutting and selling fish in Kalk Bay, and got to St James having stopped off in a rundown old stone barn in Glen Cairn, where he managed to find just enough wood to make a fire. He then *braaied* the fish heads by the tidal pool at St James and slept in a little brightly painted beach hut once the security guards had gone. I'm continually amazed by the lengths to which a heroin addict will go to feed his habit – forsaking friends, family and security in order to keep his slave driver, heroin, satisfied.

Reswell was the first young man I ever met in Manenberg. It was immediately obvious that he was incredibly bright. As a young teenager, he had been offered a scholarship to a private school in the suburbs, but the world of heroin addiction got him before he was able to attend. It's a sobering thought that had he been able to start at the school a mere matter of months earlier, he may have never become a heroin addict. Two divergent paths, two very different destinies. That said, Reswell was not only intellectually astute, but had a passion for Scripture and prayer as yet unseen in the Cru62 intakes. Having him around seemed to almost attract visible instances of God's goodness.

3.5.15

A great testimony to God's kindness happened the other day in the Cru62 house. Ashton was feeling really down, and as if he wanted to relapse. He told Reswell, who prayed for him for strength and joy (Reswell having felt like relapsing the day before). That evening, Ashton had perked up. As they were all lying in bed chatting, he and Reswell were dreaming about what it would be like to speak at church and share the gospel with people. Ashton spoke about how he feels he is growing in maturity faith-wise and would like the opportunity to lead things more. Then I knocked on the door of their bedroom, unaware of their conversation, asking if Ashton would be happy to lead devotions the next morning because I was going to be away. They both laughed and immediately saw the God-thread in the story. I was concerned Ashton would be up all night worrying about what to share etc., but he confidently said – 'No it's fine, I've got a couple of different things I want to do for devotions tomorrow'! For Reswell it was a sign that his prayers are powerful and effective. For Ashton, it was a confirmation that God hears the desires of his heart. And for me it was a timely encouragement that the boys are growing in faith and maturity.

Mother's Day

There is a pandemic of fatherlessness across the Cape Flats. I have lost count of the conversations I've had with gangsters whose fathers are either dead, on drugs, or in prison. The connection between fatherlessness and gang membership is clear. Failed fatherhood – either the absence of a caring father or the presence of an abusive one – has grave personal and societal implications. The obvious knock-on effect of this is that the relationship between son and mother becomes particularly poignant. Mothers in Manenberg are treated with a mixture of affection and abuse. On the one hand, there is a deep reverence young men feel towards maternal figures; on the other hand, such maternal figures are the first to be affected by the cruelty and manipulation of a son on drugs. With so few fathers and husbands around, mothers become providers and punchbags in about equal measure.

We had Calvin, Reswell and Ashton living with us, and with Mother's Day around the corner, after some gentle prompting from Sarah, they decided they would like to honour the strong women whom they had put through hell. We suggested a dinner party, and Sarah taught each of them something specific to cook. Invitations were sent, and flowers bought. The day arrived, and each of the boys cooked their signature dish – Reswell made stuffed chicken breasts, Calvin a potato bake, and Ashton began proceedings with a carrot soup starter. I went to pick up the mothers and brought them to Cru62. There was a nervous energy in the room as the boys hugged their mums, presented them with roses, and attempted small talk. We all sat down to eat. The food was a roaring success, if at times unorthodox. Reswell, in his excitement, had overstuffed the chicken breasts. We laughed as they emerged from the oven, with string tightly wound round each one. In appearance they weren't dissimilar to hastily tied shoelaces on a child's football boot.

Sarah, never one to miss an opportunity to affirm and appreciate, asked if any of the boys wanted to say anything to their mothers.

Silence.

And then . . . one by one, each of them opened up and shared how they felt, deep down, about the woman sitting opposite them who had given them the gift of life. Being a few months clean from drugs meant that brain connections were firing in ways they hadn't for years, and each of the boys boasted about how wonderful their mother was. It went way beyond generic plati-tudes; this was mining the forgotten recesses of the heart and revisiting moments of loss, trauma and regret. As the mothers processed the extreme levels of kindness gushing forth from each of the boys, they began to weep. We all did. By the end of the meal there wasn't a dry eye in the house. Hope emanated from the table and filled the house.

After I returned from dropping the mothers off at home, I was greeted by a beaming Calvin at the front door of Cru62.

'*Joh*, what a night!'

'Wasn't it?! You guys all spoke so beautifully to your mums.'

'I don't know how to repay you guys for arranging this evening. I've never been so happy!'

'You don't have to repay anyone. Just focus on your journey and do your best not to let your mum down.'

'Yeah, you're right. But – you know what, when I have a job, the first thing I'm going to buy is a brand new Mini Cooper. I'm going to buy one for you and one for Sarah. The newest model!'

'That's really kind of you Calvin – but you don't need to do that.'

'Then I'll buy you a house – a huge house. To say thank you!'

The more I protested, the larger and more expensive the gift Calvin said he would buy me. It was a moment of manic euphoria, utterly out of perspective, but delightfully innocent. It may have been the most endearing excitement I've ever seen in someone.

We are often asked, 'Why do you do what you do?' The events of that evening were the perfect answer. I got into bed, deeply thankful to have been able to witness such raw, honest humanity expressed in love and affection.

Not soon after, Sarah was teaching the guys how to plant bulbs in the garden. Among her eclectic collection of flowers, she had some rose bulbs. Reswell, buoyed by the warm fuzzies of Mother's Day, perked up.

'My mum's name is Rose! Could we give her one of them when they bloom?' Sarah agreed that would be a lovely idea.

A baby raised

We learned that one of the greatest distractions to an individual recovering from drug addiction is having a girlfriend. Relationships

between young people in Manenberg can often be fairly dysfunctional, largely due to the high number of broken families and the
dearth of positive older role models for young people to follow.
Reswell's girlfriend was pregnant and due to give birth in July.
As the time approached, he became noticeably agitated. Part of
his own recovery and faith journey involved dealing with the
confusing combination of violent abuse and neglect that his own
father had put him through for most of his childhood. As a result,
he wasn't at all convinced that he wanted to be part of his soon-
to-be-born child's life, let alone be present at the birth. We
eventually convinced him that it was good for the baby to have
a father, and committed to driving his girlfriend to hospital when
the time came.

The call came at about midnight. Sarah and I jumped up, woke
Reswell, and the three of us drove round to pick up his girlfriend
and take her to Hanover Park clinic. Hanover Park is next to
Manenberg, and was in the middle of a splenetic gang fight at
the time. As we drove in, it struck me how this was the complete
opposite of a scenario into which you would want to be driving
a first-time mother-to-be in the middle of the night. It wasn't safe,
it wasn't controlled, there was no guarantee we wouldn't be shot
at or mugged getting out of the car, nor much likelihood there
would even be an available bed at the clinic. Yet, such a scenario
is the sad norm in the Cape Flats and for the majority of
Capetonians, and Candice was just thankful to have a lift there.

Eventually an ambulance took her to Mowbray Maternity
Hospital, a fifteen-minute drive towards town – an infinitely better
place to be. I dropped Reswell off, with a bag full of food, a cellphone and the book he was reading – Tim Keller's *The Reason
for God*. He began to open the car door, but then hesitated, and
slowly closed it again. Something was obviously on his mind.

'You know I've been thinking, Pete.'

'Oh yeah? What about?'

'This book is really speaking to me. In the chapter I'm at, the
author is describing God's grace in different ways.'

'And what is it speaking to you about specifically?'

'Well, I've been following Jesus for the last few years, but for the first time this morning I began to understand what "grace" actually means, and how it affects us. It changes everything!'

'Go on . . .'

'The point is, I've always had this deep angst that I have to please God by doing various religious things – praying, watching my language, going to church. But today I get it – I've had it wrong these last years. I'm able to have a relationship with God because Jesus died in my place. And he forgave all my sin! And now God sees me as perfect and unpunishable, however much I mess up or make mistakes. I get it now! And it feels amazing – I've been walking around today with such joy and happiness for the first time, knowing that God's love is unconditional!'

And with that, he got out of the car and walked into the hospital waiting room, a new man. I sat in the car for a few minutes and prayed a prayer of thanks that Reswell was not only off drugs, but was going to be present at his daughter's birth and would now be able to be a gracious and joyful father to this little one about to arrive. As usual, God's timing had been exquisite.

No sooner had I got back home and into bed, we got a phone call from Reswell.

'Sorry to phone again this late, but the baby's coming and we need you to get Tree of Life praying.'

'Why, is there a problem?'

'Yes – the baby's heart has stopped mid-delivery, and the doctors are really worried we'll lose her. We need to pray life into her body *now*!'

'OK, will do!' With that, Dowayne woke the Cru62 boys and got them praying, Sarah and I prayed, and others in Tree of Life woke in the middle of the night to declare life into this tiny girl's body. We prayed, and we waited. And waited. And waited. It seemed like we waited for an age, but in reality it was just under half an hour. The phone rang. *Oh God, what's the news going to be? Jesus, Jesus, Jesus.*

'She's alive, she's alive! A beautiful baby girl!' I could hardly believe it. We started screeching and screaming for joy down the phone to each other, undone by the love of God that had intervened with a remarkable miracle.

The next evening I took Cru62 to the Deep River, the monthly city-wide worship event we'd started by accident a few years previously. It's always a time of great joy and celebration, of hope-generating testimonies and lots of charismatic shaking and whooping. Reswell got up and shared his story of the last twenty-four hours, the place was set alight, and he went and sat back down. A woman in the row behind us tapped him on the shoulder, introduced herself and gave him her business card – she owned a baby clothes store and wanted to invite him to come and fetch whatever he needed for his new daughter. He said nothing, but looked her in the eye and nodded excitedly, dumbfounded by her generosity and the favour on his one-day-old baby's life.

The weekend came and went without much drama. But then, on the Monday, Reswell started playing up. He said he wanted to leave Cru62. His reason? To be present for his baby daughter and patch things up in his relationship with Candice. We asked him to think about it for the day and not make a rash decision – we had, after all, already put in place a plan that would enable him to father well while also concentrating on his faith life, the 12-Step recovery process, and positive relationships in Cru62 – a plan he had been part of coming up with. We understood his reasons for wanting to leave, but were concerned his baby's birth was being used as a classic 'plausible but untrue' reason to leave and relapse. Monday evening came, and his mind was made up. He left, taking all his belongings with him.

A week later, we hadn't seen him in church and had heard nothing from him at all. We couldn't find him at his mum's, so went round to Candice's. He was there. Candice was first to speak.

'Please can't you guys take him back; he's causing trouble here.' One conversation later, it emerged that Reswell had been taking money for the baby and using it to buy alcohol. When we questioned him on this relapse, he eventually admitted it was true, but was incensed by my use of words.

'I've not relapsed – I was in Cru62 for heroin addiction, I've not touched that since I've been out.' The glaring blind spot in his reasoning was of course that the substance was fairly irrelevant – he was now using alcohol as his 'drug of choice' to create mess and trouble. But despite our repeated pleas, he refused to admit this was the beginning of a slippery slope, and he wouldn't come back to Cru62. All the while, he used his now three-day-old daughter as a convenient excuse to live unaccountably and self-ishly. Needless to say, a week later when we visited him he had begun to sell his own clothes for alcohol, and a week after that was back on heroin.

In some ways it was a textbook scenario. But that didn't make it hurt any less. I turned to my journal to process my emotions.

3.8.15

I've seen him battle so hard, I've spent hours and hours and hours pouring all I've got into him. I've got up at 2 a.m. and driven him around Cape Town. I've believed the best about him day in day out, I've confided in him, I've grown so close to him. I've grown to love him deeper than I thought possible. I've been convinced that each time he slips up, that that's not the final word – and yet today I sit here feeling completely hopeless for his life. I GIVE UP, GOD. I GIVE UP ON HOLDING OUT HOPE FOR RESWELL. I GIVE UP, OPENING MY HEART TO ADDICTS WHO JUST TRAMPLE OVER YOU ONCE THEY'VE USED YOU ENOUGH FOR THEIR OWN BENEFIT. I GIVE UP SOWING SEED INTO CONCRETE. I GIVE UP. ARE YOU HAPPY NOW?

Soon after Reswell left, the roses he had planted bloomed. Sarah honoured his wish and took them to his mother. Both of them sat, sobbing, as they lamented the choice he had made.

12: Gangsters, My Greatest Teachers

To desire . . . [the marginalised and broken] . . . for their own sake, to have them as the focus of respect, love and friendship in a covenant community, to honour their names and tell their stories, is a radical challenge to the church as well as to the rest of society.
(David Ford)[1]

The world doesn't need more words, not even more 'right' words. The world needs more words made flesh . . . In living among the poor, we cannot help but lower the bullet-proof shield that separates the professional service provider from the poor. Consequently, we open ourselves to good news from the poor.
(John B. Hayes)[2]

Canadian theologian Jean Vanier established the first L'Arche community in 1964 after witnessing institutionalised maltreatment of the physically and mentally disabled. Since then, L'Arche has spread far and wide, with communities serving the marginalised in thirty-seven different countries around the world, and Vanier has written extensively and vulnerably about living with one of the most marginalised demographics in society. After five decades living such a beautiful expression of faith, he is gloriously honest about his flaws, his propensity to anger, and his longing for plaudits in the middle of his shared life with the physically and mentally disabled.

> They have been teaching me that behind the need for me to win, there are my own fears and anguish, the fear of being devalued or pushed aside, the fear of opening up my heart and of being

vulnerable, or of feeling helpless in front of others in pain; there is the pain and brokenness of my own heart. I discovered something which I had never confronted before, that there were immense forces of darkness and hatred within my own heart. At particular moments of fatigue or stress, I saw forces of hate rising up inside me, and the capacity to hurt someone who was weak and was provoking me. That, I think, was what caused me the most pain: to discover who I really am, and to realize that maybe I did not want to know who I really was! I did not want to admit all the garbage inside me. And then I had to decide whether I would just continue to pretend that I was okay and throw myself into hyperactivity, projects where I could forget all the garbage and prove to others how good I was.[3]

Some of the lessons Jean Vanier has learnt from those with disabilities, I am beginning to learn from those in gangs and on drugs. In my more lucid moments I see these daily lessons as a personal gift from God. Manenberg is an 'ethical epiphany of the human condition'.[4] The constant stream of gruesome headlines serves to show how bad the normal order of things can become when systems of oppression are allowed to play out over time. Living in Manenberg teaches me new facets of the truth of the gospel – for example, that humans are more broken than we might like to believe, but that we have more potential for love than could ever be imagined. The lessons I'm taught in Manenberg – often by those rejected by mainstream culture, and who would likely feel uneasy setting foot in a church building – form the basis of my emerging life message as I return to the suburbs as an apostle (simply meaning, *someone sent out*) lovingly intent on evangelising society and the Church.

That life in Manenberg, this feared and violent place, gives me more than I could ever contribute in return is, I think, one of those treasured paradoxes of a life with Jesus. The closer I become to the young men living with us, the more I realise God is using *them* to transform *me*. High-risk youth often come to us dirty, always angry, masters of manipulation, violent in the extreme, and yet regularly they cry themselves to sleep at night. You can smell, see and touch their brokenness and pain – there's no hiding it. As we have intentionally sought friendship with these conspicuously broken young men, I feel a strong resonance with Vanier's sentiments, and I experience my own less conspicuous brokenness rising to the surface. As this happens, I realise how much pain and brokenness there is in me, and how much grace others must have to extend towards me day by day. And so my heart becomes more thankful for friends who forgive, and I'm opened up to the possibility to grow in humility and gratitude. This is a journey I hadn't ever learnt living anywhere else. I'd always thought that to be transparent about brokenness or pain would be perceived as awkward at best or, at worst, shamefully weak. God has used Manenberg to show me otherwise.

God sides with the weak

Every morning at Cru62 we worship and study the Scriptures together. It's an absolute highlight in my life. Reading the Bible with young, unchurched ex-addicts is deeply energising. While reading together about the calling of Levi in Mark 2:13–17 one day (a passage that had never particularly spoken to me before), all sorts of pennies began to drop. In the text, Jesus passes Levi sitting at a tax collector's booth and simply says, 'Follow me.' Seemingly without a second thought, 'Levi got up and followed him' (v. 14). I explained to the Cru62 boys that tax collectors extorted money from people, sometimes violently, that they operated in ganglike groups and worked for the Roman occupation – enemies of the local people.

'*Yoh*, Levi sounds like Ougat! He *moers* people who don't pay,' said one of the guys, to laughter from the others. Ougat is well known in Manenberg for being one of the more successful and violent loan sharks, lending money to the poorest of the poor and charging extortionate rates of interest. So desperate are many of his customers that he is alleged to be in possession of a large number of their SASSA cards – the means by which they are able to obtain government grants and child support – meaning if they don't pay their debts, he takes their only income for himself. We then had an animated discussion about what Jesus was thinking, calling Levi – the Ougat of northern Galilee – to become one of his disciples.

'*Nee* man, that's not *kwaai*.'

'*Miskien* Jesus didn't know who Levi was.'

'*Ja* but *die ou* was sitting by the tax booth. He's not *dom*.'

'But I thought Jesus was a *regte* guy?'

'Let's read on,' I suggested, beginning to grasp the contextual connotations of what we had just read. The passage didn't get any easier – Jesus accompanies Levi to his house for dinner, where 'many tax collectors and sinners were eating with him and his disciples' (v. 15). As we imagined the free-flowing booze and possible scenarios that could have been going on at Levi's dinner party for reprobates, Brandon piped up, 'It sounds just like Peta Court!', the corner of Manenberg where he grew up and where payday weekend often brings violence and drug-fuelled parties. Again, everyone laughed.

'So what was Jesus doing, this rabbi who called himself the Son of God, hanging out in that sort of place?' I asked.

Silence.

'Does someone want to read verses 16 and 17?'

Waydin put up his hand, and began to read:

When the teachers of the law who were Pharisees saw him eating with the sinners and tax collectors, they asked his disciples: 'Why does he eat with tax collectors and sinners?' On hearing this, Jesus said to them, 'It is not the healthy who need a doctor, but the sick. I have not come to call the righteous, but sinners.'

Again I asked, 'So why did Jesus hang out with these people?' Everyone's eyes looked at the ground. I let the silence linger.

Slowly Kevin stirs, looks up, and answers in a near whisper –
'Because they were the ones who could admit they needed help.'

Jesus lived outside the acceptance of religious authorities and
conventional structures of power. 'This shame from rejection by
the world is something that Jesus experienced and warned his
followers they should expect.'[5] John 15:18–19 reads: 'If the world
hates you, keep in mind that it hated me first. If you belong to
the world, it would love you as its own. As it is, you do not belong
to the world, but I have chosen you out of the world. That is why
the world hates you.' While such words are decidedly uncomfortable for those of us within the mainstream of society, they are
music to the ears of the young men with whom we live in
Manenberg who are used to being hated by the world.

These young men, with no prior knowledge or experience of
Jesus, can instantly resonate with him and his teaching once they
realise how hated he was among circles of 'good' people, and how
fond he was of drunkards, prostitutes and high school dropouts.
(I wonder if the more the world condemns a certain demographic,
the more that demographic becomes like, and close to, Jesus.)
Jesus lived outside the mainstream structures of the world, and
received the death penalty 'because he consistently sided with the
excluded sinner types rather than agreeing with the religious law
enforcers'.[6]

It's a source of great frustration to me that the way Jesus lived,
defiant to the domineering powers of his time, subversive in the
extreme, in communion with the despised, siding with the
excluded, dismissive of fear, scarcity and aggression, is seen by
so many 'good' Christians today as being 'bad'.

Old Testament Israel through the eyes of Manenberg

Stories from Exodus and Deuteronomy offer some reflections on
the life of addicts in Manenberg. In the first chapter of Exodus,
the Egyptians (those with power) were feeling threatened by the
growing number of Israelites (the enslaved). So the Egyptian

slave-masters oppressed the Israelites all the more, treating them ruthlessly and unfairly. 'But the more they were oppressed, the more they multiplied and spread' (Ex. 1:12). So fearful were the Egyptians that the king gave an order to kill all baby boys born to Hebrew mothers. But the midwives defied the coercion of the oppressive regime, and let the boys live. This subversive act of resistance brought blessing to them and their community – 'So God was kind to the midwives and the people increased and became even more numerous. And because the midwives feared God, he gave them families of their own' (vv. 20–21). The story of the liberation of God's people out of slavery began through the resolute courage of a group of women at the bottom of the social spectrum saying 'No' to injustice rooted in fear.

What follows is an amazing story of the liberation of the Israelites through Moses' bold advocacy and God's mighty power. However, it's not all plain sailing, and with unnerving regularity the Israelites become their own worst enemy. Having sworn to Moses that 'Everything the Lord has said we will do', they take just eight chapters to freak out. God felt distant, Moses had been gone for forty days and nights, and so they fashioned their own god out of gold. We might be tempted to think we're immune from such hypocrisy, but would be wise to remember that 'God-making, amid anxiety is a standard human procedure!'[7] And yet despite their falling at such an early hurdle and relapsing into old patterns of idolatry, God forgives them and recommits to covenant. We see this painfully clearly on a regular basis in the lives of addicts desperate to get free and love God but struggling with double-mindedness. God's response to failure and relapse, now as it was then, is renewal of covenant – the empowering of grace.

This patient grace is the model we follow at Cru62. As long as an individual is committed to change, no number of relapses preclude them from relationship and another chance to get clean and free. It comes at a cost for us each time, however, as we need to generate hope for someone who may have fallen at the same hurdle many times. There is no place for cynicism, we cannot afford to be anything less than relentlessly hopeful. In Exodus 34:1 we see God doing the same thing. He tells Moses to chisel out two new stone tablets 'like the first ones, and I will write on them the words that were on the first tablets, which you broke'. God neither pretends the first relapse didn't happen, nor withholds relationship – he is blunt with Moses, but committed to giving it another go. You can almost hear the loving sigh of a father who is relentlessly hopeful, but feels the pain each time his people fall.

Further along in the story, in Deuteronomy, Moses spends thirty chapters instructing Israel by the Jordan. Why so long? Because he knew that entering the promised land was going to be a 'high-risk venture . . . [as] prosperity breeds amnesia'[8] – Israel will be tempted to forget about dependence on God, will be tempted to autonomy, and to forget where they came from. They will be safe and happy – and will be able to enjoy a standard of living like never before – but Moses recognises that to be able to deal with plenty, abundance and comfort, they need comprehensive character formation.

Addicts and gangsters in Manenberg, exiled in a 'foreign land' through the legacy of apartheid, spend their life 'making bricks' for another, more local oppressive regime. They become slaves to local pharaohs, the murderous and money-making drug merchants, as well as to their own inner cravings for *tik* and heroin. There's no limit, no reasonable restraint, no rest, no freedom; just anxiety and coercion. The only work available is dealing for these merchants, who give them the ability to feed themselves and their families but in so doing entice them further down the road of slavery. Life is lived breaking into houses, mugging, or *skarrelling* – the complete antithesis to neighbourliness. This violation of others is epitomised by a regular rhythm of gang fights that only end when a counterfeit peace (more accurately, a fickle ceasefire) is called by gang leaders, balanced on a knife edge by the threat of damage *we* will do to *you* if *you* encroach on *our* land. It's not peace in any real sense, more of a self-serving impasse allowing both sides to rearm for next time.

The gang hierarchy dole out rewards or punishments based upon individuals' conformity and obedience to the system of oppression. There is a fixed *modus operandi*, the rites and rituals of life in the gang. If you violate the law by, for example, breaking into a house on your own gang's turf, you'll be beaten up by your 'pseudo-kin'[9] and left outside hospital. This is seen as justice – the offering of a sacrifice and shedding of blood in payment for sin. Alternatively, if you agree to take out a rival gangster you will be rewarded by handsome payment. As with any misappropriated act of worship, the rewards always seem lucrative beforehand. But idolatry never pays off. The modern-day religious idols are the logos and emblems of designer goods, branded clothes and shiny cars as signs of success and rank. All this visible polish acts to show others how you have sold more drugs (akin to making more bricks) than others. The defining of your worth is measured by how much you produce, and as such it's the very epitome of slavery, a life of frantic productivity in order to survive and grow 'respect'.

When guys in Cru62 begin to get free from this system of oppression, they can become complacent. Putting on weight, pushing past the acne outbreaks, headaches and pains as their bodies detox from the poison they have been smoking, wearing new, clean clothes, eating three meals a day – they get used to this new way of life, the prosperity breeds amnesia and they are tempted back to autonomy and rebellion. It's easy to see why the Israelites are repeatedly commanded to remember the long years of wilderness wanderings out of which they have been led. To call to remembrance the misery of living in an oppressive system is an effective way of making sure you don't go back. In Cru62 this is the role of the 12-Step programme. Sometimes the lies whisper so convincingly that the rotten past is remembered through rose-tinted lenses, and as with the Israelites then ('at least we had food and water back in Egypt!'), so with recovering addicts now ('at

least I could buy brand new sneakers back when I was dealing');
the allure of selective memory causes runaways and relapses.

Big choices

Before his second stint in Cru62, Waydin survived an attack on
his life. He had come to us having slept for months in an old car
after he was thrown out of his family home for stealing. But he
ran away five months into his first attempt at recovery and
returned to the Stupa Boys, the gang he'd been part of since he
was sixteen. Now deeper into drugs and being drawn into gang
plots against rivals, he had become a marked man. One afternoon
as he was walking home a member of the Ghetto Kids started to
chase him with a gun. Six shots were fired, from just a couple
of metres away, but none hit Waydin as he wrestled with the
corrugated iron gate to a friend's carport. This near-death experience earned him the nickname The Great Escape with those in
his street who had witnessed this miracle of bad aim from their
upstairs window. Needless to say, Waydin came back into Cru62
a great deal more humble the second time round, confident in
the fact Jesus had preserved his life and had better plans for him.

A few months in, when confidence began to breed compla-
cency, Waydin ran away again. It was at the height of a gang
fight, and as he had no money for a minibus taxi ride home, he
risked his life and walked the couple of kilometres through
various gang turfs. On the way he passed two dead bodies,
surrounded by crowds and cordoned off by police tape – gangsters shot that morning in a mindless war. As he arrived home
shaken by what he had seen, Dowayne drove round the corner.
After a long conversation in which Dowayne pointed out to him
that he was about to fall at the very same five-month hurdle,
and that these two dead bodies were a stark reminder of the
reality he would be choosing to re-enter, Waydin got in the car
and returned to us.

Not long later a well-known evangelist came to Cape Town and we took Cru62 to the conference he was speaking at. However, it wasn't the main name who had the most impact on Waydin that day, but a former Muslim called Yusuf, who came up to him in a break and said, through tears, 'I have never met you, and know nothing of your life. But God has clearly spoken to me. He told me to tell you if you leave the place you're currently staying, you will die.' A punchy prophetic word, and one that many would shrink back from giving, but it was one of Waydin's deepest encounters with the voice of God.

Waydin's journey to freedom is still being written, but now when he is tempted to 'return to Egypt', to the madness of his enslaved past, he is able to cling on to the unambiguous memory of two dead bodies, six badly aimed bullets, and a word of warning from a perfect stranger. Where rational reasoning and sound advice fall short, remembering the voice of the God who delivers from death hits home.

13: Learning to Love

We love our people whether they turn out well or not and the
successes do not vindicate our ministry nor the disappointments
nullify it. What is important is that we have loved in a real way.
(Jackie Pullinger)[1]

The main task of the church is the formation of people who see clearly
the cost of discipleship and are willing to pay the price.
(Stanley Hauerwas and William H. Willimon)[2]

In the first chapter of Philippians Paul shares one of the prayers
he's praying for the fledgling church: 'this is my prayer: that your
love may abound more and more in knowledge and depth of
insight' (v. 9). This continues to be our prayer for ourselves as we
run Cru62 – not simply that we will pour our lives out for others,
but that we will do so insightfully and with knowledge attained
from the walk of faith. It's a truism, but a useful reminder, to say
we can never really fail, only learn new ways not to do something
– and that the people who have succeeded most in life are those
who have failed the most but learnt from their mistakes. The key
is to learn and adapt – rather than continue along the same vein
using the same methods but expecting different results (which is,
incidentally, Albert Einstein's definition of insanity). The process
of learning builds our character and our trust in God and others.
It is invaluable and doesn't happen if everything comes together
with little effort or struggle and if we don't go through times of
trial. The value of trials is in the fact we would never choose them.
That he would allow in his wisdom what he could easily prevent
in his power is God's highest compliment to us, because it shows
he can trust us, and that he is taking us higher through difficulties.

In the first chapter of the book of James, we read: 'Consider it pure joy ... whenever you face trials of many kinds, because you know that the testing of your faith produces perseverance. Let perseverance finish its work so that you may be mature and complete, not lacking anything' (vv. 2–4). If trials are one of God's ways of developing perseverance in us, and if he is completely good, then behind each difficulty we face there is a new level of spiritual maturity we can grow into. Author Graham Cooke expresses similar sentiments when he asks, 'What if frustration is actually a sign that an upgrade is present?'[3] The words 'pure joy' can't presumably mean 'well, I guess there were some redeeming factors in this trial'. Surely real, *pure* joy must mean 'this is genuinely amazing and the best thing that could have happened to me'. That seems ridiculous doesn't it?! It's not some kind of masochistic exercise in self-flagellation; the joy comes from looking forward to the maturity and completeness James writes about. The joy is savouring the prosperity of soul that's waiting the other side of, and even within, the difficulty. The other side of the Jordan was the Promised Land. The other side of the stormy lake was a healed demoniac sent out as the first apostle. The other side of the cross was resurrection to new life. Likewise, the other side of trials is pure joy. God is waiting on the other side of your next faith step; there's a beautiful encounter with him the other side of fear.

The Beatitudes are a defining text on the joy that awaits those willing to encounter God through, in the middle of, and despite difficulty. They reveal the paradoxical nature of living as citizens of the kingdom of God. You're blessed when you're empty, or painfully aware of your own shortcomings, or grieving, or struggling to show mercy, or doggedly striving for peace. Because you can only be truly filled when you have been truly emptied, your shortcomings point you to the grace of the Perfect One, your grief opens the door to encounter the God of comfort, the measure of mercy you show will be returned to you, and the peace you bring to situations around you will affirm your belonging in the family of God.

What are we willing to give up?

Meekness may well be one of the most misunderstood words in the Bible. Its meaning has become synonymous with 'mild', but this is misleading. Jesus was meek, for sure, but he was definitely not mild. 'Mild' evokes an image of a bland chicken korma. Of all the curries in a curry house, the korma is the most flavourless, the safe choice, tepid, uninspiring and pointless. No, Jesus was most definitely not mild. But meek? Absolutely!

The Greek for meek is *praus*. It would be the word used in referring to a gentle breeze, invoking a sense of great power under control; or a wild animal tamed and willingly submitting. It is the fruit of an internal composure, having power but choosing not to impose it. A. W. Tozer explains: 'The meek man . . . knows he is as weak and helpless as God declared him to be, but paradoxically, he knows at the same time that he is in the sight of God of more importance than angels. In himself, nothing; in God, everything.'[4]

The Bible gives two clear examples of meekness. In Numbers 12:3, Moses is described as 'very meek, more than all people who were on the face of the earth' (ESV). And yet he is also the man who initiated and led the liberation of the Israelites from the oppression of Pharaoh. Jesus' decision to give up the glory of heaven for the mess of earth is the epitome of meekness. In Philippians 2:7 we read that he 'made himself nothing by taking the very nature of a servant'. The security within himself and his relationship with the Father to empty himself of prestige and splendour in exchange for a lowly life is breathtaking, the exact image of infinite power willingly restrained.

Those who feel the need to impose themselves on a situation, who carry some kind of 'big person' syndrome and need to be noticed are often the ones the world applauds – the driven, self-made person who climbed the ladder of ambition, towards success and power. And yet that image, of climbing ever higher, couldn't be further from the life of yieldedness and surrender that Jesus described and himself modelled.

The King and the Maiden

Danish theologian Søren Kierkegaard wrote a short parable describing the downward aspirations of meekness. A paraphrase goes like this.

Suppose there was a king who loved a humble maiden. The king was like no other king. Every statesman trembled before his power. No one dared breathe a word against him, for he had the strength to crush all opponents.

And yet this mighty king was melted by love for a humble maiden who lived in a poor village in his kingdom. How could he declare his love for her? In an odd sort of way, his kingliness tied his hands. If he brought her to the palace and crowned her head with jewels and clothed her body in royal robes, she would surely not resist – no one dared resist him. But would she love him?

She would say she loved him, of course, but would she truly? Or would she live with him in fear, nursing a private grief for the life she had left behind? Would she be happy at his side? How could he know for sure? If he rode to her forest cottage in his royal carriage, with an armed escort waving bright banners, that too would overwhelm her. He did not want a cringing subject. He wanted a lover, an equal. He wanted her to forget that he was a king and she a humble maiden and to let shared love cross the gulf between them. For it is only in love that the unequal can be made equal.

The king, convinced he could not elevate the maiden without crushing her freedom, resolved to descend to her. Clothed as a beggar, he approached her cottage with a worn cloak fluttering loose about him. This was not just a disguise – the king took on a totally new identity – He had renounced his throne to declare his love and to win hers.[5]

Why on earth was the king happy to give up royal entitlements and a quality of life to which he was accustomed? He was motivated by a greater love, a deeper longing. Everything else paled in comparison to that love. He could only be truly satisfied once he had the hand of the maiden for which he willingly and joyfully gave up everything. It is a stunning picture of meekness.

Who was it that recognised Jesus? Who 'saw' Jesus when he was on earth? Apart from the demons, it was the poor, the destitute, the forgotten – the *empty* ones. Jesus himself stated that his mission was to 'proclaim good news to the poor . . . [and] set the oppressed free' (Luke 4:18). It's as if our emptiness creates a vacuum into which Jesus pours his glory. The empty shall be filled. Surrender leads to victory. The meek shall inherit the earth.

Living with addicts leaves no room for bravado or self-confidence. Rather, each day is balanced on a knife edge, with seemingly endless scope for disaster – be it relapse, physical violence, episodes of rage, intimidation or manipulation. At times the learning curve is pretty vertical, and we fairly continually need to operate beyond our mere human capabilities, depending on God just to get through the day. This learning curve seems to bend towards meekness – whether we like it or not, it is this characteristic we are learning above and beyond any other.

If trials teach us perseverance, develop our maturity and make us complete, and if meekness is a fundamental characteristic of Jesus to aspire to, then having the opportunity to run Cru62 is possibly the most generous gift God could have given us. We've discovered that while we cannot speed up someone's recovery process, we can slow it down by being unaware of what is holding them back. We often get asked – 'What are some of the lessons you're learning running Cru62?' There have been many, but here are seven biggies.

1. It's the tiny little things

Most of the time, the big issues that come up in house life (such as confession of heinous past crimes or the processing of childhood trauma) are so serious that they act as a kind of spiritual thunderstorm, clearing out the heaviness and bringing light and life. What seems to trip up the guys are the fairly insignificant issues – arguments over who got more food, or who ripped a page out of their Bible to smoke their last tobacco, or pulling a knife on a house-mate for not letting you toast your bread first. Equally, playground-like insults have caused some to pack their bags. One day Calvin and Frikkie had a disagreement. Calvin called Frikkie '*skeel oë*' (squiffy eyes), so Frikkie retorted by calling him a '*khoikhoi boesman*' (nomadic bushman). When such a conflict does come up, the most common response is for individuals to go through a period of wanting to leave the house – they know that 'fight' isn't appropriate, so they resort to 'flight'. Bags are packed, insults are thrown, tears are shed, and then they storm out. Sometimes they are able to see past their anger and stick around.

2. The most common lie that comes up again and again is anything to do with shame

Shame seems to be the greatest stronghold that would try and keep the boys from living in their full identity. Be it the confession that they had resorted to prostituting themselves to get money for drugs, or the admission that they were sexually abused by a family member, all the dark secrets that are characteristic for a young drug addict in Manenberg take time to come out. And when they do, they are always accompanied by a lifetime of lies – 'I'm worthless', 'I'm trash', 'If I can't forgive myself, how could God forgive me?', 'This journey of healing is going to be so hard, what's the point in even trying?', 'If people knew even a fraction of what I've done, they'd never want me around.' Hard walls of protection are built around each young man's heart. They come into Cru62 thinking their problem is a mere chemical dependency, but gradually realise that this addiction is a mere symptom of having lived under the spirit of shame for as long as they can remember. Pain seeks pleasure, and the quickest fix around is self-medicating on hard drugs. Years of addiction and all that comes with it are just the tip of the iceberg; the main issue is learning to unearth shame and walk out of it.

3. Allow time to sit in the mess

Once a week we have a Board Meeting, where we discuss three aspects of each person that we've noticed. A blind spot, an asset, and a weekly goal. When it gets to you, you are not allowed to defend or justify yourself, but have to trust that whatever is brought up by others is done so in love. Then we write it on a whiteboard for all to see (hence 'board' meeting), so that we 'own' these observations others have made about us, trusting that our friends are for us and that the group's discernment is better than our own. In addition to this, twice weekly we hold a 'Burning Issues' session. This is an hour dedicated to giving space for whoever needs it to bring up a burning issue. It could be a problem with someone in particular, or an issue with the way something in the house is being run. It's about giving everyone a voice to bring up unsaid things in a controlled, honouring environment where there are rules of engagement. Such is the effectiveness of these sessions that I'm pretty convinced every marriage should do these – Sarah and I have started to!

4. Have clear boundaries

In this line of ministry, how clear your boundaries are, and how well you stick to them, will pretty much define whether you burn out or are able to keep going. Boundaries will differ from person to person, and there's not always a clear 'right' answer. For example, there's a Manchester United game on television that the Cru62 boys are desperate to watch. An incident earlier in the day where you were unreasonably harsh means this could be the perfect opportunity to patch up a relationship and show there are no hard feelings. But the game starts at 10 p.m., you're already exhausted, and have to be up tomorrow at 6 a.m. for a breakfast meeting, and are then working until 9 p.m. What's the right decision? Or, you notice the vegetable garden hasn't been watered in a week. The Cru62 boys have a watering rota they should be following, but it takes ages to work out whose turn it is and they get so moody when it's brought up that it's just easier for me to do it this week, despite the fact it will mean being slightly late for a meeting. How best to handle it? Or one of the boys' families turned up to Sunday visiting with six people, when they know only three are allowed to visit. The particular boy in question has been talking about leaving Cru62, and us creating a scene with his family might just be the reason he is looking for to pack his bags. Should we say something to the family, who have done this before but then reacted badly when we mentioned it, or just leave it? I'm learning that unclear boundaries usually (though not always) stem from me being a people pleaser. There will be another Manchester United game on at an earlier time in the evening. I will end up watering the garden forever unless I bring it up. And if someone is looking for a reason to leave the house, however petty, then it would be better for them to do so rather than hang around and bring the others down. I find that my instinctive default setting is not wanting to cause a scene or rock the boat, so I end up allowing people to walk all over me, and in the process end up burning out.

5. If you take the credit for the successes, you'll take the hit when things go wrong

When we first opened Cru62, I couldn't believe the speed of growth of some of the guys. At times it seemed almost unbelievable – the hunger to know God, the willingness to learn to cook, to improve reading skills, to absorb all we were teaching them about Jesus, life and the world. It was, and continues to be, a profound privilege. However, we've had to learn that while we're an integral part of their life, *their* healing doesn't depend on us, and *our* identity doesn't depend on their healing. About a year in to running the house I'd realised that up to that point my sense of worth had come from how successful others perceived me to be. This striving to be a 'success' was only really exposed once the very guys whose faith I'd boasted about in a newsletter gradually began to lose steam and, one by one, left the house. I was ruined. Beyond the initial pain of seeing people I had grown to love relapse and end up back in prison, I hit a level of despair that had little to do with anyone other than myself. With the numbers in the boys' house depleted, I now felt I had nothing to show for my efforts.

I drew comfort reading words from someone who had walked this road before me, Tobias Jones. He wrote:

> In the early days I used to get frustrated if things went curly with a guest, if they disappeared or fell off the wagon, or whatever. It would feel like we had failed, as if someone else's behaviour had been an illustration of how incompetent we were. Whereas now I realised their disappearance or relapse wasn't our responsibility or our failure. I wouldn't get angry with an individual for their erratic behaviour and, more to the point, I wouldn't be proud when someone got clean or well. We were still deeply sad when things went wrong, or hugely grateful when they went right – but solely for their sake, not ours.[6]

Again, it's not an easy line to tread. In one sense we need to completely disassociate from the boys (and retain an identity apart from the ministry), but in another sense we're so emotionally invested in the re-parenting process that it's impossible to remain distinct from the lives we're helping develop. It's a tension, a delicate balance that needs to continually be kept in check in case it begins to swing aggressively back and forth like a pendulum on crack listening to drum and bass.

6. It takes a village to raise a child

The number of dedicated, loving friends who help out in doing shifts in the house was the deciding factor in keeping us afloat in the first couple of years. I could have had the same conversation over and over with a boy in the house around a particular behavioural issue I'd noticed, to no avail, only for a friend coming in to cover a weekend shift to have the very same conversation and somehow see the penny drop. At the beginning this surprised me. *What have they got that I haven't?* I'd ask myself. Such arrogance! I've come to see that it's a wonderful reminder of the power of community. The faith family around us who hold us, work with us, inspire us and challenge us is not a luxury. Community is the empowering grace of God in human faces. We mustn't separate God's grace from the sustenance of fellowship with those he has put in our lives. For us, it has meant we have been able to keep going. Over the years we have witnessed others cause mess, fall apart, burn out or leave Manenberg in a cloud of disappointment. Most of the time, they have overlooked or underplayed the necessity of mutual submission, accountability and love in a community of people walking the same road. We weren't designed to 'go it alone', and thank God for that.

7. Model obedience

It's well known that those coming out of addiction need clear rules and guidelines to follow. This can sometimes extend into faith life, with rule-following legalism sometimes replacing actual faith. But, from our point of view, it also means that if there's any incongruence between what we preach and how we live we'll be called up on it in no time. It's incredibly frustrating learning what a hypocrite you are, from those you're meant to be discipling! One morning, as we were reading the story of Jesus raising Lazarus from the dead (John 11) and came to the final question, 'Is there an example to follow in the passage?', we went round the group and shared whatever stood out to us. Unsurprisingly, we were all struck by Jesus bringing his friend back to life. This was inconvenient, because it meant if we were to try and follow Jesus' example that day we would need to find a dead person. As we were talking about this, Dowayne's phone buzzed. It was a message from a friend to say a gang fight had started again, and that a Hard Livings gangster had been killed the previous night. We went about looking for the family of the dead gangster, and eventually were able to locate them, and then find the morgue where the body was – but we couldn't get access until the following day. So, our attempt at following Jesus' example of raising the dead meant first rearranging whatever plans we had for the next day.

There's something I find rather unnerving about dead bodies. The young man had been shot in the head and it looked a little lumpy, like the wound had been hastily stitched up by an only semi-proficient stitcher in a hurry to get home after a long day. I couldn't stop staring at the extent of the damage, and had to close my eyes to muster any kind of faith for a miracle. Nevertheless, we began to sing in worship, quietly at first but increasing in conviction and volume, and speak life into this body as Jesus had all those years ago. We didn't see a resurrection miracle that day. We left the morgue feeling a little deflated, and heartbroken for the family. We had been unsuccessful – and another life had been violently ended by a bullet, leaving behind a distraught family. And yet we had succeeded in a tiny way. We had stepped out in faith as we sought to follow the example of Jesus. And our faith was growing.

The only true measure of success is faithfulness to what Jesus has asked us to do. In that sense, we have a 100 per cent success rate in the running of Cru62. Daily I feel the temptation to measure our success in numbers – of people getting clean from drugs or placing their faith in Jesus. But as my depth of insight grows I have come to believe that this isn't God's way of looking at things. It's not that he doesn't long for our young men to choose faith and freedom – of course he does. But if, referring to faith, hope and love, St Paul was right in saying that 'the greatest of these is love', then the fact that each young man to have walked through the doors of Cru62 knew he was loved by us and Jesus, is enough. He may leave without a faith and with little hope, but at least love abounded.

14: High Highs and Low Lows

Love is giving someone the power to crush you,
and trusting them not to.
(Simon Sinek)[1]

Love can break your bones. But broken bones tell stories
and broken bones sing songs.
(John Mark McMillan)[2]

Tobias Jones observes that 'addicts often have a paradoxical combination of low self-esteem and massive ego'.[3] I recognise this in myself just as much as in those we live with. Life with angry, addicted gangsters teaches me more about sin, grace, vulnerability and hope than I've learnt in any conventional church setting. And witnessing Jesus do his work of transformation in the lives of some of the young men illustrates to me how imperative it is to come before God in neediness and desperation. Maruwaan was one of my greatest teachers.

Maruwaan

Cru62 ran only at half capacity for the first six months. We were being deliberately cautious in our approach, learning as we went, and wanted to establish healthy life rhythms and develop a strong faith culture among the three young men we had, before adding more people to the mix. The idea was that the 'thermostat' of healing, vulnerability and hunger for transformation would be set sufficiently high that the new guys who came to live in the house would automatically 'warm up' to the collective vibe. I took a lot of time in morning devotions directing the three house-mates to passages in Scripture relating to sonship, spiritual adoption and belonging to the family of God – all with a view to them being able to 'try out' this new way of living in front of the new guys who came into the house.

Dowayne was the best at recruiting new guys for the house. One wet mid-May morning, he asked if I wanted to come and meet Maruwaan, a young guy he grew up round the corner from and who had just filled out an application form to join Cru62. It was about midday when we got to Maruwaan's house. We knocked on the door and waited. Nothing. We knocked again, this time slightly harder. Eventually we heard someone stirring, and the door opened. It was Maruwaan. He was standing in his underwear, rubbing his eyes and squinting at the daylight. His four top front teeth were missing (he'd pulled them out – the fashion in Manenberg), and he was wearing two gold ring earrings, one in each ear. Combined with a couple of home-drawn tattoos, he had the appearance of a sleepy pirate.

'We've come to see if you're still up for coming into Cru62, and if you are, when we can come and fetch you,' said Dowayne.

'Yeah I'm keen – I can't quit this stuff on my own, I need your help.'

'Cool, well we'll come and fetch you in a couple of hours. Pack a bag, get yourself ready, and we'll see you at 2.30 p.m.'

And that was that. Walking back to the car, I asked Dowayne a bit of Maruwaan's story. 'I've known him for years – we grew up a couple of doors down from each other. He's addicted to heroin, and is part of a small gang called the *Dagga Koppe* [the Dope Heads]. He's from a Muslim family – but there are a lot of issues in the house. He's a great guy, and seems desperate enough to leave his current way of life behind so I'm excited for him to join the house.'

Much as I admired Dowayne's enthusiasm, I wasn't at all convinced. There just seemed too many 'high-risk' factors. Coming off heroin is no joke – we'd already seen that with one of the guys who was currently in the house – cold sweats, joint pain, vomiting and diarrhoea for days on end. Quite apart from the drug withdrawal process, I had questions about whether Maruwaan, being Muslim, would be willing to fully participate in Bible study and prayer, one of the conditions of staying at the house. And it all just seemed a bit last minute – like he'd made a knee-jerk decision because we'd turned up at his door and put him on the spot. However, despite my doubts he was ready and waiting when we went to fetch him.

Then the drama began.

As he lay in bed that first afternoon, he began to sweat profusely, shivering violently. Sarah had made him soup, and was sitting by his bed. The rest of us were standing around, half praying, half not quite sure what to do. Someone put on some worship music, and we began to sing along. As one song came to an end, Maruwaan groaned, 'Can you play that song again?' We just figured he liked it. As it came to an end for the second time, he asked the same question. Again and again. We asked him what it was about that song, called 'No Longer Slaves', that he liked so much.

'I don't know, it's just that whenever that song is on and everyone is singing it, my withdrawal pains go and I'm filled with peace.'

What do you reply to that? Needless to say, there was a pretty limited playlist for the next week.

We had already arranged a worship evening at *Jou Ma Se Kombuis* in which the Cru62 guys were required to participate. Sarah asked Maruwaan if he felt up to getting out of bed and coming along. He declined the first time, but when she kept asking he eventually gave in and came, wrapped up in a duvet and feeling pretty fragile. The first song we sang that evening happened to be 'No Longer Slaves' – and as it began, Maruwaan spontaneously threw off his duvet, ran to the middle of the room and asked everyone to pray for him. As we prayed, accompanied by the song, his face changed from a pained frown to a toothy grin, and finally he was totally free. His pains never came back after that. Once he surrendered his life to Jesus he came painlessly off heroin, with no additional help or medication – aided only by the power of worship and Christian community.

A couple of months into his recovery journey, during a church family gathering, Maruwaan got a fright. Just across the room from him was a guy he recognised, whom he had mugged at knife point a couple of years back. The details of the incident were vivid in his mind because of something odd the man had said to him. He hadn't struggled to resist and wasn't at all scared, but instead he smiled as he gave his phone to Maruwaan and said to him, 'You can have my phone. But know this – I forgive you for what you've done, and I'm going to pray that one day you will change your ways and come to know you're a child of God.' The man's name was Leon, one of the leaders of Tree of Life, and he was now sitting a couple of metres away from Maruwaan, praying. Maruwaan immediately looked at the ground – partly in shame, partly to look like he was praying, but mainly in an effort not to be noticed by Leon. But as the meeting went on, Maruwaan's heart began to race and he knew he needed to come clean. So, as people shared their 'good news stories' from the last week, Maruwaan added his own.

'*Ja*, my good news story is that a couple of years ago I mugged a guy. I took his phone, ran off and sold it for *unga* money. But now I'm clean and have started coming to church.' Thinking this was the entirety of his story, everyone began clapping and cheering. 'But actually the man I mugged is sitting here opposite me.' As he said this, he pointed to Leon, who looked completely baffled. And then the penny dropped.

'Oooh – I remember that – was that you?!'

It was no surprise to most of us that Leon could not remember the encounter, as he'd been through much worse. Notably, one prayer week when he walked through a gun battle, undeterred by the bullets whizzing past him because he had an appointment with Jesus in the prayer room. That's just the sort of guy he is. And so amid laughter and cheers the two of them hugged, and Maruwaan learnt the power of prophetic prayer and the beauty of being forgiven.

But what else could I tell them?

Six months later, a group of Muslim men came to our gate one evening wanting to talk to Maruwaan. They had heard there was a 'Muslim brother' living at our house and had come to invite him to mosque. They asked him about whether he was doing *salah* and praying five times a day. He replied that he wasn't. They then proceeded to tell him Allah would punish him if he didn't. He said he didn't want to go to mosque with them, and that he was part of a programme in the house, and was quite happy. To which they answered, 'If you're off drugs, then leave this prison and come to mosque with us!' and they demanded he go and fetch me.

As I went to talk to them, I realised I felt like a naughty kid on my way to the headmaster's office. While the men were fairly cordial, I immediately wondered why seven of them had come together. It felt slightly confrontational – and I was reminded of the imam's words to us before we moved in: 'Sherwood Park is a quiet neighbourhood, but the people have a very short fuse if they don't like what you're doing.'

I explained to the group that while it was sweet of them to invite Maruwaan to accompany them, we did our own 'in-house spiritual formation', and it would be unfair to show preferential treatment to one of the guys by allowing him to go to mosque. They were polite but intimidating, circling round me and telling me it's required that all Muslims must go to mosque to make Allah happy – and so I should let Maruwaan go with them. I daren't tell them he had recently decided to follow Jesus – ultimately, I didn't want a religious confrontation.

After they left I went to speak to Maruwaan to see how he was doing. He was feeling pretty unsettled about the interaction and said he felt manipulated and judged. I realised what it must feel like for people when Christians knock on their door and ask if they are going to heaven or hell. It felt like we'd been caught in a religious ambush.

Then Maruwaan brightened up and delivered a great line –
'They asked me if I believe the Bible now that I'm living with
Christians. And I said of course I believe the Bible is true, but
it's not just because I live with Christians. The fact is, I'm seeing
the things the Bible describes happening in my life and the lives
of people around me. How can it be false?' He didn't entertain
arguments about doctrine and religion – he wouldn't have known
how. Instead he pointed to what he knew and the life he lived
– the supernatural reality of Jesus healing those he prays for, of
the Holy Spirit working in his areas of brokenness, and of kingdom
family doing life together as we follow Jesus. This transcends
religious confrontation, whether done in the name of Jesus or
Allah.

Fifteen months after arriving at CRU62, Maruwaan's faith and
recovery was going from strength to strength as he matured and
grew in emotional intelligence. Numbers were growing, so we
offered him a job as house supervisor. It was then that he found
the courage and conviction to tell his family about converting from
Islam to following Jesus. He even tried bacon for the first time and
loved it, and decided he wanted to be baptised.

Beginning to burn out again

By August 2016, Cru62 had been running for eighteen months,
and during that time we had welcomed into our home fifteen
addicts, many of whom were gang members. Life was relentless
and we could begin to feel ourselves burning out.

Jayden, a friend of ours who had been back and forth between
Jesus and drugs for years, had died of a heroin overdose. It came
out of the blue. Deaths of addicts and gangsters are generally pretty
sudden, as they are usually the result of an overdose or a bullet.
However, knowing this doesn't make it any easier to deal with
when it happens. His ex-wife, Fatima, a Tree of Life member and
dear friend, asked me if I would speak at his funeral. It was an
immense privilege, for sure, but I was tired and confused as to the

sort of message I should preach. I was still feeling pretty angry with Jayden for how badly he had treated Fatima and their two boys in the final years of his life, but I was at the same time totally despondent about the tragic way his life, which for some time held such promise, had ended. I eventually chose a few verses from Romans 5 for my text – centring on verse 8, 'God demonstrates his own love for us in this: while we were still sinners, Christ died for us.' I had no idea who would be at the funeral, as Jayden led a life that veered between two extremes – Pentecostal prayer meetings and heroin-fuelled gang activity – but figured both gangsters and Pentecostals would be encouraged by the message of Jesus' love for sinners. There was a clear tension in my heart, holding the pain and despair of losing Jayden to drugs against the profound hope of the resurrection of Jesus. It became apparent, however, that the Pentecostal religion of many in attendance was unable to 'go there' – to publicly come to terms with the grief – as the first hour of the service was taken up with lots of very sad people singing lots of very loud, happy songs punctuated with cries of 'Hallelujah!'

Plausible but untrue

The danger of treating addiction in a non-holistic way is that many of the really important aspects of recovery actually happen once someone is clean. (Tobias Jones)[4]

It's usually only months into recovery when a person pursuing sobriety has the mental wherewithal to begin to broach the pain of their lacerated, broken heart. Issues that have been buried for years – being raped by a family member as a young boy, being beaten up by an abusive uncle every time you broke something, consistently being told you were stupid, or hearing your mum tell you she wished she had aborted you before you were born, witnessing friends overdose or being violently killed in gang fights – all still hurt. Recovery is the process of becoming vulnerable enough to freely admit your inner agony, and allowing Jesus' Spirit to minister to the darkest parts of your soul, as you find freedom in the acceptance and love of Father God and adoption into a new spiritual family.

The hardest thing about running Cru62 is the disappointment and rejection one feels when one of the guys runs away. They are accustomed to manipulation and lying day in, day out, to hustling for enough money for their next hit, and so have become experts at coming up with excuses for their behaviour. It always amazes me how well someone in addiction can turn the tables of a conversation to become the victim. In Narcotics Anonymous there is a term for this: 'the plausible but untrue'.

A lot of our time is spent trying to explain to the young men living with us the potentially grave consequences of bad decisions. A seemingly inconsequential issue, when undealt with, can spiral into disaster. This is often the way they end up leaving. The fact is, no one who has run away has ever had a well-thought-through reason for leaving, let alone any semblance of a plan for staying clean outside. It's usually due to lies manifesting as truth through unresolved issues of the heart – generally around pride, being unable to accept authority, jealousy towards another house member, shame from being caught lying, or just plain old cravings for a hit. Calvin left after eleven months clean due to an argument over changing his bed sheets, which had gone a gross grey/brown colour and hadn't been changed in months. He maintained that Dowayne had been unreasonable for 'telling him what to do'. In reality Calvin was unwilling to address his issues with authority. He managed to stay off drugs for a couple of months after leaving but, as is so often the case, boredom led to drinking. Alcohol is the beginning of the end for so many struggling drug addicts, and within a week or two he had relapsed back on to *tik* and Mandrax. The slippery slope was depressingly similar to how it had been before he came into Cru62. After a year of getting in fights, dealing for a local drug merchant, and house-breaking, the police finally caught Calvin and put him in jail. He had just become a father to a baby girl – another child born with the odds stacked against her. All because Calvin wouldn't change his sheets.

A diary entry summed up some of the feelings I was processing at the time. This time it was a double whammy; two of the Cru62 guys who seemed to be doing really well had run away, having plotted together for weeks.

17.08.2016

My primary emotion is a sense of deep hopelessness and futility. I feel like we have invested as much as we possibly could. The money, the time, the love, the strategising and planning, the patience and forbearance, the encouragement and prayer, the sharing of our home and our lives, the coaxing out of dreams for their future, the introducing them to our friends and supporters, the changing our plans at the drop of a hat to accommodate their wobbles and hang-ups – all of this has often got us to the point of exhaustion and near burnout. But we've done it because we're convinced that what we are doing is ultimately worth it. To work and live for the transformation of a community on the brink of perpetual civil war, where the strongest economy is the drugs trade, and to specifically target the worst of the worst in such a community – that is taking on a hell of a lot of principalities and powers and a whole lot of darkness. There is inevitably going to be a toll it takes. I get that. But the pain comes from these situations where those you were pretty sure were fighting on the same side as you then take off their mask, take their money and run.

The question I keep asking is, do I honestly have the legs and the perseverance and the faith to keep going with Cru62? Do I have the patience to build people up for 11 more months, only for them to use us for whatever they can get and then up and leave at any point they so wish, breaking our hearts again? How do you maintain tough skin and a soft heart in this business? How do you make sure you're not easily offended and knocked sideways by the disastrous decisions of broken people around you, and yet keep your heart believing and hoping for fruit that lasts, and transformation of an entire community?

A week or two after Jayden's funeral, we were busy with the logistics of organising lifts, sorting out dorm-room allocations and preparing talks and ministry times for our first Tree of Life church weekend away. Despite everything that needed doing – most of which was new to us, as a small, fledgling church – there was a real buzz and sense of expectation of what the Holy Spirit had planned for our time away. No sooner had we arrived at the campsite, we heard the news that Muneep, a young guy who'd attended group counselling and worship sessions a couple of years previously and whom I had discipled for a short time, had been shot dead. He was an American gangster and had recently gone on the run for losing one of the gang's guns, a mistake punishable by death. We hadn't been particularly close for a year or two by then, but it still hurt.

The church weekend turned out to be a roaring success. Amid continual laughter and fun, it saw the establishing of new friendships and a kids' ministry. At the end of the weekend, Maruwaan and Keeba, a new church member, were baptised in the river. Both had glorious testimonies of what Jesus had done in their lives, and how the Holy Spirit had changed them completely.

Keeba was born into a Muslim family and had a difficult upbringing. She lives down the road from Fatima, and when she was in trouble or in need of something to eat she knew Fatima's door would always be open. Fatima is a natural evangelist, and having also been born into a Muslim family, she would grasp every opportunity to tell Keeba about Jesus. These conversations began to happen more regularly, as Keeba's physical hunger was allayed but her spiritual hunger grew. Their friendship flourished so much that Keeba and her beautiful little daughter, Zeeha, moved into a Wendy house with Fatima and her two sons.

And then something strange began to happen.

Whenever they spoke about Jesus, Keeba would begin to overheat, and would need to take off her sweater. She couldn't explain it, but as they spoke and prayed together she would heat up and tears started running down her face. Having understood and experienced the love of God over her, and received Fatima's love and hospitality, it wasn't long before Keeba made a commitment to follow Jesus, and was baptised by Clare and Fatima.

Dowayne and Leon baptised Maruwaan as the rest of the family watched from the banks of the lagoon, singing the words to his anthem, 'From my mother's womb you have chosen me, love has called my name. I've been born again into a family, your blood flows through my veins. I'm no longer a slave to fear, I am a child of God.' It was only as they were walking back to shore that we all realised the poignant link – that five years previously, Leon had prophesied freedom and salvation over Maruwaan, and now he was waist deep in freezing water baptising the young man who'd mugged him at knife-point but was now following the same Jesus.

Back home, devoid of any specific answers to the many questions we had about how to run Cru62 sustainably, we kept soldiering on, and a couple of weeks later a new guy we had met through Waydin came into the house.

Shayne

Shayne was heavily tattooed. He had a tattoo of a hand with a raised middle finger (the symbol of the Rude Boys gang) on his neck, a stars and stripes flag on his calf (the American gang symbol), a figure 2 and a figure 6 on each knee (meaning he was also a prison gangster), and two dollar signs on his left hand (a symbol associated with the 26 prison gang, who, in prison gang folklore are said to be robbers and 'money lovers'). He also had multiple knife wounds all over his chest, fake gold teeth, and a constant scowl on his face. It was as if I was looking at a carica-ture – his appearance bore all the hallmarks of the quintessential 'high-risk youth'. I immediately felt a strong sense of affection for him.

Chatting to him in our first mentoring session, I grew to like him even more as I peppered him with various questions to get him to open up a bit about how he ended up so physically marked, so entrenched in gangsterism, and what on earth made him start smoking *tik* while at primary school. I was stunned to hear he lived with both parents, who were married and still together. This fact made him the first gangster I'd ever met who comes from a stable family home with a healthy father figure.

In answer to why he started smoking *tik*, he told me he started before he'd even tried a cigarette – and was intrigued to try it because the older friends he was hanging around with swore by the high it gave. All of these older friends were members of the Rude Boy gang and so, aged thirteen, *tik* addiction and gang membership came in a two-for-one package. Shayne's habit was unknowingly funded by his mother, who would lovingly give him pocket money. It was only when he was fifteen that his mother found out her son was a drug addict and gangster.

'How did she react to the news?' I asked.

'She hit me. A lot.'

The inevitable anger towards adults that followed being kicked around by his mum was channelled into carrying out violent acts for the gang. Stabbing and shooting enemies of the Rude Boys became the most effective way to express his emotions, as well as fuelling his growing *tik* addiction, because the gang paid him in *tik* and Mandrax – thereby adding another substance to his system.

I'm often asked, as someone who hasn't ever been addicted to illegal drugs, if I can really understand or help the young guys with whom we work. I've always maintained that we're all in the same boat when it comes to sin. My time with Shayne that mid-August morning confirmed this when he answered my next question.

'What was your reason for joining the Rude Boys?'

'I didn't want to miss out on the fun my friends were having. I didn't want to be alone.'

'So you wanted to be part of the group and wanted a place to belong?'

'*Ja* – we were all together, all looking out for each other, having fun, talking *kak* and that. That's why I joined and got *tjappies*.'

'What about when you went to prison?'

'I joined the 26 gang because after a while being a *frans*, I was getting beaten, ordered around, told I must do this, do that – and I was scared because I had no one to defend me.'

'So you joined the 26s in order to feel safe?'

'*Ja*. After that, I had no problems. I wasn't committed to the gang, I wasn't high up, I just needed protection.'

Having been so remarkably vulnerable so early on, it was sad that Shayne left us just two days later, unable to deal with his drug cravings. Our conversation reminded me that to be safe and to belong in a community is a natural human need. It's actually a sign of emotional health. And yet, for the teenager growing up in Manenberg there are serious predators waiting around every corner, ready and willing day and night to meet such needs in the most warped and destructive way one could imagine. It was to these predators that Shayne had decided to return.

15: The Walk

———————

Step out beyond anxious waiting and into the storm of events, carried
only by God's command and your own faith; then will freedom
exultantly cry out to welcome your spirit.
(Dietrich Bonhoeffer)[1]

'I know a cure for everything. Salt water.'
'Salt water?' I asked him.
'Yes,' he said, 'in one way or the other. Sweat, or tears, or the salt sea.'
(Isak Dinesen)[2]

In contrast to the grinding cycle of setbacks that seemed to epitomise this season of Cru62 life was the emerging story of Maruwaan. By now he had been clean from heroin for fifteen months,
had become a full-time Cru62 staff member and was headed to
Johannesburg with Jonathan to raise awareness for a project they
were starting, which aimed to address the failing education system
in Manenberg. They planned to do this by walking the 1,494 kilometres back home over sixty days, stopping off at communities
and churches along the way and advocating for Manenberg's high
school students. It was the most high-profile initiative we had ever
attempted to pull off and, among the questions – *Will they make*
it? Will they raise the money they need? What might go wrong?
Where will they sleep? – there was much excitement and strong
support. Maruwaan and Jonathan had travelled to Johannesburg
two weeks before the walk began to share their back story with
churches around the city. They had appeared on radio shows, spoken
to newspaper reporters, launched a website and crowdfunding page,
and received an impressive amount of donated equipment,
comprising items they would need along the way. The weekend

before they set off was Maruwaan's twenty-first birthday. He had never been so far from home in his life and, while excited about taking part in the walk, was understandably sad not to be able to celebrate with friends and family back in Cape Town. So Jonathan organised a party, Sarah flew up and surprised him, and our church community gave money towards his first smartphone, enabling him to stay in touch throughout the walk.

From time to time, Jonathan sent through videos of Maruwaan preaching, the two of them training together, and even a few prophetic words people had given them as they prepared to embark. One of the words Maruwaan received was that God had anointed his feet for the walk and would look after his family while he was gone – and that he needn't worry about them as they were in God's hands. This was apt, as Maruwaan's mother was in hospital, there were other serious issues among his family members, and there was a daily struggle to put food on the table.

The day of the walk came, and they set off from Hillbrow at 4.30 a.m., anxious to make the minimum of 25 kilometres a day to reach Cape Town as planned sixty days later. Beyond the inevitable blisters and aching limbs, there were no significant complications. By early evening they arrived at Emthonjeni, a community with whom they were to stay, near Sebokeng in the south-west of Johannesburg, and got an early night.

The next day, accompanied by some of the community members, they started walking again bright and early. Mid-morning I received a WhatsApp message from Maruwaan:

Can I ask you a favour?
Sure – what?
Could you send me a Bible passage every morning so I can lead devotions with whoever is walking with us?

He was adamant that this walk would change lives – not just in Manenberg, but along the road. He was determined that all he encountered should hear about the phenomenal story of how he had met Jesus and been transformed. I sent him Isaiah 35, having prayed it over him and Jonathan the day before. I was especially drawn to verses 8 to 10:

> And a highway will be there;
> it will be called the Way of Holiness;
> it will be for those who walk on that Way.
> The unclean will not journey on it;
> wicked fools will not go about on it.
> No lion will be there,
> nor any ravenous beast;
> they will not be found there.
> But only the redeemed will walk there,
> and those the LORD has rescued will return.
> They will enter Zion with singing;
> everlasting joy will crown their heads.
> Gladness and joy will overtake them,
> and sorrow and sighing will flee away.

Having sent him his Bible passage and said a few words of prayer for him and Jonathan, I got on with my day – building a wooden fence in the front garden of the boys' house with Waydin and Frikkie.

At that point I was blissfully unaware it was about to become the worst day of my life.

About an hour later Sarah called to me.

She was sitting in the car in the driveway looking as white as a sheet.

'Hi love, what's wrong?' She was obviously agitated and was breathing heavily.

'There's been an accident.'

'An accident where? What do you mean?'

'With the walk.'

'What?' My heart started to race and my mind immediately started imagining various hypothetical scenarios.

'I just got a call from one of the friends they're with. A car ran into the group as they were walking. I don't know the exact details – but . . .'

'But what?'

Sarah paused. Silence.

Then, in a whisper, 'They said there's a body.'

We both sat there, panicking and trembling. None of the scenarios I'd imagined had involved a body. I began to think of all the different people I knew were walking with Jonathan and Maruwaan that day. Friends from Hillbrow, community members from Enthonjeni – many of whom I didn't know.

The phone rang again. A deafening hush filled the car. Sarah picked up, and put the phone on loudspeaker so I could hear.

'Sarah? Are you there?'

'Yes, I'm here with Pete. What's going on?'

'Guys, I'm so sorry . . .' The voiced trailed off.

'What? Sorry about what?'

'I'm so sorry. The body is Maruwaan.'

Sarah screamed.

A long, piercing scream of a mother who had lost a child. I sat in silence, stunned, unable to speak or let out a sound. The friend at the other end of the phone repeated over and over, 'I'm just so sorry.' Sitting in our car parked in our driveway, neither of us could comprehend the news. In desperation, we demanded a doctor officially declare Maruwaan dead. But for our friends at the accident scene it was obvious. He had taken the full force of a car hurtling into him at 120 kilometres per hour while standing on the hard shoulder. Killed instantly. A bright light snuffed out on the spot. One of the most promising lives we'd ever encountered, gone. Just like that. Finished. Over. Dead. Not only that, but Jonathan was in a critical condition – the crash had catapulted the parked car into his and sent him flying. Jonathan had sustained multiple internal injuries; it was touch and go as to whether he would survive.

That day it felt like my hope died. No words of comfort, no

theological explanations (and boy there were many – well meant, but entirely misguided), no meditating on Scripture or time of prayer made any dent in the total and utter hopelessness I felt. And the guilt.

Guilt fuelled from never having lost anyone before their time, and not knowing how to deal with it. Guilt from holding to warped subconscious theological assumptions that anything other than external optimism and inner joy was prohibited. Ultimately, a naive refusal to acknowledge the feelings of nihilism and numbness that can surround, swamp and slowly suffocate you in a time of trauma and grief. An accusing voice repeatedly condemned me for my despair. *You say Jesus is hope in all circumstances – what about now, then? How can God honestly be good if he allowed this? Where's your faith, you spineless fraud – the one time your faith is meant to make a difference, you fall to pieces. What would people think if they knew what you're really like?*

The next day I found myself on a plane to Johannesburg. Officially, we were going to identify Maruwaan's body and make arrangements to bring it home. But really we were going to pray for him to rise from the dead. We weren't sure how to do it, but were convinced that it is as theologically orthodox to raise the dead as it is to love your neighbour. After all, at least nine people are clearly presented as being raised from the dead in the Bible. In the New Testament alone, Jesus raised a widow's son (Luke 7:11–17), a religious leader's daughter (Mark 5:35–43), and his friend Lazarus (John 11:38–44), and then empowered us to do even greater works than he had done (John 14:12). Accordingly, Peter and Paul each raised a dead person (Acts 9:36–42 and 20:9–12), and Jesus himself rose after being crucified. In direct contradiction to those who counselled me that it was 'obviously Maruwaan's time to go home', we had pages of prophecies over his life that he was only just beginning to step into. Promises from the mouth of the Father wrapped up in embodied, earthly adventures for his son to discover. Maruwaan carried so much of the light, love and power of Jesus that Satan took him out, pure and simple. It was a robbery. Manenberg, South Africa and the world were robbed of the hope he exuded.

So Sarah and I, Leon, Maruwaan's mum and cousin, and Jonathan's sister got into a rental car and drove to Emthonjeni, the community where Maruwaan had stayed for his final night before the accident. I was on my phone non-stop, making arrangements in a city I didn't know, booking cars, thanking people I'd never met for letting us max out their credit card on flights – I felt like a traumatised tour manager arranging a holiday from hell, full of distraught, weeping people. It was the absolute worst experience I've ever been through.

And then, late in the evening, we got to Emthonjeni. We were hours late as I had botched the arrival arrangements, but Trevor Nthlola, the inimitable leader of the community, had arranged a most tender-hearted welcome for us. We were each met at the door by a personal hugger, mamas with their arms wide open, and were enveloped and held as we each wept like babies. Singing began, accompanied by *djembe* and piano, and we joined in with our brothers and sisters whom we had never met, but whose embrace was helping soak up our grief, in the most spine-tinglingly beautiful time of worship I'd ever been part of.

As if the evening couldn't get both sadder and more epic, people began to share stories of Maruwaan's effect on their community in the short time they had known him. Each shared testimony of the ways in which Maruwaan had touched their heart. 'He was such a gentle spirit.' 'He had a father's heart.' 'When I heard his past, I couldn't believe the man standing in front of me.' 'He was a walking miracle.' And so the stories went on. His last words were a joyful affirmation of the word he'd been given before the walk began – 'My feet are anointed!' I turned to look at Shanaaz, Maruwaan's mother. She was sitting in the corner of the room, deeply affected and crying quietly, until she piped up – 'I think my son was like Steve Biko or Nelson Mandela! He died for the people!'

We prayed for resurrection for five days straight. Our Tree of

Life community met in Manenberg for hours on end, worshipping and speaking life into Maruwaan's body, while declaring the prophetic words spoken over his life. It just seemed like the most reasonable thing to do. Yes, we were desperate, but we figured it was humanly impossible one way or the other to raise Maruwaan – and it didn't become less likely the more time wore on. But by the fifth day we needed to let go. Sarah anointed his feet with oil, and we left the undertakers, distraught and finally coming to terms with the fact we'd never see him again.

Back in Cape Town, there was a funeral to organise. Newspapers had picked up on the accident and were writing up the story with various degrees of inaccuracy. We decided to allow news cameras at the funeral, as ever since Maruwaan was a young boy he had wanted to be famous. Now he would be – and for all the right reasons. A significant issue arose that some of his family wanted to bury him in accordance with Muslim rites. An aunt was offering to cover the entire funeral costs as long as his mother agreed to bury him a Muslim. This would have been a travesty, and completely against Maruwaan's own wishes. And having heard so many testimonies while we were in Johannesburg of Maruwaan's transformation, Shanaaz recognised that, however embarrassing Maruwaan's conversion may have been to some in the family, his new-found faith in Jesus was both profound and authentic.

Common sense prevailed, and arrangements for a Christian service began. Never before had I seen so many Muslims and gangsters in a church building. The place was jam-packed, with not even standing room left. I remember preaching about Maruwaan's life, and highlighting that the church was bursting at the seams in part due to the fascination many had towards the turn-around he had made. Many just didn't understand the remarkable shift that had happened. And as I stood next to his lifeless body, looking around the congregation, I realised that the most potent form of evangelism is fascination – 'Christianity should not only persuade with truth, but it should also attract with beauty.'[3] What Jesus had done in Maruwaan was stunning, and this beautiful metamorphosis had attracted the curiosity of scores of people from across Manenberg and beyond.

This beauty was juxtaposed with ugliness. In a display of unmindful obliviousness, the press behaved badly and thrust cameras in mourners' faces. But then at the graveside, the beauty returned as four of Maruwaan's Cru62 brothers lovingly lowered his coffin into the ground as the rest of us sang his song through distraught tears. 'From my mother's womb you have chosen me, love has called my name. I've been born again into a family, your blood flows through my veins. I'm no longer a slave to fear, I am a child of God.'

The day Maruwaan was killed I told God I was demanding many, many souls in exchange for this dear life, with Tertullian's famous adage 'The blood of the martyrs is the seed of the church' front and centre in my mind. We began to see a shift soon after. A few short months after the funeral, members of his family asked to receive this same Jesus whom Maruwaan had come to love into their own lives. We baptised his mother and two younger siblings in the ocean at Muizenberg. A proportion of the money given towards the healing journey of the families affected by the accident was put towards the same two siblings' school fees, and his family became part of Tree of Life – all in line with the prophetic word Maruwaan had been given days before the accident, that God would look after his family while he was gone.

Meanwhile

Somewhere at the back of the crowded funeral, away from the television cameras and suit-wearing gangsters, a man was praying a prayer of surrender to Jesus. Nkosinathi Mbuyazi, a friend of mine and Sarah's and a pastor of twelve years, had only met Maruwaan briefly once, but came to the funeral to support us. As the service unfolded, and story after story was shared describing Maruwaan's impact on people as a follower of Jesus for fifteen short months, Nathi became progressively convicted. It felt like his life was little more than a small cog in a large machine, propping up the bureaucracies of a large denomination, while here was a young man who had given his all to the adventure of living out the great commission. As Nathi stood pondering this existential angst at the end of the service, a stranger approached him and gave him a prophetic word.

He was to pioneer something new. The time was now.

The next week we met together and Nathi poured out his heart – questioning his job, his life, his ultimate purpose, and the effectiveness of cumbersome event-oriented church machinations. It was all very exciting.

'What are you doing at the end of October?' I asked.

'Let me check the dates . . . Nothing.'

'Come with me to Switzerland!'

'Umm, okaaaay. Why? And how?!'

And just like that, six weeks later Nathi was on a plane to the 24–7 Prayer International gathering in Geneva. I met him there, having spent a week or so in England speaking at various churches about some of what Jesus was doing back in Manenberg. A few of us had made a short film about Maruwaan. We had filmed his entire testimony for a promo film for the walk, and so had a good amount of footage of him to cut together with Dowayne, Leon, Sarah and I all telling stories of the last couple of years of his life – and in particular, his miraculous turnaround once he had been delivered from heroin withdrawal pains. The film was shown at the Geneva gathering to gasps and tears, and was followed by a spine-tingling altar call led by Dowayne, for those willing to give their lives to serving the poor and broken. And so, over the course of four days, as Nathi heard the story of the movement, met some heroes of the faith, received unnervingly accurate prophetic words from perfect strangers in line with the word at Maruwaan's funeral, he had his heart reignited for revival and decided that this was his people. Not long after, he became the national director of 24–7 Prayer South Africa.

Fighting dirty

The first night we ever publicly showed the film, at an event in London, all hell broke loose. Dowayne, Leigh and I were staying with my family, and arrived back from the event late in the evening. We went straight to bed, shattered, having only landed that afternoon. The next morning I woke up and looked outside to see Diego, my brother-in-law, taping up a broken car window. It had been smashed during the night – the first (and only) time that had ever happened. As I boiled the kettle to make coffee my phone buzzed. It was Sarah. She had bad news. Back in Manenberg there had been an incident. In the early hours of the morning, Reswell, whom we had bailed out of prison just two weeks earlier and who was in Cru62 for a second time, detoxing off heroin, had broken into Dowayne's room where all of Maruwaan's clothes and belongings were. We had never had anything like that before. He took everything, including Dowayne's laptop and computer console, and also cleaned out the kitchen cupboards. Sarah had been woken at 4 a.m. by Waydin, telling her the news. She had later shown phenomenal determination in catching Reswell, handing him over to the police, through tears, and had even recovered most of the stolen goods. But she was traumatised, heartbroken and emotionally finished. Later on that day, I received another message informing me that Nick and Cate's home had also had an attempted break-in that night.

It was only then that I saw the pattern.

Not only had Maruwaan's life been cut short by a freak accident, but there even seemed to be a backlash against the very telling of his story after he was gone. It was both disconcerting and affirming at the same time. Disconcerting because we had obviously taken on some fairly hefty principalities, but affirming because spiritual opposition can often be a sign of having an impact for the kingdom. We continued to show the film wherever we went, watching it with gritted teeth and hearts racing, praying silently in tongues. Months later, the evening we showed the film in an open-air event in the part of Manenberg in which Maruwaan grew up, Nick's computer – the one used to edit the film – was stolen in a break-in. A part of me felt retrospectively that we should have seen it coming. It was a stark reminder that we are in a battle. There is no neutral ground in spreading a narrative of hope.

New boys' camp

A couple of months after Maruwaan died, and upon our return from Geneva, we decided to close the Cru62 house for a short while to allow us time to heal. The last two house-mates, Frikkie and Waydin, had both been hit hard by Maruwaan's death, and lost hope for their own journeys. Both had left Cru62 in the maelstrom of the last month and returned to drugs. Much as we wanted to pursue them and persuade them to come back, we knew we needed time to recover. It was sad and rather disorienting. When you have worked for five years to get something up and running and then given your all into seeing it succeed, day in, day out, for the last two years, taking a step back seemed rather counter-intuitive. I battled most days with purposelessness. I also had to repeatedly tell myself that deciding to close for a few months wasn't indulgent or selfish. Far from it, in fact, as a friend reminded me – if we wanted to be doing this for years to come we needed to step back a bit in the short term.

Apart from highlighting my worryingly task-and-success-oriented issues, this season enabled us to establish new friendships with other addicts and gangsters – all with a view to having a longer 'run-up' into them joining Cru62 when we reopened. I was rereading Jackie Pullinger's *Chasing the Dragon* at the time, and had just finished a chapter in which Jackie took a whole bunch of heroin addicts camping. She tells how it rained and rained, and how stressed she was most of the time, but the story ended (as most of hers seem to) with all the new boys encountering Jesus, praying in tongues and painlessly withdrawing from heroin.

Right, that's what we'll do – we'll take the new guys camping. Why didn't I think of this before? We can make fires and put up tents, sleep under the stars, tell our stories, and all of them will get filled with the Spirit and detox effortlessly. If it worked for Jackie Pullinger, it should work for us too. Easy peasy!

Dowayne booked us a spot three hours' drive from Cape Town at an organic mango farm in the middle of a remote expanse of the Cederberg mountains. The far-flung location precluded anyone running away, and it was so isolated from anywhere that we really didn't have a plan B if any of the detoxers began to freak out. In my mind it was a perfect set-up for God to move powerfully.

We had driven roughly a minute and a half from Manenberg when the first fight began – between Devrino and Boytjie, over which song should play next on the Bluetooth music box one of them had brought. Devrino demanded to go home then and there, on the garage forecourt, throwing a hissy fit a three-year-old toddler would have been proud of. We split them up in different cars and carried on.

Having arrived and set up the tents, conflict again surfaced as it emerged the local drinking water came straight from the river and was light brown in colour. This was unacceptable to Boytjie, who announced he wasn't going to drink it. For three days. In 35-degree summer heat. I figured this wasn't an argument worth having – he wouldn't need persuading in a few hours when he was thirsty.

As the day went on, it became more and more draining being around these new guys. I began to kick myself. We had only known them a few weeks, they were all still living utterly chaotic lives back home, and it was completely unrealistic to have expected anything else from them on camp. An example of this was personal hygiene. Milo had very pallid, grey skin. He spent his life selling second-hand bricks he had procured from the building site across the road. At 50 cents a brick, Milo only needed to sell forty or so to buy a hit of *tik*. This didn't take long, so his mornings were spent wheeling other people's bricks home, stacking them appealingly outside his house, and waiting for buyers. By lunchtime he had usually sold his quota and his work for the day was done – he would go inside and sit in front of the TV smoking *tik*. At camp, he hadn't showered the first evening. It was only when it came to the end of the second day that we discovered he had no soap and wasn't completely sure what to actually do in a shower. As Dowayne, in the next shower cubicle along, coached him through how to wash, Milo let out a surprised grunt. It appeared his grey complexion was in fact layers of dirt that had built up over such a long time that it was now dropping off him like a melting ice cap.

With Milo now looking a much healthier colour, we had dinner. The conversation around the fire that evening was as shocking as it was depressing. Someone would start talking about gangs. Then drug use. Then violent crimes they had committed. Then sexual encounters. Then back to gangs . . . and the cycle would continue. Every time one of Dowayne, Brandon or I intervened and changed the subject, it would take less than five minutes for the conversation to gravitate towards a mixture of gangs, drugs, violence or sex. When Boytjie began to explain the meaning of a tattoo on his back – 'it's a person holding a decapitated head in their hands, I got it after beating someone to death with a steel pipe' – I began to realise we had not organised any prayer covering for our time away, and I began to pray for the dark atmosphere to lift.

The third morning of camp eventually came, and I packed up my tent before breakfast as I had to be in Cape Town a day earlier than the others. I can't say I was sad to leave, there were no post-holiday blues as I drove home – I was just thankful to be alone. It had been a disproportionately exhausting time away largely spent nannying grown men. No sooner had I arrived back in Manenberg than my phone rang. It was Dowayne. My heart sank. We had agreed that no news was good news – he would only phone if something was up.

'Pete?'

'Yes? How are you guys getting on?'

'We've had to pack up and are being asked to leave. We've got to go this evening.'

'What?! Why? Who's asking you to leave?'

'The manager of the campsite. He said he's not happy us being here any more.'

'Why? What's his problem?'

'Well, when we were swimming earlier, there was a family of tourists in the river, and Devrino did something silly.'

'Uh-huh. What exactly?'

'He pulled his pants down in front of the children and the parents complained to the manager.'

'Ah.'

I couldn't say I disagreed with the campsite management's decision. Devrino exhibited a rather unnerving combination of narcissism and intense rage. He was clearly a very troubled individual. It was a sad end to a rather disastrous camp, not at all the powerful spiritual experience I had hoped it would be, and nothing like I'd read in Jackie Pullinger's book.

Her addicts got clean and saved.

Our addicts got weird and sent home.

The most positive aspect of the whole fiasco was the conversation I had with Dowayne and Brandon late that evening when they arrived home exhausted and looking shell-shocked.

Sitting slumped on the sofa, Brandon remarked, 'Working with addicts is just so hard. Those guys are *hectic*. They're the *worst*!'

'Yeah,' said Dowayne. 'I can't actually handle the sheer amount of issues they come with. I mean, come on!'

I then proceeded, with great delight, to remind them that they'd each been in a much worse state when we met, than any of these new guys were. And we all looked at each other and burst out laughing.

16: Family is the Revolution

The most creative social strategy we have to offer is the church. Here we show the world a manner of life the world can never achieve through social coercion or governmental action. We serve the world by showing it something it is not, namely, a place where God is forming a family out of strangers.
(Stanley Hauerwas and William H. Willimon)[1]

Sometimes the obsession with finding solutions can get in the way of forming profound relationships of mutual understanding, and sometimes those relationships are more significant than solutions.
(Sam Wells and Marcia A. Owen)[2]

When missionaries start with the needs, hoping they will one day get to know poor people personally, they are likely to be found 10 years later, still addressing the need. They are welcome, even necessary, outsiders, but outsiders nonetheless.
(John B. Hayes)[3]

It seems to be an innate instinct in those of us who grew up in privilege yet want to 'help' those who are 'poor', to develop relationships characterised by detachment and power. We keep our distance, but still offer advice about problems our less privileged friends might be going through, presumptuously expecting them to take it. I have found that many will venture into poor communities and hand out a combination of food, hugs and opinions, but very few will keep quiet and just *be with*. In their book *Living Without Enemies*, Sam Wells and Marcia Owen write about how this impulse to offer solutions actually represents an emotional withdrawal:

. . . to avoid being present in the pain among the people experiencing that pain. The host of explanations for why people get shot
and killed – it's poverty, it's racism, it's the educational system,
it's the parents' fault, it's a bunch of drug addicts, it's just criminals
killing criminals – are all, in the end, justifications for such withdrawal. And so presence is in itself a form of protest against such
explanations and such legitimized withdrawal.[4]

This notion of 'presence as protest' might sound radical to our
contemporary ears, but sharing life with different people is really
quite a normal thing to do. It's worth reiterating – what we are
trying to achieve, and how we aspire to go about it, is a basic and
logical response to the message of the gospel. We can see this
through some interesting parallels between the book of 1
Thessalonians and our Tree of Life community in Manenberg.
Five particular values stand out.

1. Living together

*. . . we lived among you for your sake. You became imitators of us and
of the Lord . . . And so you became a model to all the believers . . . your
faith in God has become known everywhere.* (1:5–8)

*Because we loved you so much, we were delighted to share with you
not only the gospel of God but our lives as well.* (2:8-9a)

A lot of Christian ministry is conducted at arm's length, done *for*
people with little interest in inviting participation or encouraging
agency. This can be seen both within the Church, and in the
Church's outward expression of mission. Church meetings can be
prime examples, with a polished performance from the band, a
slick talk from the preacher on stage, and surface-level chitchat
afterwards. The only participation required is to put money in

the collection. And then it's back home to carry on with life as normal. Outside of church meetings, an example would be packing food parcels for 'poor' people in one's city – actually meeting those to whom the food is sent can seem a bit too much like hard work. Then another level up would be going out on to the streets of 'poor' neighbourhoods to do evangelism or feed the hungry – all done in short, convenient bursts.

There's a word for this – *assistencialise*. To assistencialise simply means 'to treat people as passive Objects worthy only of benev-olent gestures, rather than active Subjects capable of transforming their world'.[5] Assistencialised approaches tend to view ministry as a one-off event where poor or unbelieving people are seen as problems to be solved or a captive audience to be preached at, and who have nothing to contribute to the encounter. This really does more damage than good in the long term. Harsh? Maybe. True? Absolutely. The saddest part is that some part of us is really convinced this kind of approach is making a difference – and so we keep on doing it, and the Church yet again becomes a dispenser of goods and services to 'people not like us'. *But what about the ones who get saved?* Well, it depends. You wouldn't allow a new-born baby to lie outside alone in the cold, would you? Then what is your plan to nurture life, growth and relationship in that new believer? Without life-on-life discipleship the evangelistic initia-tives of the Church will merely give birth to spiritual orphans. The scary thing is, we have devised whole ministries perfectly crafted at creating spiritual backsliders. But at least we've ticked the boxes.

In living among the Thessalonians and sharing his life with them, Paul demonstrates that discipleship is a relational and reciprocal process over and above a dogmatic, diarised event. The close connection he enjoyed with the Thessalonian church, over a long period of time, was the very thing that enabled them to imitate him, a mature believer, as he followed Jesus. There is no sense of this approach to ministry feeling like a sacrifice – completely the opposite. In fact, he was 'delighted' to share his life with his dear friends. For Paul, a 'dip in, dip out' approach would have made no sense – to share the gospel was synonymous with sharing his life too. The natural overflow of this was that the Thessalonians' faith was so grounded and inspiring that news of them spread far and wide.

Jackie Pullinger talks of new converts saying to her, 'I'll believe in Jesus and then I'll come and live in your home.' They had witnessed their friends meeting Jesus, being completely changed, and going to stay with Jackie. Naturally, they wanted the same. There was no notion that one might believe in Jesus and *not* move into a community house. New faith, new family. That's what was modelled, and it worked. New believers, especially those from vulnerable backgrounds, don't need well-oiled church programmes, or to be drafted into a middle-class home group. They don't need meetings, they need family. As a friend of mine, Aaron White, once said, 'The poor don't need sandwiches and shoes, they need a place at your table for the next twenty years.'

Opposition

> . . . *for you welcomed the message in the midst of severe suffering with the joy given by the Holy Spirit.* (1:6)

> *For we wanted to come to you . . . again and again – but Satan blocked our way.* (2:18)

Opposition can be blindingly obvious or insidiously subtle. It can manifest through individual people, or through entire systems and structures. In Cape Town, a city that continues to manifest a spirit of apartheid, it should be expected that any shared life between people of different races will be met with various forms of resistance. Sarah and I sometimes refer to the 'I told you so' police – those who, when a crisis hits Cru62 or something bad happens within our church community, see this as proof that the life we have chosen is naive, idealistic or futile. *Somebody relapsed/stole something/let you down/became violent?*

I told you that moving into Manenberg was a bad idea – what did you expect? We find ourselves in good company, however, as one of the most recognisable hallmarks of Paul's apostolic life was suffering.

We hold 24–7 prayer weeks every quarter, when as a community we pray non-stop for 168 hours (a whole week), day and night. Something always seems to come up. Once a bullet came through our office window as we were sitting in the next room sharing communion together. Another time, a community member's brother was stabbed badly. Other times it has been a family member taken sick, or a Cru62 run-away. All during prayer weeks. And yet if our prayer week begins during a gang fight, it is not unusual for a truce to have been called by the end of the week. Over the course of running many prayer weeks we've seen numerous signs of God's presence among us. Drug-addicted Muslims have experienced heavenly visitations during Ramadan, ex-gangsters received the gift of tongues, a young girl on the brink of death from a suicide attempt recovered fully.

One particular prayer week Shihaam was feeling very nervous. She was a new believer and was fired up in faith for miracles, but had no idea how to fill an hour talking to Jesus. She made sure she had learnt the Lord's Prayer by heart, and made a list of things to ask God for. But that would only last a couple of minutes – and then what was she meant to do? She admitted to being a little confused as to the point of these long-drawn-out times sitting alone in a room, and was pretty intimidated by the whole thing. The day came, and she opened the door to the prayer room. The next hour was a blur. The moment she entered the room, she fell to her knees and started to weep. As she lay face down in front of the wooden cross in the corner of the room, she could only utter one word, 'Hallelujah'.

The same prayer week, a young Hard Livings gangster who was addicted to *tik* had just been stabbed in the face. Neither his family nor his gang 'brothers' had gone to visit him in hospital, but Clare spent hours sitting with him in the ward as he recovered. And having been discharged from hospital, during the small hours of the morning he could be heard weeping uncontrollably as he sang along to worship music being played. Out of the public eye this angry gangster became a sobbing son resting in the arms of his Father. Someone who was there described it as 'the most beautiful thing I've ever heard'.

They are tiring, a logistical headache, utterly inconvenient, and spiritually opposed, but these weeks of prayer have become an integral part of our life.

2. A local theology

Theology has to arise out of an oppressed community as they seek to understand their place in the history of salvation. – (James H. Cone)[6]

Thinking Christianly . . . is simply examining where we're standing, and then understanding how exactly those positions and locations shape our everyday faith and practice. – (David P. Leong)[7]

A friend of mine once asked me how he could pray for me and the ministry in Manenberg. I thanked him and replied that we would appreciate his prayers as we grapple with what it looks like to develop a local theology arising from the different voices in our community. He wrote back slightly puzzled, saying he wasn't sure he agreed with the idea of a *local* theology, but that he would pray for us to come to greater understanding of a *biblical* theology. For him, there was an obvious dichotomy between the two. For us, they are one and the same. Each informs the other. A local theology acknowledges that not everyone reads Scripture in the same way or prays in the same way – and it celebrates that. It exposes the narrow-minded definition of what constitutes 'biblical' (so often dictated by men in pulpits, ignorant about the diversity of culture, language, outlook and tradition of the rest of the world). But it goes further, exploring how best to follow Jesus in among the variation of personalities, stories, backgrounds, languages and cultures in a group. The Bible informs our reading of the world around us, and that starts with our home, our street, and our local community. Christians will often talk about 'kingdom culture', but unless the culture of a church reflects that of those it comprises, it will just be a flat-pack copy of another version of church seen elsewhere or read about in a book. Imagine what church would look like if all we had to go on was the book of Acts and our own local community. No mega-church podcasts, no spotlights and smoke machines, no courses and training material, no weird Christian phrases like 'loving on people' and 'getting blasted by the glory'. Reduced down to its skin and bones, local theology is simply doing whatever the apostles did in the book of Acts, *in* and *with* your local community. End of.

Local theology in Manenberg has to address addiction and recovery

[M]ake it your ambition to lead a quiet life: you should mind your own business and work with your hands, just as we told you, so that your daily life may win the respect of outsiders and so that you will not be dependent on anybody. (4:11–12)

In Tree of Life our conception of God, forgiveness and freedom has to include issues relating to addiction – because that's a huge local issue where we are. The Thessalonians were to become self-sustaining, not relying solely on others. They were to find jobs, avoid getting caught up in extraneous affairs and, in so doing, earn respect from those who didn't even know them, for living lives of integrity. In these verses Paul succinctly sums up the values needed in a journey out of addiction – humility, focus on self, a job, healthy self-sufficiency. Leaving drugs behind is a process of co-liberation through collaboration. It's not much use doing it in isolation. Fellowship and accountability with other believers is not only an intrinsic part of the Christian faith but is a vital component to recovery from addiction.

This means our church in Manenberg needs to offer a holistic approach to spiritual formation. Bill Johnson expresses this powerfully:

> People are turning to believers, not because they want to get saved, but because they want answers for their problems. The church has a habit of answering questions people aren't asking. We justify by saying we're answering questions they should be asking. They should be asking about eternity and peace with God and the purpose of their life. They're not. They're asking how to keep their kids off drugs, how to be successful in business, how can they reconcile a conflict with a relative . . . What we have to do is take the zeal we have for heavenly things, and let it transfer into our hope for earthly things – the practical – and come to people with answers. And when we start serving them for where their heart beats, suddenly we get positioned to start helping to define the real reason they're on the planet.[8]

It simply won't do to just hold church services or run endless home groups, no matter how good they might be. Those struggling with addiction, or reeling from sexual abuse, or living in abject material poverty, or suffering with drug-induced psychosis, or growing up in a gang-affiliated family, or living in continuous trauma – they aren't asking the 'standard' Alpha course questions about why Jesus died, or how to read the Bible. Commonly, questions asked by addicted young people in Manenberg revolve around why they are going through such hell, how to survive another day penniless without stealing or prostituting themselves, whether social services will give their baby back, or how come this God people talk about has forgotten them. This should be the role of any church. But issues will be specific to location and will have a local form. Which is what a local theology specifically needs to speak to.

3. Rooted in place

Cape Town is 'one of the most – if not the most – unequal cities in the world [in the most consistently unequal country in the world', meaning], more than any other city in South Africa, well-to-do residents can live a life that is largely separated from their socioeconomic 'other'. (David A. McDonald)[9]

To be at all – to exist in any way – is to be somewhere, and to be somewhere is to be in some kind of place . . . nothing we do is unplaced. How could it be otherwise? (Edward S. Casey)[10]

'Both the history of the forced removals in Cape Town and the Old Testament narrative of the Israelites involve an exiled people, displaced, alienated from the place which gave identity and security . . . on the way to a land whose name . . . [they] do not know'.[11] The Cape Flats are located on sandy, barren, desolate land. People of colour were banished to areas far from centres of power and with substandard infrastructure. However, despite the barrenness of a journey to and through wilderness, there is hope for a forsaken community in the words of Exodus 16:12 – 'At twilight you will eat meat, and in the morning you will be filled with bread.' When the land offers nothing, God's presence is able to transform the situation. His presence among his people is the decisive factor that made 'for landless Israel an environment as rich and as nourishing as any landed people had ever known. Yahweh is transformer of situations. The surprise is that landlessness can become nourishing.'[12] Like the coloured experience during apartheid, the Israelites had enjoyed bread, land and security in Egypt under an oppressive regime. In the wilderness, they were 'free' but had neither land nor security. Instead they had a promise of bread from heaven, 'bread from an economy Israel did not know or understand, bread given and

not planned, received and not coerced, bread . . . as a sacrament
of glory', reframing their situation from one of despair to one
of hope.[13]

And so, while 'slavery' and 'wilderness' are both words long
associated with ancient Israel, one could equally well associate
them with the spatial history of Cape coloured people. The suggestion that 'wilderness is presented as a place where desolation is
as much psychological as physical' certainly rings true in relation
to the psychological trauma of forced removals. And yet, biblically
speaking, the wilderness was the place where, time after time,
Israel met with her placeless God. This suggestion that God
especially likes to communicate with humans in the wilderness,
invites us to consider the prophetic nature of the poor and
marginalised, and asks whether the very last thing a human
would choose for themselves (isolation, rootlessness, poverty,
disempowerment) might be *the* significant factor in close
communion with God. If this is even partly so, then the coloured
ghettoes of the Cape Flats are positively sacred places. What we
are confronted with is an unknown land, a passage through a
desert, testing and discernment. But, as Gustavo Gutiérrez
suggests, in this same land, 'from which God is not absent, the
seed of a new spirituality can germinate'.[14]

The issue of place was significant to Jesus too. In the fourth
chapter of John's Gospel, he is on his way from Judea to Galilee.
To get from one to the other, you would logically pass through
Samaria. But such was the animosity felt towards Samaritans and
the intensity of ethnic conflict, Jews usually chose to take a circu-
itous route around Samaria. Characteristically flouting the social
norms of the time, Jesus 'had to go through Samaria' (v. 4). He
chose to go where others like him intentionally avoided. In doing
so, he opened himself up to a prophetic encounter with a
Samaritan woman who, so deeply struck by their conversation,
would become a 'key person in the salvation and redemption of
an entire Samaritan community, paving the way for cultural others
to encounter the living God'.[15] If only we would be willing to go

a different route and to different places from the majority from time to time, we might discover opportunities to share in the love of God with 'those not like us'.

4. Oriented around family

Re-parenting

. . . we were gentle among you. Just as a nursing mother cares for her little children . . . (2:7)

. . . we dealt with each of you as a father deals with his own children, encouraging, comforting and urging you to live lives worthy of God, who calls you into his kingdom and glory. (2:11–12)

Paul *re-parented* these new believers – he describes being like both a mother and a father to them, reflecting the different aspect of mother-father-God's nature.[16]

This has been absolutely crucial for us to understand as we seek to 're-parent' high-risk youth. We are fierce advocates for the way to freedom being found in belonging in a faith family. Sarah and I sometimes find ourselves disagreeing over things we allow the Cru62 guys to do. I mostly push for more freedom for the guys, Sarah is much more cautious not to put them at risk. I like to encourage risk and adventure, Sarah likes to nurture and protect. Sometimes people caution us not to blur the boundaries between personal and professional, though judging by these verses I don't think Paul would have understood such sentiments. For him, the boundaries between 'work' and 'play' seem gloriously fuzzy, as every experience and emotion it elicits gives the opportunity to guide, nurture and instruct the Thessalonians in the ways of the kingdom.

The reason we focus on the family model for transformation is that there simply aren't macro-, aid-based, economic or political solutions to the problems Manenberg, or any community, rich or poor, faces. 'As followers of Jesus we are not called to campaign for a political solution – for ultimately there is none – but to demonstrate an authentic Christian alternative.'[17]

Most outsiders come in and bang on about job creation. It's not an awful idea – jobs will help some, for sure. But jobs will also impede others. (Mainly the thing that grates is the assumption that we haven't already thought about such an obvious point.) Frikkie's life is a prime example of this. He had a full-time job working as a panel beater for a large local contractor, earning about R4,000 (£200) a month – which he later admitted was more money than he knew what to do with. He was a *tik* addict and so, after first giving some of his earnings to his mother, he smoked the rest of his earnings away. He described his twenty-first birthday to me as getting through R1,200 worth of *tik* in one big binge (one hit of *tik* costs roughly R20). But one day, after a heated argument about a pair of flip-flops, his fifteen-year-old brother stabbed him so severely in the shoulder that he lost all movement in his right arm. Did his job sort him out, get him on the straight and narrow, teach him how to budget and use money, or to deal with conflict, his inner pain and fatherlessness, or help with his addiction? No. It exacerbated every pre-existing issue in his life. Job creation in a place with rampant drug use, outside of belonging within a community that offers accountability, guidance and spiritual development, will most likely become a curse rather than a blessing.

I witnessed another example of solutions not founded on relationship one scorching summer afternoon (I'm sure it's happening all over the place, I just happened to witness this instance first hand). I arrived at our offices in Manenberg to the unexpected sight of banners and posters hung on gazebos advertising free HIV tests, and emblazoned with the name of the funders responsible. While watching from our office window, Jonathan and I noticed a group of five notorious young men, queuing to get tested. The line was right around the block. Not only was the sweltering weather making their long wait decidedly uncomfortable, but as Jonathan pointed out, there was a disproportionate number of drug addicts and gang members queuing to be tested. This was surprising to say the least, as gangsters and addicts in Manenberg are generally fairly apathetic towards matters of health. Jonathan sighed with frustration, but I still hadn't understood what was going on – until he pointed to where people went after getting tested. There was a person handing out R5 mobile phone credit vouchers as an incentive for people to get tested and, no doubt, help fulfil funder-driven objectives in the number of HIV/AIDS tests carried out. The five friends in line had a plan – grouping together, receiving their airtime vouchers and immediately selling each one for R4. The half-hour wait was well worth it, earning them R20 to buy a small packet of heroin. And so everyone is happy – the drug addicts smoking their next fix, their friend getting a deal on mobile phone airtime, and the anti-HIV funder ticking its boxes. Meanwhile, the drug dealers' pockets are being inadvertently lined by an international aid agency.

A futile picture on so many levels. Yet it is only compounded when one looks at statistics for drug-related crime on the South African Police Service (SAPS) website. While the level of crime in South Africa is generally decreasing across the board, that's not the case everywhere. In Manenberg, official police statistics showed a 600 per cent increase in drug-related crime between 2004 and 2014, and it's only getting worse. So what's the solution?

Healthy, loving relationships

To be oriented around community as a family-on-mission together means choosing what some might see as a 'radical' or 'intense' way of doing life. It means a refusal to differentiate between your task (mission) and your relationships (family). There's no need to sacrifice the health of your kids in order to 'succeed' in ministry. In fact, no ministry could ever be truly successful (where success equals faithfulness to God's calling) if it were founded on the sacrifice of a healthy family. Equally, the spiritual development of those you are discipling needn't be put on hold because you choose to spend time with your kids. It involves cultivating deep, unguarded relationships with each other above and beyond the mere completion of tasks, and it exposes the irony that 'doing ministry' is often Christians' greatest obstacle to growing proper friendships.

There is a compelling case for close-knit relationships as the most effective rehabilitation for addicts. Which means (at least in theory) our approach is the precise antidote to addiction. As Scott Larson writes, 'if the root of the problem is rejection, then the solution must be acceptance'.[18] This premise that 'the opposite to addiction is connection'[19] rings true in what we have come to discover in Paul's approach to discipleship. To be oriented around family means to re-parent the unparented, to commit to vulnerability in relationships, and to place belonging and connection at the heart of this Christian alternative to limited state-ordained solutions.

5. Embracing those at the margins

The long-term consequences of this abandonment [of those at the margins], barring radical interventions, are likely to be disastrous not only for the youth, whose situation is already dire, but also for society as a whole. (Tony Roshan Samara)[20]

We believe that God puts the poor first because the world puts them last . . . Poverty, we know about. It's poor people we do not know; but it's knowing poor people that enables substantive change and authentic empowerment to take place. (John B. Hayes)[21]

For now we really live, since you are standing firm in the Lord. (3:8)

This world we inhabit is meant to leave us unfulfilled. It's not our home. We've all heard a variation of the classic evangelistic sermon where the preacher passionately implores the listeners to give up searching for Jesus in the things of the world – the new car, the bigger pay cheque, the beautiful spouse, the huge house – moth and rust will destroy it all, and none of this will fill the Jesus-shaped hole in your heart. This is true, of course – the main problem is that this is where most believers are left – having made a commitment to 'life in its fullness', but finding out that so often that means little more than abandoning friendships with 'unsaved' friends and signing up to serving in church day in, day out, in the confident knowledge they are bound for heaven.

C. S. Lewis wrote, 'If we find ourselves with a desire that nothing in this world can satisfy, the most probable explanation is that we were made for another world.'[22] I have found in my relatively short time on earth that the one thing – one thing – that satisfies me, fills me with more joy than anything else, affirms my own destiny and purpose, and induces worship, awe and praise more than anything else is watching those into whom I've poured my life, my prayers, my time, my love, maturing in faith, standing firm and following Jesus with all they've got. The words Paul chooses, that we only '*really* live' if we see those we have discipled 'standing firm in the Lord', seems to suggest you can be a follower of Jesus Christ and not 'really live'.

Like, *really* live.

Paul links this fullness, this true, deep, incomparable reality with one thing – life-on-life discipleship bearing fruit that lasts. For us in Manenberg, this primarily looks like sticking around. Staying put. Making home. Being present. Sharing life. The simple prerequisite for discipleship is: not leaving. But it goes beyond that, to a commitment that each church member actively disciple a handful of non-believers or new believers. Some of us have been discipling individuals on and off for eight, nine, ten years. A minority of them are standing firm and following Jesus, but most aren't. But we don't give up because we know that when someone gets reborn and is transformed (either dramatically and instantly or slowly over time), then we are really living.

If it's true that there's a dynamic interrelationship between the health of marginalised communities and the general social scene, then it's fair to say the city of Cape Town will never change until Manenberg has been transformed. And, if the most sustainable way to bring about change is by 'being with' rather than 'doing for', then establishing and growing dynamic, locally led communities of faith outside of centres of power may well be *the* most important thing people could give their lives for in this city, and in any city. Incarcerating the 'preferably unheard' is the most effective anti-development strategy imaginable. Sadly, the South African system tends to see incarceration as the most effective solution for those living out the social effects of exclusion. In a world of growing inequality (where there are now such huge and growing divisions between rich and poor that a term has been coined – 'global apartheid'), establishing a shared worship life with those who don't look, speak, smell, pray or eat like you is possibly the most important, subversive and generative thing you can give your life to. Just don't expect those in power to get it.

Define success

A combination of providential factors ended up bringing Helen Zille, premier of the Western Cape, and some of her government ministers to have tea and cake at *Jou Ma Se Kombuis*, our Manenberg coffee shop, to learn about our approach to social transformation. I thought to myself, *This is it! They're going to come and hear inspirational stories of bad kids turned good, get fired up and start bouncing off the walls from a cupcake-induced sugar high, throw loads of money and resources at us to help us replicate our model all over the Western Cape and then we'll see thousands upon thousands get free from gangs and drugs.* I admit it, I got a little over-excited. But it genuinely felt like we might be on the cusp of something significant.

In the days preceding the visit, we had a security team come and view the space in which we'd host the premier and her ministers – to check for bombs, and how to evacuate rapidly in case of nuclear meltdown. Or something. I chatted nervously with the head of security about how much we were looking forward to the visit, remembering to underplay the gang fight that was going on at the time and that he kept asking about. ('Oh no, that's all going down on the *other* side of Manenberg. This is *upper* Manenberg.')

The day of the visit came, and I found myself standing in front of this esteemed group, feeling both nervous and energised by the adrenaline. Dowayne spoke before me, telling his story eloquently and movingly. The politicians looked interested and engaged. So far, so good. I then spoke about who we are, and explained a few of our core values, giving examples of how that played out day to day, and some of our hopes and dreams for Manenberg. I then gave our guests an opportunity to ask questions.

During the questions that ensued it became evident that there was a clear disparity in values between us and our visitors. I was asked how many addicts we had 'successfully helped', how much money it took to get someone off drugs, how quick the rehabilitation process could be made to be, and how scalable our approach was. These are all valid questions, coming from those who are involved in finding macro solutions to society's problems. But, strange as it may seem, such questions showed that these educated politicians had completely missed the core motivation behind *what* we did because they had failed to understand the *why*. In their searching for a silver bullet solution to Cape Town's drug problem, they had severed the heart, and so the most human of pursuits had become disembodied. They didn't seem to understand that drug addiction is, at best, a secondary issue, an inevitable fallout of a city divided against itself. They seemed unable (or unwilling) to accept an approach whose foundation was relationship rather than outputs, depth rather than width, and quality rather than quantity. Here was a group of influential people seeking answers for one of Cape Town's biggest problems but who couldn't grasp that the opposite of addiction is not sobriety and employment (both of which are resulting outcomes) but belonging and connection. For them, it seemed that the only indicator of success (such a subjective term in itself) or justification for what we do in Manenberg was numbers. The notion of cultivating a family of families from different races, socio-economic and theological backgrounds, choosing to do life together in a violent, marginalised community – thereby epitomising the reconciliation so desperately needed in this divided nation – was lost on them. Unless our 'model' could be replicated throughout the province, using as little government funding as possible, with as high a profile as possible, and as quickly as possible, it didn't seem to interest them.

Signs over solutions

I was so grateful they came. The meeting had served as an invaluable learning point. That evening, as I reflected on our hour with the leaders of the province, I unearthed a quote from one of my favourite theologians, Stanley Hauerwas, that spoke directly into what I was feeling:

> . . . the church must serve the world on her own terms . . . the first task of the church is not to supply theories of governmental legitimacy or even to suggest strategies for social betterment. The first task of the church is to exhibit in our common life the kind of community possible when trust, and not fear, rules our lives.[23]

Elsewhere he describes the primary task of the Church as not *having* a social ethic but *being* a social ethic – not of rolling out countless programmes to improve society, but in cultivating communities that epitomise the values of the kingdom of God, and thereby rewiring the very values of society – by *being a sign* above *offering a solution*. That, he suggests, is a more powerful form of witness than anything else – and those who love and follow Jesus are to do this not primarily because it's effective, but because it's true. Think about two different ways of finding the route to a certain destination. Either you can follow Google maps on your phone, giving you your step-by-step directions to your lostness, or you can follow signs and maybe stop and ask people along the way. One offers a convenient individualistic solution, the other invites agency, collaboration and interaction into the process. It is infinitely more generative for the Church to offer society signs rather than solutions, because signs invite input, whereas solutions don't; signs give us clues *how* to think, solutions prescribe to us *what* to think.

The next day, I received a phone call from the Premier's Office. No offer of any assistance to open a house for young addicted girls (as we had explained in depth was what Manenberg desperately needed). Instead I was asked if I had seen the morning headline in *Die Son*, an Afrikaans tabloid. I hadn't. The article, provocatively entitled 'Zille Drink Tee in Gangsterland', was written after an enraged self-proclaimed community leader had found out about the visit and gone straight to the papers, criticising Zille and her 'American delegation' (there were no Americans in the group) for not visiting her. Of course, nothing came of the article, and the details were mostly false, but it did serve to show the anger felt by many in Manenberg towards the government. It also alerted us again to the difficulty of working alongside one or two of the 'mayors of Manenberg' in the community, who had elected themselves as spokespersons and decision makers, judge and jury for all and sundry. Once I had got over my initial anger I reminded myself that this person, just like anyone else, needs to feel significance and connectedness, and that the leaked story to the newspaper was probably an indication that they felt little of either.

17: Looking Back to Look Forward

It takes some serious revising of scripture to picture a Jesus who was the advocate of orderly tradition. With his small band of followers, he started a revolution . . . an uprising that eventually led to a worldwide movement that spread to all nations . . . a missional movement that transcends culture, tribe, race, age and gender.
(Floyd McClung)[1]

If you want to build a ship, don't drum up people to collect wood and don't assign them tasks and work, but rather teach them to long for the endless immensity of the sea.
(attrib. Antoine de Saint-Exupéry)[2]

Azusa revisited

In 1906 William J. Seymour, a thirty-four-year-old African American, one-eyed son of freed slaves, was invited to speak at a church gathering in Los Angeles. Undeterred by his apparent disadvantage, he preached over the course of five weeks about the Holy Spirit and speaking in tongues. Listeners were stirred by Seymour's message, and meetings were held in homes as people gathered to pray and fast to receive the gifts of the Holy Spirit. One evening weeks later the first few people began to speak in tongues, followed by many others. Jennie Evans Moore, William Seymour's future wife, spoke in six different languages under the anointing of the Holy Spirit. She even had an interpretation for each one – though she'd never uttered a foreign word in her life. Instances such as this meant the crowd grew in number and desperation to such an extent that the front porch of the house collapsed, so a new venue was found and gatherings continued, at an abandoned old church located at 312 Azusa Street.

As things grew there were critics from both within the Church and outside. Journalists were critical of this new 'sect' jabbering away in incomprehensible utterings, and conservative Christians pronounced it unbiblical and tried to have the police shut it down. None of this served to slow down the growth of what God was up to – quite the opposite, in fact. With no publicity, funding or formal organisation, multitudes began to flock to this inconspicuous revival and powerfully encounter Jesus through receiving the same Holy Spirit. Alongside charismatic experiences, the revival was characterised by a political progressivism way before its time. Baptism of the Holy Spirit, ecstatic encounters, speaking in tongues and physical healings took place in among the intermingling of people of different races and socio-economic standing decades before the civil rights movement and the empowering of female leaders – who weren't even able to vote at the time.[3] As Richard Foster puts it, 'by the power of the Spirit, a revolutionary new type of Christian community was born.'[4]

The revival continued unabated for a number of years. Such zeal was galvanised during this time that scores of missionaries were sent all over the world, contributing to the fastest-growing denomination the world has ever seen. This wave of the Spirit 'from the ghetto to the world' was so significant that today it is estimated there are over 500 million Pentecostals worldwide.

Bringing it Home

It was only when Sarah and I were visiting Bethel Church in Redding, California, in 2016 that we learnt about Azusa Street. We had vaguely heard the name, but knew next to nothing about what had gone on. Sitting in on some of the classes at the School of Supernatural Ministry, we were unaware that it was coming up to the 110th anniversary of the revival. During one particular session, as some of the history of Azusa was being shared, I recalled the many conversations I have had with South African Christians about the Cape to Cairo revival prophecy. I found myself frantically scribbling down various thoughts about what South Africa's equivalent of the Azusa Street revival could look like in the here and now.

> *It will be a revival bringing offensively counter-cultural and subversive conciliation across races. It will raise up South African leaders and be locally led (by a racial representation of the country as a whole). It will value the presence of God above all else and lead South Africa into a new era of revival, seeing 100,000s of souls saved. It will spring up from deep wells of worship in different tongues, languages and styles representing the heavenly diversity of South Africa, and mustn't be hijacked by white, suburban charismatics if it is to carry power nation-nay-continent-wide. It will talk TO, and hear FROM Jesus more than it talks ABOUT Jesus: i.e., it will be founded on intercession and 24–7 prayer. It will empower the previously/currently marginalised – they will be at the centre of the vision and will carry it further. In this way, it will realign cities, and centres of power and influence. It will emphatically address injustices, including white privilege, land issues, restitution, economic inequality, violence and crime. It will necessarily champion living among the poor and disempowered and will mix things up colour-wise and money-wise. Finally, it will ride the wave of the personal prophetic to fuel the systemic prophetic (i.e., it won't just be angry activists screaming about injustice, it will be guided by the personal prophetic stemming from intimacy with Jesus).*

The word 'revival' has been hijacked by the religious right and prosperity preachers, obsessed with politicised hot-button topics and financial wealth. The true meaning of revival is in danger of being lost to a prevailing evangelical faith culture of polarised opinion, 'moral' outrage, and blithe promises of 'your best life now'. Instead, maybe we should use the word 'transformation' – because if something doesn't transform society, is it really revival? In the case of Azusa, it seems that the meaning of revival is found in God taking what has already been formed (racial segregation, inequality, disempowerment of women) – and *re*-forming it – so that it is *trans*-formed. So to answer the question 'What would revival in my city look like?', one would need to look at what has already been formed, and how it could be re-formed towards transformation.

FORMATION → RE-FORMATION → TRANS-FORMATION

If it is centred on the transformation of society through recon-ciling all things to Christ, then revival is necessarily fluid, it is not a static end state. Nor is it some homogenised, marketable flat-pack formula; we would be foolish to try to simply copy the *form* of Azusa Street and expect the same *power*. Religion is doing twice what the Holy Spirit did once. God looks at what's in the hands of his people *here* and *now*, and uses whatever he finds to redeem situations brought about by the past actions of others.

South Africa is a unique context. Cape Town is regularly on the 'top places to visit' lists for tourists. From high-end travel companies to newspaper supplements to backpacker blogs, people across the world continually call it heaven on earth. There is also a deeply embedded history of violence and segregation, along with the greatest inequality between rich and poor in the world – part of the reason we also have one of the highest crime rates. (A teenager in Cape Town is statistically more likely to be shot to death than die in a traffic accident or of natural causes.)[5] The rich minority cling to the side of Table Mountain in their beach-front villas, but for the majority of Capetonians life here is not heaven on earth, but hell on earth. While we see certain trends across the world (inequality and violent crime are generally two sides of the same coin, wherever you go), the 'DNA' of each locale

is unique. To deny that, is to fail to recognise that every place
has its own story.

Part of Manenberg's story is that it is alarmingly over-
evangelised. Over the years we've come to see that the high crime
rate, widespread poverty and prevalent gang presence holds a
certain allure to hardcore preachers, 'bringing' Jesus to Manenberg
as if he isn't already there, preaching about how they are bringing
Jesus' light to a sinful, godforsaken place, without realising the
pretty offensive socio-political connotations of what they are
saying. What they often mean equates to shouting at predominantly Afrikaans-speaking people in English, about getting saved
by praying a prayer of repentance. I can count on one hand the
people in Manenberg I've chatted with over the last eight years
who were *unwilling* to pray such a prayer. Does that mean
Manenberg is more 'spiritually open' than other places, as some
have told me? Possibly. But there is a lot more going on.

The fact is, Manenberg is a worshipping community. Official
statistics state 60 per cent are Christians and 40 per cent Muslims.
For the vast majority of people here, whether passionate or
nominal in faith, the notion that one wouldn't believe in God is
absurd. So if you're sitting on a beer crate on a street corner in
the middle of the day because you are unemployed, wearing dirty
clothes, not knowing where your next meal is going to come from,
worrying about your addicted teenage child, then you'll probably
say yes to a random, white foreigner walking up to you and asking
if you would like to 'make a commitment to God' or 'give your
heart to Jesus'. You're going to say yes by default – you have
nothing to lose and don't want to offend this person you've
historically had to obey. Plus, there may be a few perks – maybe
some money for food, or a brand new Bible you could sell. Have
you definitely understood what you're saying yes to? Probably
not. However, if someone does genuinely have a life-changing
encounter with Jesus, which we also see happen (and love it when
it does), these same visitors generally leave a week or two later,
unable to commit to the long-term task of discipling new believers.

To some, this will sound cynical and even judgemental. Some may be thinking, 'But we are commissioned to preach the good news – stop trying to second-guess whether someone has actually encountered Jesus or not – it's not your job to decide who's genuine!' To others, it will seem blindingly obvious. They may be thinking, 'It's just so frustrating this even needs to be said.' Either way, to ask such questions is, I believe, a prerequisite for a more informed, loving, God-and-people-honouring way of spreading the good news. And if it is that, then it's probably more full of the Holy Spirit too. If we are worried we will have less to show for our 'mission' efforts if we don't get lots of people to 'pray the prayer', we should spend more time dealing with our fear of inadequacy than handing out gospel tracts.

We are learning that the best thing we can do is to 'nail our feet to the ground' – simply, not leave. If God 'freely chose the insignificant, the unimpressive, the foolish to show forth his glory' (Richard Foster again) at Azusa Street then, while it will always look different, Manenberg seems well placed to glimpse the glory of God. I'm convinced that if we stay in Manenberg and give our life to serving the community and loving the people, we will not fail to see a powerful move of God that transforms many lives. But the fact is, a life lived in love is the epitome of a move of God, regardless of any subsequent 'results'. In describing the battle between darkness and light, Lisa Sharon Harper takes us back to the creation narrative in Genesis. 'God does not obliterate the darkness; rather, God names it and limits it – puts boundaries on it. The boundary is the light.'[6] And in fact, the overarching promise of Genesis 1 is this: 'darkness is limited by the light. Suffering is not in perpetuity. The light may take generations to come, but it will come. There is always hope'.[7] That's surely worth repeating.

It may take generations to come, but it will come.

There is always hope.

I'm beginning to learn how to cope with the news that another Cru62 boy has run away. Whatever the reason, be it verbal conflict, emotional pain or physical cravings, it always hurts. One

of the saddest parts is that they never say goodbye. Shame will
not permit them to look us in the eye, give us a hug and leave
well. I suppose it's impossible to leave well if we all know that
within an hour they'll be self-medicating against the emotions
that briefly surfaced in the house, through getting high with
their old gang friends. But if we have a long-term mindset towards
those struggling to get free from drugs, we won't view any runaways as a failure but as the next chapter in someone's unfolding
story towards freedom. Relapse is so often part of recovery. And
if we are committed to Manenberg for the long haul, then it's
not unlikely we will encounter each runaway again one day. They
may well have a job, a kid, a gunshot wound, a gang tattoo, or
have been in jail since we last saw them, but there will always
be the opportunity to reminisce about Cru62 days and point
them back to Jesus. Jackie Pullinger has been loving gangsters
in Hong Kong for over half a century. She, of all people, has
learnt about perspective. So valuable is her insight that it is worth
quoting in full.

> And then there is time. If God meant a child to grow slowly and
> safely in a loving family for up to eighteen years why should we
> be angry at those who do not change at our pace for the sake of
> statistics, furlough or, sadly for some, funding? All the unreason-
> able benefits came for me after nearly twenty years. People I had
> spent time with so long before never forgot even though we lost
> each other for a while. Suddenly someone from the past appeared
> again and turned out that he had not killed the memory of a love
> that was so extraordinary that the giver spent Himself in giving
> until He died. So we have been the delighted, sobbing represent-
> atives of the Father whose prodigal son crawled or rushed home
> after all. (Jackie Pullinger)[8]

Things came full circle for Jackie after twenty years, whereupon
some of those who had left her to return to drugs were only
now starting to come to faith. When Harley, the Hard Livings

gangster who broke into my house, was shot dead I thought there was nothing redemptive to come out of the story. He was gone, and I had missed the chance to share the love of Jesus with him. But seven years later, when we reopened Cru62, his younger brother Kevin came to the house to get clean from the drug habit he had developed to numb the pain of his grief from losing his older brother. Kevin's story continues with its ups and downs, relapses and recovery – but our friendship gives me hope, and reminds me of something Augustine once said: 'It is easy to hear Christ, easy to praise the gospel, easy to applaud the preacher: but to endure till the end is peculiar to the sheep who hear the Shepherd's voice.'[9] If we are to endure, if we are to remain focused and faithful to the call of God on each of our lives, we need to know we have heard the voice of the Shepherd.

False dichotomies

Hearing Jesus' voice will enable us to navigate theological difficulties as well as persevere in our calling. In some places within the evangelical church there has emerged a false dichotomy between two camps. We have tried to separate the two sides of the coin. I love both camps, and one of my deep-set passions is to see the gap disappear – I will call one Revivalism and the other Activism.

The stream of belief I'm referring to as Revivalism would emphasise the righteousness side of the coin and has many beautiful strengths. These include expectant, excited faith that champions supernatural signs, wonders and miracles, in bringing heaven to earth. It invests in joy-filled worship with a high value for prophecy, words of knowledge, gifts of the Spirit and spontaneous praise. Revivalists will often assert that 'God is in a good mood!' – by which they mean he's not angry with us or disillusioned with his world, but loves us as his children. Revivalism often displays an inspiring dependency on hearing from God, a strong emphasis on evangelism, and high regard for personal purity.

Activism emphasises the justice side, and also has a whole lot going for it. A central focus is on faith expressed through action. Active engagement with the world – including politics, sustainable development, advocacy and solidarity with the poor, fuels its embrace of learning and theory, and seeking to understand the complexities of issues. As such, it is well equipped to speak truth to the world in ways accessible to those outside the Church, as well as readily acknowledging the beauty of lament, mystery and doubt as crucial to faith. Over and above the personal prophetic, it stresses the systemic prophetic – such as fair trade, environmental awareness and subversive protest against unjust power. It would also tend to talk more about the systemic nature of sin (e.g., the banking system, colonial hangovers, white privilege) than personal piety.

Both sides of this unnatural divide have their blind spots.

It could be said of Revivalism that it is overly simplistic, focuses too much on personal prosperity, and sounds uncomfortably similar to the self-help movement (*my* journey, *my* encounter with Jesus, *my* anointing). There is an implicit 'West is best' feel to some of the teaching in this largely white male-led stream of Church. Equally, the 'God is always in a good mood' mantra simply doesn't get anywhere near to conveying the empathetic character of a God who weeps with the families of the 29,000 children (largely in the developing world) who die of preventable diseases each day. In this, and in the use of rather strange religious jargon (recent ones I've heard – 'getting swirly' and 'dropping revvies'), it can end up losing respect from those outside of the Church in relation to, well, pretty much anything.

Activism generally struggles with a fairly deep-set critique of the Church – it's too materialistic, or hypocritical. It often reacts so strongly to perceived theological error that it could be more accurately termed 're-activism', focusing more on what's wrong rather than what's missing. This is seen in propagating a 'call out culture' where if someone isn't 'woke' enough or using the most politically correct vocabulary, they are written off as racist, colonial, bigoted. In this way, it breeds a sense of 'lone prophet in the wilderness syndrome' among its subscribers, and as such can easily spiral into hopelessness, anger and cynicism. Ultimately, it can become rooted in pride, masquerading as false humility. And if Revivalism leaves little room for doubt, Activism tends to see doubt in any and every circumstance as a core virtue.

Do you see how ridiculous this is? Both camps evidently represent some of what revival looks like. We desperately need more of both. If the Church is going to be authentically together, we need a prophetic vision for cross-pollination between different Christian streams. The personal prophetic blending with the systemic prophetic, physical healing combined with healing of memories, demonic deliverance coupled with deliverance from allegiance to powers of this world, and a next-world-focused evangelism weaved together with this-world-focused advocacy and action. The fact is, the reason the Azusa Street revival came to an end was because it was shut down by white supremacists who 'could live with glossolalia [speaking in tongues] but not with the revolutionary interracial fellowship that Seymour insisted flowed from it. They abandoned love and reconciliation. The movement split irreparably along racial lines.'[10] The Church at the time was unable to cope with the idea that God was making society new by giving it a foretaste of a racially reconciled people. It was inconceivable to them that the gift of speaking in tongues was a means to bringing about radical shifts in social relationships and breaking unequal power dynamics. The prejudice of the few cost the rest.

In Jesus' time there were two main religious sects within contemporary Judaism – the Pharisees and Sadducees. They spent a good part of their time constructing and arguing about their version of the dichotomy we still see today.

A good example of this in action is found in John 12:27–29. God spoke from heaven and the Sadducees, believing in natural explanations, thought it was thunder. The Pharisees, with their over-emphasis on the spiritual, thought it was an angel. Both filtered God's voice through their predetermined worldview. This is fairly inevitable, but as long as we are aware of this we can chart a way forward.

Manenberg was conceived of and constructed by the spirits of racism and division similar to the climate around Azusa Street. If God always manifests in the opposite spirit to that of the prevailing powers, then it makes perfect sense for our small church to comprise a mixture of coloured, black, white, English, Scottish and Irish people from Manenberg, and coloured people from outside of Manenberg. Some have always had all they need. Others have only ever known lack. Some have grown up in religious environments, others in gangs. Some used to be Muslims, others still are Muslims. Some have happy memories of childhood, others were abused. We spend time asking what they were taught about education, Jesus, race, expressing emotions, power, money, sex and the family unit when they were growing up.

Out of such discussions, in our efforts to retell the story that has already been told, we have adopted certain ways of living out Jesus' love towards others. This is part of seeking a third way between polarising theological dichotomies as well as racial division. We have come to see that theology should not be viewed as a noun, nor a detached, ivory tower pursuit. It is a verb, lived out among others. (Anyone can theology, and indeed everyone does. It's more than just talking about God, it is the worldviews and things we value that inform our actions, and thus tell back to us and the world what we believe about God. We all theology every day, whether we believe in God or not.) We are a multiracial community that reads Scripture together and commits to each other through the ups and downs of life with friends who don't look and speak exactly like we do. This has become our story, and as new chapters are written we have found that there are certain things we all say a big 'yes' to: putting relationship above task; sharing in the upbringing of our children; choosing to have difficult conversations despite the awkwardness it can create; emphasising belonging before believing or behaving – along with mutual submission; dealing with offence; a flat leadership structure; making sure everyone's voice is heard; and celebrating diversity as a strength that fuels unity.

In cultivating our 'yes', we have also discovered some of our 'no': male-only leadership; assuming 'West is best' and 'white is right'; judging people by their appearance or smell; religious rule-making; ignoring or maintaining financial inequality; perpetuating the myth of redemptive violence (either personally or systemically); and playing the numbers game and worrying about 'outputs', replication or scalability. We get it wrong a whole lot of the time and there is a long way to go, but we know what we are aiming at, and it represents the fertile ground we believe the Holy Spirit gets excited about sowing into.

Two sides of the coin

One afternoon we were hosting a mission team doing street outreach in Manenberg. They were full of expectation for miracles and exuded enthusiasm for reaching the lost. After a couple of hours of worshipping on the streets, preaching the gospel and praying for the sick, we returned to the Manenberg Peoples Centre, our rendezvous point, and began to share stories and testimonies of what we had seen God do. As we were chatting together in the car park, a number of older people emerged from the building – a man had his arm in a sling, and some were walking with crutches. Instinctively, our visitors jumped up and offered to pray for them. One lady, who had been hobbling along on crutches, received prayer and let out a yelp as the pain immediately left her legs. She jogged around the car park smiling and hugging her new friends.

'You lot must come again and pray for more of us!'

'We would love to!'

'I'm leader of the Manenberg disabled people's group – maybe you could come to one of our meetings?'

We made a note to get in touch, as our offices were in the same building. As we were driving home later we saw her walking along the road, crutches under her arm. There was a spring in her step, and as she saw our car she laughed and waved – thankful for Jesus' healing touch.

Another experience was having lunch with three elderly nuns at their inauspicious house on Manenberg Avenue. Sarah and I had been invited by the then priest of the local Catholic church. 'Come and meet my special friends,' he said. We were glad to accept the invitation. The women were part of an order called the Little Sisters of Jesus. Over a simple lunch of lentils and rotis they described to me and Sarah what this meant. Inspired by the life of Charles de Foucauld, and as a response to the ordinariness of Jesus' years in Nazareth, communities of Little Sisters live among the poor and marginalised all around the world.

It all sounded rather, well, ordinary. I was sure there must be more to it, so I made the naive mistake of asking what their ministry in Manenberg looked like.

'What do you mean, dear?' replied the most elderly nun.

'Well, what do you actually *do*?'

'Every morning we have adoration together at 5 a.m. Then the younger two go to work, and I look after the garden.'

'Yes, but what *ministry* do you do in the community?'

'I just told you – adoration, work, and gardening.'

It didn't make much sense to me. I was sure the sweet old lady must be forgetting something important, so I asked some more questions, this time to the younger, more switched-on-looking one.

'So how do you spend your evenings?'

Her face lit up.

'We play Scrabble,' she said, smiling.

'Who is the best?' I replied, trying to stir the pot, looking for some semblance of ambition or competitiveness.

'What do you mean?' she replied. How didn't she understand, it was a pretty simple question, wasn't it?

'Well, who usually wins?'

She laughed. Not unkindly, but in a such way that I immediately recognised I'd asked a silly question.

'We all do!' She replied. 'We add our scores together and see how we did!'

Two stories. Both beautiful. Both illustrating God's heart, both involving humble, elderly women filled with the joy of knowing Jesus. Both rather different from the other. Whether we choose to emphasise the dramatic, supernatural healing power of Jesus, or the ordinary, menial humility of Jesus – both are beautiful expressions of the *shalom* of God's kingdom, and as such there is plenty of room for both.

The key is being fully committed to being Jesus' hands and feet here on earth. We need to be prepared to give our whole lives – whether as *answers* to individual needs, as in the first story, or as *questions* prompting people to re-evaluate their outlook, as in the second story. Either way, 'the greater the mission is, the clearer the vision must be, because huge assignments usually require high levels of sacrifice and/or risk to see them fulfilled'.[11] Spirit-empowered transformation of your city or country will cost you. It may cost you your felt entitlement to your money, or your house, your social life, or your comforts. The widely quoted *Message* translation of John 1:14 tells us God's big plan for saving the world was to 'move into the neighbourhood'. Jesus swapped the privilege of heaven for the limits of human existence, and walked the earth as an ordinary human in right relationship with God.

In other words, God's way of saving humanity was to move towards danger, violence, injustice and poverty. As I've heard Sarah say many times to people, if you're worried that if you invite a homeless person into your house they'll steal your belongings, what should you do? Get rid of your belongings! If we spend our life moving in the opposite direction to Jesus, towards ease and comfort, can we really say we are following him?

William Seymour's leadership came under criticism for being weak, because he didn't stand up to the power-hungry 'professionals' whose racism and misuse of power eventually shut down the Azusa revival. But this couldn't be further from the truth. Seymour's problem was that 'his leadership was too effective, too successful. He had called for an all-inclusive community of loving persons beyond the colour line. In 1906 Seymour's way was a direct challenge to the prevailing white supremacy. Indeed, if continued, it could well have meant a martyr church.'[12] The early church understood what it meant to take up their cross and follow Jesus and be a martyr church. They understood, better than anyone, the tension of living kingdom-minded lives within a power-obsessed society. The Epistle to Diognetus, written sometime in the second century, expresses the beautiful witness of the Church to the world.

> As citizens, they share in all things with others, and yet endure all things as if foreigners. Every foreign land is to them as their native country, and every land of their birth as a land of strangers... They have a common table, but not a common bed. They are in the flesh, but they do not live after the flesh. They pass their days on earth, but they are citizens of heaven. They obey the prescribed laws, and at the same time surpass the laws by their lives. They love all men, and are persecuted by all. They are unknown and condemned; they are put to death, and restored to life. They are poor, yet make many rich; they are in lack of all things, and yet abound in all; they are dishonoured, and yet in their very dishonour are glorified. They are evil spoken of, and yet are justified; they are reviled, and bless; they are insulted, and repay the insult with honour; they do good, yet are punished as evildoers. When punished, they rejoice as if quickened into life; they are assailed by the Jews as foreigners, and are persecuted by the Greeks; those who hate them are unable to assign any reason for their hatred.[13]

Is it any surprise that this was written at a time when the Church was growing exponentially? To see Azusa now, or to live even remotely as the early church, it will take nothing less than a giving of one's entire self in pursuit of *shalom* in the world, and in so doing unifying Jesus' Church in leading all cultures, tribes and tongues from, and on, a heavenward trajectory. There is nothing more costly, nothing more rewarding, nothing more exhilarating, nothing more subversive, and nothing more God-honouring. And we are privileged to get to give it a go.

18: How Then Shall We Live?

The real question is whether the gospel of Jesus Christ is like aspirin or like dynamite, whether it is a gospel of pacification or a gospel for revolution, whether it is a gospel of the status quo and the Establishment or a power for the liberation of the oppressed.
(J. Deotis Roberts)[1]

We are simply a tiny sign, among thousands of others, that love is possible, that the world is not condemned to a struggle between oppressors and oppressed, that class and racial warfare is not inevitable. We are a sign that there is hope, because we believe that the Father loves us and sends his Spirit to transform our hearts and lead us from egoism to love, so that we can live everyday life as brothers and sisters.
(Jean Vanier)[2]

It is better to fail in a cause that will finally succeed than to succeed in a cause that will finally fail.
(Bill Arlow)[3]

In Cape Town there is a cold insensitivity towards those who struggle with drug addiction – which is, I believe, symptomatic of the prevailing fear in which many live. One of the things I find saddest is when those who have no clue about another person's story make a moral judgement about them. There's a line that says 'your enemy is just someone whose story you haven't heard'. In the same vein, Henry Wadsworth Longfellow suggested that 'if we could read the secret history of our enemies, we should find in each person's life sorrow and suffering enough to disarm all hostility.[4] If choosing to live in Manenberg has taught me anything, it is just that. We will probably never know the amount of pain those even closest to us carry – let alone someone we meet in a fleeting encounter dealing heroin on the corner or shooting a gun at someone. Various negative circumstances have somehow led them to that point of desperation, and for whatever reason they've not decided, or been able, to choose another path. Therefore, as each person we meet is likely more broken than we would imagine, shouldn't we aim to be kinder than others think is reasonable? Besides, if it boils down to choosing one over the other, how much better to be unreasonably kind, and risk being naive, than to be only reasonably kind and risk being cynical. My problem is that while being kind can be pretty simple, I don't find it particularly easy.

Two of my greatest struggles are the crippling fear that I'm wasting my life, and the seductive pull to be seen as a success. Whatever questions both of these bring up in me, I'm determined to live life sowing into the only ultimately successful cause – being faithful to Jesus' call. Many people spend their lives succeeding in causes that will finally fail – 'delivering programs that produce good statistics but only reinforce inequalities, launching initiatives that only institutionalise humiliation and making grand statements that only disable genuine relationships'.[5] However, 'what will finally succeed is years and years of "being with", building trust, caring about people for their own sake, expecting to see the face of God in them for the wondrous creation that they are. It may not look like much, but it is the way Christ spent most of his incarnate life.'[6]

Why do you pray?

I need to remind myself of this regularly. It reawakens me to the danger of artificial self-sacrifice, where our life in Manenberg could become 'an exercise in social science to be pursued only to the extent that it works'.[7] We don't do what we do primarily because it's effective, we do it because it's true. This relates to prayer as well. Why do we pray? To see revival break out, on earth as it is in heaven? To see lives and neighbourhoods, cities and nations get reborn? For sure – but that's secondary. Ultimately we pray because Jesus is beautiful, and through prayer we see his face and become more like him. Through prayer we meet with God and discover our true selves. The extension of this is that that which is true should ultimately affect lives – and it does. At some point in the future we believe that there will be a natural tipping point where the sheer number of lives touched in Manenberg reach such a depth of transformation that a whole community will be changed. We live and breathe the hope that emanates from that prophetic vision. But that's not necessarily the reason we do it. 'Success' in these terms is not the driver. Because if it was, and if in many years' time not much seemed to have shifted, I should dearly hope you wouldn't find us harbouring bitterness towards God or stewing with self-condemnation, because we'd know that we are living the truest lives we could imagine in response to the glorious gospel of Jesus.

It can't be emphasised enough that it may not look like much to choose to simply 'be with' and journey alongside the hurting. I regularly struggle with the anxiety of 'this doesn't look like much'. If only things would develop quicker, if only people would just heal faster, if only the Holy Spirit would work more dramatically, if only we employed more people, planted more churches, saw more miracles, had more money . . . the list could go on and on. These 'if only' desires are largely rooted in my own brokenness and the attachments I've allowed to influence my motives. If I genuinely think that more addicts will find freedom through me simply trying harder or being more organised or impressive, then I've made the whole thing about me. Once I admit the pride behind these longings, and remind myself that only through an encounter with Jesus can a person or community be truly transformed, then the heat is off, the burden is lifted and I can get on with doing what God has asked me to do.

Likewise, the Church in Cape Town could feel the pressure of the weight of expectation from all these prophetic words spoken about revivals starting on the southernmost tip of Africa. That would be to miss the point entirely, assuming we're the centre of the story. When, in the 1990s, this prophecy was being shared again and again, something remarkable began to happen.

The nations of Africa began to flood to Cape Town.

Words were about things originating and going *from* Cape Town, and God began to seemingly do the opposite. Whether fleeing genocide, as the Rwandese and Burundians were, or escaping Mugabe's mess in Zimbabwe, or running from the militia of the Eastern DRC, the inhabitability of Somalia or sectarian violence of Nigeria, the list went on and on. The prophecies were of a fire starting in Cape Town and spreading across the continent, and no sooner had the words been uttered than thousands upon thousands of people from many different countries made their way to Cape Town. It is not dissimilar to the politically conceived upheaval of people at the time of Jesus' birth, ensuring he was born in Nazareth as the prophecies had stated, six hundred years before.

If it's a thing – if God, using the unfolding political turmoil of the world, sent people from many nations, tribes and tongues to Cape Town; and if prophecies have been accruing around the fire going from Cape Town through Africa; and if the vast majority of refugees want to return home one day – then there seems to be a thread of the Spirit here, with obvious connotations. What if the wave of revival throughout Africa is the returning home of scores of people who have been loved, equipped and discipled while living in Cape Town? What if loving the marginalised, displaced alien is the key to unlocking the destiny of nations? (This would make sense, of course, as throughout the Bible it is exactly what followers of Jesus are called to do.)

I'm naturally impatient. I want to see multitudes of lives changed, and I want to see it now. But every day in Manenberg we get up and choose again to give ourselves to a cause that, however slow it may seem, however unimpressive it may look, will finally succeed. God, in his love and wisdom, gives us just enough encouragement at just the right time to keep going. Whether we're talking one small community or one huge continent, the approach is ultimately the same. Love.

Three stories I've been privileged to witness portray the values of everyday revival bringers in the lives of those around them. One involves a friend's relationship with a prostitute, another is set on a farm in the Palestinian West Bank, and the third charts the progress of a heroin den in Manenberg.

1. New Hope

Around the time I was living alone with Dowayne for the first time, my mate Jake had newly come back to faith. A couple of years of booze-filled partying had left him underwhelmed and unfulfilled, and amid much soul searching he had recently encountered Jesus afresh. He was still finding his feet in church, and trying to work out how to live a Jesus-filled life. One Saturday night while driving home from our friend Bolly's house, he saw a woman sitting on the side of road, head in her hands. He drove on, but found himself weighed down by this picture of despair etched in his mind. Guilt began to convict him. Here he was, on his way home to a warm bed, stomach full, having spent an evening with friends – the polar opposite of this woman sitting alone on the curb. If his new-found faith meant anything, if saying he had 'the love of Jesus in his heart' (or some other Christian platitude) was remotely true, then ignoring her was not an option. There was no audible voice from God, no profound moment of revelation, just a gnawing realisation that he didn't want to be a hypocrite any more. He turned the car round and drove back.

Wandiswa was a sex worker. As Jake sat with her and listened, she told him her story and how she had ended up where she was now. Not knowing how he could help her besides buying her food, Jake suggested she accompanied him to the 7–11 where he could get her some dinner. As he scanned the aisles for things to buy, he noticed she had disappeared. It was only once he was at the till about to pay that she rushed up to him carrying four litre bottles of crackling – cheap wine.

'I didn't know what to do, but was adamant I wasn't going to be *that* guy who decides he knows what the person in need should have. She wanted wine, so I bought her wine. And a sandwich.'

They chatted a little longer and Wandiswa said she would like to go to church with Jake the next morning. 'I was out of ideas, and figured maybe it was a good thing to do,' Jake remarks.

The next morning Jake returned. But Wandiswa was nowhere to be seen. 'To be honest, if I was out drinking a load of alcohol on Saturday night, the last thing I'd have wanted to do the next morning was get up and go to church. I totally got it!' There was a group of people standing around. They were friends of Wandiswa and asked if they could come to church with Jake. So he packed a load of people into the car and went to church. It wasn't *unbearably* awkward, but nor was it particularly comfortable having six homeless sex workers accompany him to his 'white middle-class, big flatscreens and free filter coffee and brownies' type of church. 'I'm not sure many of the congregation had ever sat next to a homeless person in church before. And I'm sure a prostitute would never have stepped foot in that church. Ridiculous, really.' The next week Jake picked up more people and did the same thing, 'though I began to see that really it was more beneficial for those in the church than it was for Wandiswa's homeless friends. It made the Christians feel uncomfortable – which was no bad thing! If homeless people aren't welcome in church then where are they welcome?!' (Why was it beneficial to Christians to sit next to a homeless person or a sex worker at church? Because it opens the church up to people living a different experience of life and so challenges the injustice of the mono-racial white suburban Cape Town church. It offers the possibility of reciprocal friendship on an equal footing, and in so doing disarms the spirit of fear and learnt habits of paternalism. And frankly, it's just something Jesus would do.)

After a month of this, Bolly and Jake began to realise there must be more to it than just taking Wandiswa's friends to a church where they felt out of place. So every week they would cook and share a meal with those they had met on the streets, enabling them to get to know each other and share stories. Numbers began to grow, and soon home groups in Jake's church wanted to start a new initiative to the homeless. So Bolly helped them set it up and began meeting more people on the streets who wanted help getting sheltered accommodation. He would take a group to the shelter once a week to pray together, and in winter they shared meals indoors. This went on for four years, and Bolly became good friends with managers and residents in the shelters. Wanting to empathise on a deeper level, he decided to live in a homeless shelter for a week, to raise funds and awareness. 'In many ways, it was dangerous and self-righteous, was easy for others to criticise and had the potential to draw attention to myself.' But he spent the week journaling his experiences, learning about life in a shelter and the obstacles between homelessness and employment. 'I really didn't want it to be an isolated PR stunt. So afterwards, we looked at ways of advocating for the needs of those living in shelters, and working in solidarity with them.'

Bolly decided to formalise things, and established a ministry called New Hope. When he joined a different church, which was already sharing dinner with the poor and addicted on the streets, he found a new level of co-operation. Now he was able to get people not only into shelters, but also into rehabs. 'We raised R30,000 from one Facebook post to help an addicted friend go to rehab. He is currently over a year clean from heroin and has started studying and doing a welding course.' At the time of writing, New Hope is a registered voluntary association, and has eleven people giving their time to help the addicted and homeless.

All because Jake stopped to talk to a prostitute.

2. A City on a Hill

In mid-2016 I went to Israel-Palestine as part of a group organised by the Telos Group, an organisation looking to 'build a transformative pro-Israeli, pro-Palestinian pro-peace movement'. I was embarrassingly ignorant of the complexities of the Israeli-Palestinian conflict, but was given an immediate foretaste at Johannesburg airport. My flight was with El Al, the Israeli airline, and I have never witnessed such . . . (let's be kind) *thorough* security checks. My bags were searched, every book and journal was flicked through, emails were scrolled through and WhatsApp messages inspected. I was asked the same questions again and again by different officials, who then had whispered discussions with each other as my answers were cross-examined. Thankfully, I was wearing a shirt with long sleeves, which I rolled down to hide the Hebrew tattoo on my forearm. The classic evangelical guy going to the Holy Land, with his Hebrew tattoo – I have never felt like more of a cliché!

While the entire trip was paradigm shifting – in that it introduced me to my own ignorance around the conflict – there was one particular visit to a farm that affected me the most. Driving from Jerusalem to the West Bank (a Palestinian territory on the western side of the River Jordan, occupied and controlled by Israel) that day, I couldn't help but notice how many checkpoints we had to stop at. (I later learned there are over five hundred Israeli-controlled checkpoints throughout the West Bank.) Israeli Defence Force soldiers would hop into the bus carrying machine guns, and look us in the eye, checking to see if anyone dared eyeball them back. The intimidation of such a move hardly seemed accidental. And as we drove, looking out of the window we could see the hurried construction of new (UN-condemned and illegal) Israeli settlements on every hilltop. Only upon returning to South Africa did I read that these settlements 'are erected either on the top of hills, at crossroads, or next to natural resources, providing the maximum level of control' and psychologically 'looking down'

on Palestinian villages, and that this intentional connecting of
Israeli settlements along lines of resources and control simultaneously disconnects the Palestinians, making the aim of
'establishing a Palestinian state a de facto impossibility'.[8] It struck
me, a first-time visitor with little knowledge of any of the context,
let alone conscious bias for or against either 'side', that currently
Israel seemed to more closely represent Pharaoh's relentless
Egyptian empire rather than the Hebrews crying out for liberation.

There were obvious parallels between the land through which
we were driving and the historical and current reality of the
country I now call home, South Africa. The 'them' and 'us' narrative; the primal fear of the other through the demonising of
specific people groups or ideologies; the violence; the international
sanctions; the support of oppressive empire by evangelical
Christians; the 'God is on our side, not yours' taunts; the land
grabbing of those in power; checkpoints and control of movement;
safety sought through intimidation and high walls. I was feeling
decidedly hopeless as the bus stopped and we arrived at a heap
of rubble.

'This is us! Everyone out, we're walking the last few hundred
yards.'

Daoud Nassar is a Palestinian Christian whose family has owned
their farm on the West Bank for over a hundred years. They are
located on top of a hill, surrounded by newly built Israeli settlements, and with no vehicular access ever since the road to the
farm was blocked by rubble dumped by the settlers. The Nassar
family have had entire orchards uprooted by Israeli bulldozers
– the fruit of over a decade, gone in a day. They have suffered
intimidation, have been prohibited from developing their land,
have been subject to armed soldiers' midnight raids, and have
been embroiled in a legal battle for over twenty-five years to keep
what is legally and rightfully theirs. They are regularly goaded
and pushed to the limit, in the hope that either they will resort
to violence (and then be locked up) or they will flee. Their
response? 'Nobody can force us to hate. We refuse to be enemies.'

They champion non-violence and peace-building, holding camps for Palestinian children who have grown up in the urban chaos of refugee camps, to come and discover the gift of space and of the land. The sign at the entrance to their farm states their hymn of extremist love, declaring boldly, 'We refuse to be enemies with anyone.'

That afternoon as we sat around a table, Daoud spoke to us about the Beatitudes. He described some of the feelings that come up in him on a fairly regular basis – fear, anger, sadness – but that he always comes back to the person and teaching of Jesus.

> Blessed are the peacemakers,
>   for they will be called children of God.
> Blessed are those who are persecuted because of
>   righteousness,
>   for theirs is the kingdom of heaven.
>   (Matt. 5:9–10)

St Francis de Sales, a man known for his gentleness, once said 'nothing is so strong as gentleness, nothing so gentle as real strength'. I felt the familiar sensation of hope rising within me as we sat at the feet of Daoud and his family, who through supernatural reservoirs of inner strength were gently trailblazing a third way in the midst of polarised rhetoric and virulent animosity. I had met a man and his family who left my head spinning by the depth to which they exude the heart of Jesus. Through their uncompromisingly peaceful pursuit of peace in the face of violence and intimidation they showed 'the incontrovertible truth that without struggle and pain, sacrifice and hopeful endurance, systemic transformation and redeemed politics, justice will not become reality'.[9]

The Nassars' farm is a 'city on a hill' in every sense of the word. And as Jesus said, it 'cannot be hidden' (Matt. 5:14). Amid the hysterical screaming of polarised theologies, ideas or mindsets, it reminds us all that there is another way. There is another option

beyond empire-building or angry revolt. This third way isn't
aligned to a political ideology, and is often overlooked as it is not
showy, loud or 'big'. It doesn't grapple for the airwaves; it is not
interested in profile, numbers or celebrity endorsement. It is
invariably creative, never aggressive or violent, nor manipulative
or co-optive. It doesn't justify cruelty or domination for a far-off
'greater good', but pursues peaceful ends via peaceful means,
exposing the brittle idol of nationalism.

To model the third way involves extreme sacrifice and the
cultivation of the heart of Jesus. It is classic Beatitudes. The third
way is the furthest from blanket tolerance or resigned middle
ground you could imagine. It is vehemently intolerant of anti-
Christ ideals and as such comes at huge personal cost, and with
criticism from those wedded to empire. It is the embodiment of
imaginative protest shown not by slogans uttered, events attended
or causes fought, but through lives lived. As such, it is kingdom
through and through. The third way will never seem 'enough' for
either side of the polarised divide. As such, those who follow its
narrow path open themselves up to perennial misunderstanding
and false accusation. But it is obstinately expectant that as, like
the Nassars on top of their hill deep in the West Bank, you 'let
your light shine before others . . . they may see your good deeds
and glorify your Father in heaven' (Matt. 5:16).

3. The Casino

As a seventeen-year-old *unga* addict, Dowayne was repeatedly
thrown out of the house for stealing. It wasn't unusual for him
to sleep outside next to the front door. As winter came, however,
this wasn't sustainable even for an *unga* addict, so he decided to
build himself a home in his mother's back yard. He was used to
skarrelling the streets for scrap metal he could sell to buy drugs,
so he just added wooden planks to his list of sought-after materials. In no time at all he had all he needed to construct a small
shack and provide a roof over his own head.

When other addicts found out about Dowayne's new shack, they flocked to it like moths to a flame. His new home swiftly became a drug den and a hive of illicit activity affectionately named the Casino. It even had its own security camera, alerting drug users to police raids. This arrangement didn't last long as it was a stolen camera for which Dowayne didn't have a licence, and so the police removed it. Undeterred, and ever the home-maker, Dowayne upgraded his security measures through more creative means. He put a roof over the metre gap between his and the neighbours' shacks, and then made an opening in the outer wall of his shack, placed a cupboard in front of it and a board behind it. Now when the police turned up, whoever was carrying the drugs would just slide the cupboard to one side, climb through the hole in the wall, slide the cupboard back and wait in the gap between the two shacks. In addition, the roof over the gap had a loose panel, so if the police did move the cupboard, you could have already climbed through the roof, walked along the top of the other shacks, and been half-way down another street by the time the loose roof panel was discovered.

As is typical in any space given over to using heroin, the visitors usually ended up staying the night, satiated and semi-comatose as a result of their obsessive relationship with their fickle friend *unga*. As some slept, passed out and sprawled on top of one another, others would gamble late into the night. Coins would be scattered around the floor as they played, but wads of notes were tucked behind their shoelaces, enabling them to run off with most of their money in the event of a police raid. The winners of the dice and card games would leave briefly with their winnings, braving the cold, and dodging bullets, pockets stuffed full of notes, only to return with more *unga*. And as the sun came up the next morning, a hunger would kick in. Hunger not for breakfast, but for another hit to take away the early onset of withdrawal pain. Indeed, the only item ever on the menu – breakfast, lunch and dinner – was *unga*.

For five years the Casino flourished. But after Dowayne had

finally got clean from *unga* and returned to Manenberg, aged twenty-two, he realised he needed to make amends for the things he had done while on drugs. One of his chief concerns was sorting out the mess he had created in his mum's back yard. By now the Casino was being used for Hard Livings' gang meetings, which caused a long list of unwanted issues for his mother. Top of the list was physical safety. During gang fights the Clever Kids, a neighbouring gang, would run across the roofs of the back-yard shacks shooting down through the thin corrugated iron sheets. A number of Hard Livings gangsters had been killed this way, although such an indiscriminate and haphazard strategy often meant a high number of innocent people were also injured or killed.

So Dowayne cleared out his old one-roomed home and fumigated it of gang presence. The Casino was no more. It was chained shut and stood empty. We didn't think about it much for the next few years. For me it brought up a lonely chapter in my life of chasing after an addicted friend whom God had told me to pursue, but who didn't seem to want help. For Dowayne, it signified the darkest, most traumatic season of his life.

Three years later, with Dowayne, Sarah and I running Cru62 together, our church community had grown. We decided to multiply into three groups and plant into people's homes across Manenberg. I had been contacted by a growing number of people around Cape Town who were interested in joining our church family in Manenberg, having become bored of monotonous suburban church life. But we still felt like we were just starting out, had no desire to become the next flavour of the month among church commuters, and were clear among ourselves of wanting to be *in* Manenberg, *of* Manenberg and *for* Manenberg. This meant growing through local people coming to faith, not bloating from being joined by dozens of disillusioned suburbanites. We figured that smaller regular gatherings in homes full of local people, rather than a large weekly event in a big hall full of strangers, was more likely to reach those least likely to come to church.

We formed three teams to lead the house churches, gave people the choice of which group to belong to, and got thinking about which homes to meet in. The first two locations were pretty clear – Leon and Cynthy's place in the Americans' gang territory, and Clare and Lloyd's new home in Sherwood Park, the Muslim corner of Manenberg – but where would be best for the third location? And then it struck us. Dowayne's shack! We let it sink in. Almost ten years before, a drug addicted seventeen-year-old with no faith had constructed a church building in his mum's back yard – he just hadn't realised what it was really for. And so it was decided – the Casino would become Tree of Life's third house church!

Today it is no longer called the Casino. We now call it the *Hok* (shack). The walls have been whitewashed to hide the old gang signs and symbols, wooden planks lie on top of old beer crates to make benches, and there are no Narnia-style wardrobe tricks for evading police. The physical space, while ostensibly fairly unchanged, has become a place of worship and prayer, and with that, a redemptive sign of God's faithfulness.

Look East

The great British theologian Lesslie Newbigin tells a story from his days as a missionary in India. On an early morning journey to a distant village, setting off in darkness, and walking west, he describes meeting a group of people travelling the opposite way with a faint glow on their faces, reflecting the light of the sun. He writes,

> If we stop and ask them: 'Where does the light come from?', they will simply ask us to turn around . . . and look towards the east. The church is that company which, going the opposite way to the majority, facing not from life to death, but from death towards life, is given already the first glow of the light of a new day. It is that light that is the witness.[10]

That 'first glow of the light of a new day' – in Jake's face as he edges up to a distraught stranger on the side of the road, or in the bright eyes of Daoud as he explains the power of forgiveness, or in the redemptive action of Dowayne renovating the *Hok* – is the personal revival in the ones and twos that could just be the foundation of something even more far-reaching.

And so, what of the future? Where does this story end? God only knows! But for us back in Manenberg, it looks like sitting with Jesus and asking for more and more dreams to come to reality. Skatties, the Tree of Life pre-school that doubled in size to reach more toddlers and their addicted mothers with Jesus' love; Basila, the home for teenage girls coming out of addiction and abuse, changing the trajectory of disempowered young lives. Manenberg Media Company, bringing reconciliation through reframing narratives. A reintegration house for Cru62 graduates to live and work in secondary recovery in Manenberg, recruiting the next intake for healing and freedom. Across South Africa and Africa, communities of 24–7 Prayer drawing on and learning from all the mistakes we've made in Manenberg and teaching us a thing or two as they multiply throughout townships and rural communities. The list could go on, and it will – way beyond us.

The majority may think we're naive idealists, and that a community like Manenberg can never change, but we have a sneaking suspicion that God has other ideas.

Nevertheless, I will bring health and healing to it; I will heal my people and will let them enjoy abundant peace and security. I will bring Judah and Israel back from captivity and will rebuild them as they were before. I will cleanse them from all the sin they have committed against me and will forgive all their sins of rebellion against me. Then this city will bring me renown, joy, praise and honour before all nations on earth that hear of all the good things I do for it; and they will be in awe and will tremble at the abundant prosperity and peace I provide for it . . . there will be heard once more the sounds of joy and gladness, the voices of bride and bridegroom, and the voices of those who bring thank offerings to the house of the LORD, saying:

'Give thanks to the LORD Almighty,
  for the LORD is good; his love endures forever.'
        (Jeremiah 33:6–9, 106–11)

Acknowledgements

The deadline for finishing these acknowledgements crept up on me. Quite honestly, I didn't really know who to thank. As in, there are so many people I could thank that I didn't know where to start. So I put it off. And then, the evening I was meant to be emailing it to Katherine the inimitable editor, I thought I would take a drive through Manenberg en route to Jerry's Burger Bar, a 15-minute drive away – where I could catch the end of happy hour and get writing.

I should have known that most drives through Manenberg are more eventful than planned. This was no exception. Manenberg Avenue was buzzing with people. Some were carrying wooden planks, others doors, still others corrugated iron roof sheets and galvanised gates. I pulled up to the corner where the avenue hits Swakop Road, and stopped under the 'caution: mothers and children' road sign that's peppered with bullet holes, outside the old rent office building. It was a ruin. In just two days it had been completely stripped and looted of all its materials. Various groups of people were chiselling away at the external walls, and passing the loose bricks to friends with trolleys who were then carting them off to sell. The roof and rafters had gone, and there was even a group of young men attaching a rope to a safe, while waiting for an accomplice to bring his *bakkie* to drag it out of the building. There was a vague feeling of celebration in the air. All of this was going on in broad daylight, with scores of others just watching on. A government-owned building, ransacked in a matter of hours.

I hopped out of the car and walked around chatting to people – trying to get a handle on how this was happening.

'The city of Cape Town hasn't done anything with this building for a couple of years – it's been standing empty. It was only a matter of time before this would happen.'

'Right. And are you OK with that?'

'Yes! Why not? The police came earlier, and after shooting at people they decided there was nothing they could do, so they gave permission to tear the building down. The gangs have been making sure people work together!'

As another trolley was pushed past, the whole thing struck me as deeply sad. Just a year earlier we had put together a proposal for use of the space that included a workshop, classrooms, a coffee shop and vegetable garden, a music recording studio, counselling rooms and offices, and ample room for other organisations to have office space. Ultimately, endless bureaucracy and political umm-ing and aah-ing resulted in the process reaching an impasse, and we decided to let go of the dream. The dream that would have been housed in the structure now being carried away in wheelie bins and shopping trolleys.

And as I drove to Jerry's it struck me how easy it had been to tear down that building.

Building it would have required forethought, drawing up plans, financial capital, and expertise in the building trade. But demolishing it took no skill at all. Building it may have taken years, but destroying it had taken 48 hours. The irony of the gangs helping to co-ordinate the destruction of a community asset wasn't lost on me – works of darkness can never be creative, they can only destroy what good already exists.

To tear down and destroy is easy and can happen in an instant. But to build and create can be difficult and often takes time.

It took me a rather long time to write this book. Many hours of planning, writing, editing, copyediting, checking and double checking have gone into it. I have not done it alone. What has been constructed could not have come about without the generosity, kindness and proficiency of people around me. The work of many has gone into this. Because, let's be honest, is anything written ever truly original, and from only one person's mind? Nothing I've read, no people I've spent time with, no experience I've been through hasn't left a mark. Really there are too many to acknowledge. But I may as well give it a go . . .

My sincere thanks go to:

Rene August, Ruth Padilla DeBorst and Idelette McVicker for organising the Robben Island weekend that got me writing in the first place.

My big sis Claire Casagrande for sharing advice, expertise and friends, and for cheering me on.

Katherine Venn, for taking a punt on this rookie, for believing there's a story to be told, and for your endless patience and skill in making my rambles readable.

Jessica Lacey, for your eye for detail and willingness to explain everything to me multiple times!

Andy, for getting me to South Africa in the first place. I will always be thankful for that first year of brotherhood.

Jonathan, for imparting your passion, faith and vision for a community, and holding my hand back in the early days.

Dowayne, for permission to tell some of your story. This book wouldn't make much sense without you. I'm deeply thankful for our friendship, wherever life takes us.

Adam and Juli Cox, for always being available, either thousands of miles away in Kansas City or in our home, to listen, encourage, prophesy, pray and model what relentless hope looks like.

The Warehouse community in Cape Town, for the indelible mark you made on me the years we were part of you.

The 24–7 Prayer movement and communities all around the world, for championing us, inspiring us and sharing with us. Tree of Life wouldn't be the same without you – we have found our tribe!

Bill and Joyce, Anthony, Cathy and Renita, for the gift of your homes to write in.

Simon Middleton – for accidentally coming up with the title for the book!

Cynthy and Yoli, for reading the manuscript, making suggestions and correcting my wayward Kaapse *taal*.

Cate, for the words to that beautiful song.

Tree of Life – my faith family. For being part of this funny life we lead, for sharpening me, for encouraging me, for teaching me all about the priceless kingdom of God. It is impossible to overstate my gratitude.

Sarah, for . . . well, everything. You are soft as feathers and hard as nails.

Glossary of Terms

Americans	gang in Manenberg, generally seen as the main rivals to the Hard Livings
bakkie	pick-up truck
braai	barbeque
broe	brother/friend
Cape coloured	people of mixed racial descent, generally but not exclusively originating in the Western Cape
Clever Kids	gang in Manenberg
Darkies	racist/offensive slang for black people
die ou	'the guy'
dom	stupid
frans	non-gang-affiliated prison inmate, often viewed as weak
gangetjie	thin alleyway between courts of flats
Hard Livings	Manenberg's largest gang, established by twins Rashied and Rashaad Staggie
hok	shack or shed
Jarre	term of surprise, akin to 'Oh God'
Jester Kids	gang in Manenberg
kak	shit, rubbish
kerk broe	a churchgoing man
klopse	Cape Coloured minstrel troupe
kwaai	cool, amazing
lollie	a perspex pipe used for smoking crystal meth
Mandrax	tranquiliser with psychotic side effects, one of the most widely used drugs in Manenberg. Mandrax comes in

tablet form, is crushed, mixed with marijuana and the mixture smoked in a glass bottle neck. It is alleged the apartheid government flooded the townships with Mandrax in order to quell to political uprisings

merchant	drug lord
miskien	maybe
moer	to beat up
naartjie	tangerine/satsuma
The Number	South African prison gangs. There are three gangs that operate in prison, the 26s, 27s and 28s. The Number are not directly linked to specific street gangs, so you could have two 28s who are allies in prison, but in different street gangs. The Number speak a gang language called Sabela, a mix of Afrikaans, English, Xhosa and Zulu. Sabela also includes symbols and colours designating different gang loyalties
Pan African Congress	a black nationalist political party (also known as PAC), originally led by Robert Sobukwe
PTSD	post-traumatic stress disorder (referred to as shell shock during the Second World War)
regte	morally upstanding
skelm	manipulative liar, someone up to no good
skollie	thug, gangster
skarrel	scavenging the street for things to sell, often to fund a drug habit
smaak	craving drugs
tik	crystal meth, smoked in a *lollie*
tjappie	tattoo
twak	rolling tobacco
unga/ whoonga	street heroin, often highly contaminated with chemicals such as rat poison
Wendy house	self-built home, often made of wood and in someone's back yard; sometimes called a *hok* or shack

Notes

Preface and Introduction

1 C. S. Lewis, *Christian Reflections* (Grand Rapids, Cambridge: William B. Eerdmans, 1967), p. 41.

2 Arundhati Roy, *The Ordinary Person's Guide to Empire* (India: Penguin Books, 2006), p. 330.

3 Chimamanda Ngozi Adichie at TEDGlobal 2009: www.ted.com/talks/chimamanda_adichie_the_danger_of_a_single_story?language=en

4 J. Kameron Carter, *Race: A Theological Account* (Oxford: Oxford University Press, 2008), p. 3.

5 Cornel West, *Prophesy Deliverance!* (Philadelphia: Westminster John Knox Press, 1982), pp. 48-65.

1: Early Days

1 Richard Holloway, extract from the speech he gave at the Catholic Renewal Conference at Loughborough in April 1978. Quoted in John Stott, *Why I am a Christian* (Illinois: IVP, 2003), p. 76.

2: The Stirring

1 Jackie Pullinger, *Chasing the Dragon* (London: Hodder & Stoughton, 1980, 2010), p. x.

2 John Ortberg, *If You Want to Walk on Water, You've Got to Get Out of the Boat* (Grand Rapids: Zondervan, 2001), p. 83.

3 Francis A. Schaeffer, *Art and the Bible* (Illinois: IVP, 2006), p. 91.

4 'If God's will is to heal *all* disease, why do people die even when they have been prayed for?' Those who have either seen a loved one die, or are themselves holding out for healing and not seeing God visibly do anything often ask this question laden with emotion and understandable disappointment. There are no easy answers to this question. Books I have found helpful on this topic are *When Heaven Invades Earth* and *The Supernatural*

Power of a Transformed Mind, both by Bill Johnson. While Bill has seen many, many miraculous healings, his father died of cancer, and his son Eric is partially deaf. *God on Mute*, by Pete Greig is also a wonderful book that goes into the process of trusting God through mystery and pain.

3: Knowing Your Place in Cape Town

1   Tony Roshan Samara, *Cape Town After Apartheid: Crime and Governance in the Divided City* (Minneapolis: University of Minnesota Press, 2011), p. 2.

2   David A. McDonald, *World City Syndrome: Neoliberalism and Inequality in Cape Town* (Oxford: Routledge, 2008), p. 44.

3   Don Pinnock, *The Brotherhoods: Street Gangs and State Control in Cape Town* (Cape Town: David Philip, 1984), p. 99.

4   www.warehouse.org.za

5   www.dailymaverick.co.za/article/2016-04-08-beyond-khayelitsha-just-how-unequal-is-distribution-of-police-in-south-africa/#.WT6yoxOGORs

6   Bob Ekblad, *A New Christian Manifesto: Pledging Allegiance to the Kingdom of God* (Louisville, Kentucky: Westminster John Knox Press, 2008), p. 52.

7   John Western, *Outcast Cape Town* (London: George Allen & Unwin, 1981), pp. 146, 149.

8   Brian Barrow, quoted in Don Pinnock, *Gang Town* (Cape Town: Tafelberg, 2016), p. 14.

9   Norman Hanson, town planner, speaking at a planning conference in 1938. Quoted in Don Pinnock, 'Ideology and Urban Planning: Blueprints of a Garrison City', in Wilmot G. James and Mary Simons (eds), *The Angry Divide* (David Philip: Cape Town, 1989), p. 44.

10 Richard Rive, *Buckingham Palace: District Six* (Cape Town: David Philip, 1986), p. 127.

11 Pinnock, *The Brotherhoods*, p. 56.

12 *Ibid.*

13 *Ibid.* p. 101.

14 McDonald, *World City Syndrome*, pp. 1, 6.

15 www.un.org/sg/en/content/sg/articles/2003-12-04/search-new-un-role

4: A New Home

1   Theodore Dalrymple, *Junk Medicine: Doctors, Lies and the Addiction Bureaucracy* (Harriman House: Petersfield, 2007), p. 6.

2   Tobias Jones, online essay: https://aeon.co/essays/recovering-addicts-need-to-get-dirty-before-getting-clean

3 Zimitri Erasmus, 'Re-imagining Coloured Identities in Post-Apartheid South Africa' in Zimitri Erasmus (ed.), *Coloured by History, Shaped by Place: New Perspectives on Coloured Identities in Cape Town* (Cape Town: Kwela Books, 2001), p. 14.

4 Mohamed Adhikari, *Not White Enough, Not Black Enough: Racial Identity in the South African Coloured Community* (Ohio University Press, 2005), p. 25.

5 James Matthews, 'Black Voices Shout!' in James Matthews and Gladys Thomas, *Cry Rage!* (Johannesburg: Spro-cas Publications, 1972), p. 64.

6 James Matthews, 'An Autumn Afternoon: An Excerpt from an Unpublished Novel', *Realities* (Cape Town: BLAC, 1985), p. 7.

5: Early Impressions

1 Don Pinnock, *Gang Town* (Cape Town: Tafelberg, 2016), p. 193.

6: Tea with the Gang Leader and Other Stories

1 Saul Alinsky, *Reveille for Radicals* (New York: Vintage Books, 1969), p. 60.

2 Lisa Sharon Harper, *The Very Good Gospel: How Everything Wrong Can Be Made Right* (New York: Waterbrook, 2016), p. 61.

3 Strictly speaking, he is the right-hand man of the overall leader of the Hard Livings, Rashied Staggie. Staggie had made headlines in the early 2000s for allegedly turning his life around and coming to faith in Jesus, and was put on a stage in front of thousands of people and told his testimony at a national day of prayer. Though at the time I had the vision about this particular leader, Staggie was in jail for the alleged kidnapping and rape of a seventeen-year-old girl.

4 Jason Upton, (accessed 11 December 2018) www.instagram.com/jason_upton/

5 Caitlin Moran, *Moranifesto* (London: Ebury Press, 2017), p. 158.

7: You'll Die Alone

1 M. Scott Peck, *The Road Less Travelled* (London: Random House, 1978), p. 3.

2 Pete Greig, 'When life is tough...' (accessed 11 December 2018) https://twitter.com/PeteGreig/status/957550267272237056

3 Bill Johnson, *God is Good: He's Better Than You Think* (Shippensburg: Destiny Image, 2016), p. 117.

4 Shane Claiborne, *The Irresistible Revolution: Living as an Ordinary Radical*, updated and expanded (Grand Rapids: Zondervan, 2016), p. 357.

5 www.christianaid.org.uk/resources/churches/reflections/do-you-believe-in-life-before-death.aspx (last accessed 10 March 2016).

8: Asking, Seeking, Knocking

1 Pete Greig, *The Vision and the Vow* (Kingsway, 2005), p. 14.
2 Gustavo Gutiérrez, *We Drink From Our Own Wells: The Spiritual Journey of a People* (London: SCM Press, 1984), pp. 95, 98.
3 James H. Cone, *God of the Oppressed* (Maryknoll, New York: Orbis, 1997), p. 88.
4 James H. Cone, *A Black Theology of Liberation* (New York: J. B. Lippincott Company, 1970), p. 29.

9: Placed with the Displaced

1 Stanley Hauerwas and William H. Willimon, *Resident Aliens* (Nashville: Abingdon Press, 1989), pp. 24, 28.
2 Albert Einstein. A variation on his words can be found in 'The significant problems we face cannot be solved at the same level of thinking we were at when we created them', *The New Quotable Einstein* (Princeton University Press, Princeton and Oxford, 2005), p. 292.
3 Heidi Baker, *Learning to Love* (Maidstone: River Publishing, 2013), p. 65.
4 Matthew Parris, 30 May 2015: www.thetimes.co.uk/article/we-fool-ourselves-that-weve-all-got-a-future-j5m555z3c9r
5 Floyd McClung, *You See Bones I See An Army* (Cape Town: YWAM Publishing, 2008), pp. 200-201. Used with permission from YWAM Publishing.

10: Cru62

1 Kris Vallotton, *Heavy Rain: How You Can Transform the World Around You* (California: Regal Books, 2010), p. 55.
2 Oswald Chambers, 'My Utmost for His Highest' (accessed 11 December 2018) utmost.org/classic/getting-there-3-classic/
3 Tobias Jones, online essay: https://aeon.co/essays/recovering-addicts-need-to-get-dirty-before-getting-clean
4 McClung, *You See Bones*, p. 101.
5 Claiborne, *Irresistible Revolution*, p. 293.
6 Some thoughts on why prison will never do anything to solve the issue of gangsterism:
• Institutions don't change people; people change people. This shouldn't surprise those of us who profess to following Jesus, because he tells

us the heart of the human problem is the problem of the human heart.

- Pro-social change comes about when inner core beliefs are altered in a person. Punishment, or fear of punishment, will never change someone's core beliefs. At best, it might bring about behavioural change – but when all those around you are dragging you down, your polished behaviour won't last long.
- Retributive justice never gets to the root issue behind a crime. For example, poverty, sexual abuse, hopelessness, trauma, absent or neglectful parents, etc. The epitome of hopelessly misguided retribution is, of course, the death penalty – 'we are killing you in order to show that killing people is wrong'.
- Because prison gangs run the prisons, to be incarcerated in South Africa is often synonymous with becoming more deeply embroiled in gang activity. Not only does prison rarely help, but it actually serves to criminalise you more.

7   Alinsky, *Reveille for Radicals*, p. 59.

8   Bill Johnson, *Dreaming with God* (Shippensburg: Destiny Image, 2016), p. 89.

9   Richard Foster, *Streams of Living Water: Celebrating the Great Traditions of Christian Faith* (London: Hodder & Stoughton, 2017), p. 264.

11: Young Men Will See Visions

1   Bill Johnson, *When Heaven Invades Earth: A Practical Guide to a Life of Miracles* (Shippensburg: Destiny Image, 2013), p. 165.

12: Gangsters, My Greatest Teachers

1   David Ford, *Christian Wisdom: Desiring God and Learning in Love* (Cambridge Studies in Christian Doctrine, 2007), p. 359.

2   John B. Hayes, *Sub-merge: Living Deep in a Shallow World* (California: Regal Books, 2006), p. 118.

3   Jean Vanier, *From Brokenness to Community* (Mahwah, N.J., Paulist Press, 1992), p. 19.

4   I borrow this phrase from Dr Anna Rowlands, who uses it in describing refugees and forced migrants. Anna Rowlands, 'On the Temptations of Sovereignty: The Task of Catholic Social Teaching and the Challenge of UK Asylum Seeking', *Political Theology*, 12:6, 843-869 (2011), DOI: 10.1558/poth.v12i6.843.

5   Ekblad, *New Christian Manifesto*, p. 56.

6   *Ibid.*

7   Walter Brueggemann, *Sabbath as Resistance: Saying No to the Culture of Now* (Louisville, Kentucky: Westminster John Knox Press, 2014), p. 35.

8   *Ibid.*, p. 37.

9   Pinnock, *Brotherhoods*, p. 100.

13: Learning to Love

1 Pullinger, *Chasing the Dragon*, pp. 236-237.

2 Hauerwas and Willimom, *Resident Aliens*, p. 48.

3 Graham Cooke, online article: 'Every Negative Thought Has a Heavenly Counterpart', http://brilliantperspectives.com/every-negative-thought-counterpart/

4 A. W. Tozer, *The Pursuit of God: The Human Thirst for the Divine* (Wingspread Publishers: Camp Hill, 2007), p. 107.

5 Based on a story in Søren Kierkegaard, *Philosophical Fragments*, ch. 2; readingtheology.com

6 Tobias Jones, *A Place of Refuge: An Experiment in Communal Living* (London: Quercus, 2015), p. 330.

14: High Highs and Low Lows

1 Simon Sinek, 'Love is...' (accessed 11 December 2018)twitter.com/simon-sinek/status/963782657246195712?lang=en

2 John Mark McMillan, lyrics from 'Guns/Napoleon' Written by John Mark McMillan, Lionhawk Records, 2014.

3 Tobias Jones, *Online essay: https://aeon.co/essays/recovering-addicts-need-to-get-dirty-before-getting-clean*

4 *Ibid.*

15: The Walk

1 Dietrich Bonhoeffer, *A Testament to Freedom: The Essential Writings of Dietrich Bonhoeffer*, ed. Geffrey B. Kelly and F. Burton Nelson (San Francisco: HarperSanFrancisco, 1990), pp. 542-3.

2 Isak Dinesen, *Seven Gothic Tales* (Vintage, Random House: New York, 1991), p. 39.

3 Brian Zahnd, *Beauty Will Save the World: Rediscovering the Allure and Mystery of Christianity* (Florida: Charisma House, 2012), p. 60.

16: Family is the Revolution

1 Hauerwas and Willimom, *Resident Aliens*, p. 83.

2 Sam Wells and Marcia A. Owen, *Living Without Enemies: Being Present in the Midst of Violence* (Illinois: InterVarsity Press, 2011), p. 30.

3 Hayes, *Sub-merge*, p. 181.

4 Wells and Owen, *Living Without Enemies*, p. 77.

5 Ana Freire, Foreword to Margaret Ledwith, *Community Development in Action: Putting Freire into Practice* (Policy Press: Bristol, 2016), p. viii.

6 Cone, *God of the Oppressed*, p. 6.

7 David P. Leong, *Race and Place: How Urban Geography Shapes the Journey to Reconciliation* (Illinois: IVP, 2017), p. 18.

8 Bill Johnson, speaking at a Bethel Conference (televised by Bethel TV 2016).

9 McDonald, *World City Syndrome*, pp. 42, 44.

10 Edward S. Casey, *The Fate of Place: A Philosophical History* (Berkeley, California: University of California Press, 1998), p. xi.

11 Walter Brueggemann, *The Land: Place as Gift, Promise and Challenge in Biblical Faith* (London: SPCK, 1978), pp. 6, 8.

12 *Ibid.*, p. 33.

13 Brueggemann, *The Land*, p. 34.

14 Gutiérrez, *We Drink From Our Own Wells*, p. 19.

15 Leong, *Race and Place*, p. 55.

16 If you have issues with God being referred to as mother-father-God, you might find the following female images of God interesting: www.women-sordination.org/resources/female-images-of-god-in-the-bible/

17 Zahnd, *Beauty Will Save the World*, p. 15.

18 Scott Larson, *At Risk: Bringing Hope to Hurting Teenagers* (Gainesville: Praxis Press, 1999), p. 36.

19 Johann Hari from a TED talk: https://www.ted.com/talks/johann_hari_everything_you_think_you_know_about_addiction_is_wrong

20 Samara, *Cape Town After Apartheid*, p. 187.

21 Hayes, *Sub-merge*, pp. 79, 71.

22 C. S. Lewis, *Mere Christianity* (New York: Harper Collins, 2001), p. 137.

23 Stanley Hauerwas, *A Community of Character: Toward a Constructive Christian Social Ethic* (Notre Dame, Indiana: University of Notre Dame Press, 1981), p. 85.

17: Looking Back to Look Forward

1 McClung, *You See Bones I See an Army*, (YWAM Publishing: Cape Town, 2008), p. 200-1. Used by permission.

2 Antoine de Saint-Exupery, possibly derived in translation from a passage in *Citadelle* (*The Wisdom of the Sands*) (1948).

3 Of course, this makes total sense in light of the Pentecost story in Acts 2 where, when the Spirit came through flames of fire, the importance of diversity and culture was celebrated by the speaking in and comprehending

of many different languages. Thus it is clear that some of the hallmarks of a work of the Spirit are cross-cultural communication, the embracing of diversity, and a vision to unite rather than divide or separate.

4 Foster, *Streams of Living Water*, p. 117.

5 Medical Research Council, in Samara, *Cape Town After Apartheid*, p. 45.

6 Harper, *Very Good Gospel*, p. 21.

7 *Ibid.*, p. 20.

8 Pullinger, *Chasing the Dragon*, p. 237.

9 Quoted in Foster, *Streams of Living Water*, p. 194.

10 Foster, *Streams of Living Water*, p. 123.

11 Vallotton, *Heavy Rain*, p. 181.

12 Foster, *Streams of Living Water*, p. 124.

13 www.ccel.org/ccel/schaff/anfo1.iii.ii.v.html

18: How Then Shall We Live?

1 J. Deotis Roberts, *A Black Political Theology* (Louisville, Kentucky: Westminster John Knox Press, 2005), p. 144.

2 Jean Vanier, *Community and Growth* (London: Darton, Longman and Todd, 1979), p. 312.

3 Bill Arlow, cited in Wells and Owen, *Living without Enemies*, (Illinois: IVP, 2011), p. 46.

4 Quoted in Wells and Owen, *Living Without Enemies* (Illinois: IVP, 2011), p. 46.

5 Henry Wadsworth Longfellow, *The Complete Works of Henry Wadsworth Longfellow*, (Scholarly Publishing Office, University of Michigan Library, 2005).

6 Wells and Owen, *Living Without Enemies*, p. 46.

7 *Ibid.*

8 Hayes, *Sub-merge*, p. 121.

9 Mitri Raheb, *Faith in the Face of Empire: The Bible Through Palestinian Eyes* (Maryknoll, New York: Orbis Books, 2014), p. 59.

10 Allan Boesak, *Pharaohs on Both Sides of the Blood-Red Waters: Prophetic Critique on Empire* (Oregon: Cascade Books, 2017), p. 36.

11 Lesslie Newbigin, *Mission in Christ's Way: Bible Studies* (Geneva: WCC, 1987), p. 21.

Bibliography

Alinsky, Saul D. *Reveille for Radicals* (New York: Vintage Books, 1969).

Baker, Heidi. *Learning to Love* (Maidstone: River Publishing & Media Ltd., 2012).

Boesak, Allan Aubrey. *Pharaohs on Both Sides of the Blood-Red Waters: Prophetic Critique on Empire* (Oregon: Cascade Books, 2017).

Brueggemann, Walter. *The Land: Place as Gift, Promise and Challenge in Biblical Faith* (London: SPCK, 1978).

——. *Sabbath as Resistance: Saying No to the Culture of Now* (Louisville, Kentucky: Westminster John Knox Press, 2014).

Carter, J. Kameron. *Race: A Theological Account* (Oxford: Oxford University Press, 2008).

Casey, Edward S. *The Fate of Place: A Philosophical History* (Berkeley, California: University of California Press, 1998).

Claiborne, Shane. *The Irresistible Revolution: Living as an Ordinary Radical*, updated version (Grand Rapids: Zondervan, 2016).

Cone, James H. *God of the Oppressed* (Maryknoll, New York: Orbis, 1997).

Ekblad, Bob. *A New Christian Manifesto: Pledging Allegiance to the Kingdom of God* (Louisville, Kentucky: Westminster John Knox Press, 2008).

Erasmus, Zimitri. *Coloured by History, Shaped by Place: New Perspectives on Coloured Identities in Cape Town* (Cape Town: Kwela Books, 2001).

Foster, Richard. *Streams of Living Water: Celebrating the Great Traditions of Christian Faith* (London: Hodder & Stoughton, 2017).

Greig, Pete. *Dirty Glory: Go Where Your Best Prayers Take You* (London: Hodder & Stoughton, 2016).

——. *Red Moon Rising* (Eastbourne: Kingsway Publications, 2004).

Gutiérrez, Gustavo. *We Drink From Our Own Wells* (London: SCM Press, 1984).

Harper, Lisa Sharon. *The Very Good Gospel: How Everything Wrong Can Be Made Right* (New York: Waterbrook, 2016).

Hayes, John B. *Sub-merge: Living Deep in a Shallow World* (California: Regal Books, 2006).

Hauerwas, Stanley. *A Community of Character: Toward a Constructive Christian Social Ethic* (Notre Dame, Indiana: University of Notre Dame Press, 1981).

——. and Willimon, William H. *Resident Aliens* (Nashville: Abingdon Press, 1989).

Johnson, Bill. *God is Good: He's Better Than You Think* (Shippensburg: Destiny Image, 2016).

——. *When Heaven Invades Earth,* Revised Edition (Shippensberg: Destiny Image, 2003).

——. *Dreaming with God* (Shippensberg: Destiny Image, 2016).

Jones, Tobias. *A Place of Refuge: An Experiment in Communal Living* (London: Quercus, 2015).

Larson, Scott. *At Risk: Bringing Hope to Hurting Teenagers* (Gainesville: Praxis Press, 1999).

Leong, David P. *Race and Place: How Urban Geography Shapes the Journey to Reconciliation* (Illinois: IVP, 2017).

Lewis, C. S. 'Christianity and Culture', *Christian Reflections* (Grand Rapids: Eerdmans Publishing Co., 1995).

——. *Mere Christianity* (New York: Harper Collins, 2001).

Matthews, James. 'An Autumn Afternoon: An Excerpt from an Unpublished Novel', *Realities* (Cape Town: BLAC, 1985).

——. 'Black Voices Shout!', *Cry Rage* (Johannesburg: Spro-cas Publications, 1972).

McClung, Floyd. *You See Bones I See An Army* (Cape Town: Struik Christian Books, 2008).

McDonald, David A. *World City Syndrome: Neoliberalism and Inequality in Cape Town* (London: Routledge, 2008).

Newbigin, Lesslie. *Mission in Christ's Way: Bible Studies* (Geneva: WCC, 1987).

Ortberg, John. *If You Want to Walk on Water, You've Got to Get Out of the Boat* (Grand Rapids: Zondervan, 2001).

Peck, M. Scott. *The Road Less Travelled* (London: Random House, 1978).

Pinnock, Don. *The Brotherhoods: Street Gangs and State Control in Cape Town* (Cape Town: David Philip, 1984).

———. *Gang Town* (Cape Town: Tafelberg, 2016).

Pullinger, Jackie. *Chasing the Dragon* (London: Hodder & Stoughton, 2010).

Raheb, Mitri. *Faith in the Face of Empire: The Bible Through Palestinian Eyes* (Maryknoll, New York: Orbis Books, 2014).

Rive, Richard. *Buckingham Palace: District Six* (Cape Town: David Philip, 1986).

Roberts, J. Deotis. *A Black Political Theology* (Louisville, Kentucky: Westminster John Knox Press, 2005).

Samara, Tony Roshan. *Cape Town After Apartheid: Crime and Governance in the Divided City* (Minneapolis: University of Minnesota Press, 2011).

Tozer, A. W. *The Pursuit of God* (Camp Hill: Wingspread Publishers, 2007).

Vallotton, Kris. *Heavy Rain: How You Can Transform the World Around You* (California: Regal Books, 2010).

Vanier, Jean. *Community and Growth* (London: Darton, Longman and Todd, 1979).

———. *From Brokenness to Community* (Mahwah, N. J.: Paulist Press, 1992).

Wells, Sam and Owen, Marcia A. *Living Without Enemies: Being Present in the Midst of Violence* (Illinois: InterVarsity Press, 2011).

West, Cornel. *Prophesy Deliverance!* (Philadelphia: Westminster John Knox Press, 1982).

Zahnd, Brian. *Beauty Will Save the World: Rediscovering the Allure and Mystery of Christianity* (Florida: Charisma House, 2012).

TREE of LIFE
MANENBERG

Tree of Life is a church family committed to a life of following Jesus together in Manenberg. We don't primarily aim to offer solutions to all of Manenberg's problems, we simply seek to be a sign that another reality is possible when love is put at the centre. Our expression of church comes from our understanding of the first community of disciples in Acts 2. We believe that through our pursuit of this shared mission and lifestyle we will have an impact on our community, and that Manenberg will be revived.

We are part of the global family of churches and communities associated with the 24–7 Prayer movement, and are committed to a lifestyle of prayer, mission and justice.